The Se

to

Beyond the Known:
REALIZATION

A Channeled Text

Eagles

Ligt filering Tru Tree Canopy

Book One of the The moon
Shoting stars Light
BEYOND THE KNOWN
Trilogy

* climb ing the Lader
To the uperrooms

Paul Selig • Re

Lisening to Crikits
frgs
A wakening to th
Shakti

ST. MARTIN'S ESSENTIALS

RAinbows Thuder Litinig

Thunder Humming birds
SAILRS

First published in the United States by St. Martin's Essentials, an imprint of St. Martin's Publishing Group

For information, address St. Martin's Publishing Group, 120 Broadway, New York, NY 10271.

www.stmartins.com

Designed by Steven Seighman

The Library of Congress Cataloging-in-Publication Data is available upon request.

ISBN 978-1-250-20422-6 (trade paperback)
ISBN 978-1-250-20423-3 (ebook)

Our books may be purchased in bulk for promotional, educational, or business use. Please contact your local bookseller or the Macmillan Corporate and Premium Sales Department at 1-800-221-7945, extension 5442, or by email at MacmillanSpecialMarkets@macmillan.com.

First Edition: August 2019

10 9 8 7 6 5 4 3 2 1

Contents

Foreword

I consider myself an open-minded skeptic. When my friends and mentors Ted Dekker and Duncan Trussell recommended that I listen to the channeled teachings of Paul Selig, I casually tuned into a podcast. Paul seemed like a humble, genuine guy. I noticed no indication of bravado or any desire to wear the mask of spiritual master. It was when he started the process of channeling everything became very interesting. He would quickly mumble parts of a sentence and then repeat them again clearly and audibly. As I listened further, I became more and more intrigued. The message that he was offering was, well . . . impeccable. I had never heard a more salient expression of Truth from any spiritual teacher, alive or dead. I was astounded. It was enough to put me on the path to discovering more.

I immediately dove into his channeled books. That is when the teaching really started to shift my perspective. I began to comprehend my own potential to grasp highly evolved concepts. My experience with this work in a few short months had been more profound than anything I had known prior.

I was determined to meet Paul in person. I invited him to come to my office for a podcast at the Onnit headquarters in Austin,

Texas. While Onnit is focused on the body and the mind-set of peak performance, my personal passion is the expansion of consciousness, and this often takes me deep into the unchartered realms of spirituality.

This was the start of a genuine friendship with Paul, and a dedication to learn as much as I possibly could from the teaching of the Guides. I was fortunate enough to get an early copy of *The Book of Freedom,* which took me even further in my understanding of my questions of who I am, what I am, and how I serve—perhaps the most important questions of any spiritual philosophy.

Learning from the Guides has not only taught me a great deal, it has also provided a language for many of the truths that I have discovered from over twenty years of experiential work. Everything I have come to know from my dedication to plant medicine, breathwork, yoga, and meditation was all consistent with these teachings. The goal of my personal work has always been to become free. Free to experience love and the bliss of existing in true presence. Free to experience pain without the mental resistance that creates suffering. Free to experience the connection to everyone and everything around me, without judgment. Free to know myself beyond my personal history and identity.

So when Paul asked me if I would like to read his latest work, *Beyond the Known: Realization,* and write the introduction, there wasn't a moment's hesitation. Not only was that a great honor, it was a treat to get an early copy of his latest manuscript. This book is the most audacious of the Guides teachings to date. It describes how anyone who chooses can claim the true expression of who they are; what the Guides call the Divine Self, the True Self, or the Christed Self.

From my personal experience it is important to take your time with the teachings. Trust that your path will follow the perfect timing and teaching for you, and you alone. And while you are in the process, recognize that just because you are doing this work, it doesn't make your path any better or worse than anyone else's.

Those are all judgments that you can't bring with you on this journey. We're all together in the school of life.

I can't say that after reading this book that I am a permanent resident of what the Guides call the Upper Room. But I have gazed out of those sun-soaked windows for a few moments, moments that in Zen Buddhism they would call satori. And having seen that view, I find myself happier, less fearful, and much more abundant in love. I hope you have the same experience. I have no doubt that you will.

—Aubrey Marcus,
New York Times bestselling author of *Own the Day, Own Your Life* and founder and CEO of Onnit

The following are the unedited transcripts of recordings of channeled lectures delivered through Paul Selig in workshops and seminars held in New York City, New York; Atlanta, Georgia; London, England; Ann Arbor, Michigan; Rhinebeck, New York; Madison, Wisconsin; Santa Barbara, California; Portland, Oregon; Seattle, Washington; Boone, North Carolina; and Calgary, Alberta, between May 19, 2018, and August 26, 2018.

Prologue

DAY ONE

Now the ambassador of truth, come as you, will claim a world in a new vibration, the ambassador of truth being the one who knows who she is and has affirmed her place in the Kingdom, the Kingdom being the awareness of the Divine in all she sees.

The manifest world is more than a projection. In some ways, it's the collective agreement to be what it needs to be at the level of vibration that it has been confirmed in by name. The names you have gifted things claim form—a chair, a rock, a tree, a roof. These are all things that have been named that confirm the names they have been given. But a treetop may be something other than what it's been conceived of. A house may be a house, not for man, but for clouds. Everything you see may be known anew from the high vantage point where we intend to take you.

The right to be was gifted to you at the inception of your soul. The right to be cannot be taken from you. It is not dependent upon the life you live, the adherence to rules, the diplomas on the wall, the pedigree of birth. It is not dependent on what you have believed yourself to be. The right to be is confirmed by the octave that you find yourself expressing in, and by *octave* we mean the level of resonance and energetic accord that you have bound yourself to. As we lift you, one and all, to the high room, to the high level of agreement that can be understood and experienced while embodied, we will take you where you can go for the sole purpose of realization.

"What does it mean," he* asks, "that we can know?" As long as the body is in density, there are levels of awareness that will preclude you from admittance. But, as the body expresses itself more and more in the high vibration, even those become apparent to the eye. The reclamation of the Divine as *what,* in form and field, is the teaching you receive. And, in order to enter the Upper Room, you cannot leave the body behind, the body that seems to fail you, that doesn't look as it should, that is riddled with cancer, or in fear of what could happen to it. Nothing can be released until it is known. Nothing can be re-known until it is first considered at the level of vibration that it has claimed for itself.

So we intend to bring you all, wherever you sit, whatever you sit as, to the level of agreement that may hold you and support you in perceiving the self, in acknowledging the self as an inhabitant of the Upper Room. Now, what the Upper Room is, in some ways, is a creation. Everything, in fact, that exists and may exist or could exist one day is a creation of consciousness. Nothing exists without this. So the idealization of the Upper Room, while unnecessary, may support you only in one way. It is where you arrive to in consequence of the vibratory accord that you have claimed an alignment to.

Imagine you have a jukebox and you punch two numbers in. A certain song will play. The coordinates for the Upper Room are as present as thus, and you may return here whenever you claim it. But to abide in the Upper Room is to maintain the vibration that has brought you here, and not collect the old, the twigs of the past

---

* Paul.

fires, still broken, and attempt to ignite them in the higher place. The smoke from them will evacuate you quickly. You only bring to the Upper Room what you carry, and what you don't need will be brought back to where it came from, in the oasis of this plane that has known itself in all kinds of ways.

The crisis you may face here, if you have to have one, is that what you seek as a small self may not be found here. "Bring me to the place of no pain, to no awareness, or bring me all awareness, as long as the awareness feels good." From the perspective of the Upper Room, you will actually be of benefit to your world, but you will also see with new eyes what man has done to man, what humanity has wrought through fear, and how you have claimed yourself as a small self as a separate entity from the Source of your being, and the perils you have claimed for humanity and this plane of expression that you may call earth.

Now, as we sing to you—and by *song* we mean resonance, and the language we endow with purpose, expression, and accord—we sing for you to bring you to us at the level of agreement that you can adhere to. To bring you to the Upper Room simply requires you to consent and to be lifted. To have the simple experience of it is to align the self to the presence of what already is. You are not making anything happen. You are accepting what is, exists, at the top of the stairway in the Upper Room. The claim you make, "I am free, I am free, I am free," as sung through the resonant field, is what will reclaim you here, because this is the room of freedom where you are not bound by what you have thought or consented to as a small being in consent with others who are consenting to the same.

"What does that mean?" he asks. Adherence to law. Adherence to the prescriptions of time. Adhering to what you have been taught to expect at the denial of what is. These are the things you no longer align to in the Upper Room. They are present in lower octave, may be understood there, played out there, seen through there, and to *see through* means to claim to completion. To align to the higher at the cost of the old is to begin to have an experience of no limitation, of freedom beyond the known, beyond what you've consented to as an individual living in a tapestry or an echo that is in fact a shared creation.

So when we do this with you, we do this for several reasons. Because we prefer to teach now without the opposition that the small self likes to claim, we invite you to the place where such opposition is not present because the fear that would be at its basis is not present in the Upper Room. And, as we teach you here, and, as you learn here, as you are reclaimed here, the seeking of justification for the old ways begins to peel from you. Imagine shingles falling from an old roof, the attic is exposed, the Upper Room is exposed, and there is nothing to separate you from the great sky beyond. The great sky beyond. All that is of God and may be known as God exists all around you in the cloud of love, the cloud of remembrance that supports you in lifting again and again to what may be realized beyond the known.

The song we sing for you today, and will continue to sing, will be heralded in the new text, *Beyond the Known*. And, as we sing it, as we announce the text in language, in tone, we support you each in your reliance on the Divine that is you, that has always been you, that can only be you, that is here, that is here, that is here.

As we lift you each to the Upper Room, where this class may convene again and again, we offer you the opportunity to say, "No, thank you. I wish to abide in the lower floors. I wish to stay where I have been in the resonant field of fear, in the opportunities that fear brings me to learn in the old ways." You may choose to stay where you are. You are loved as you are. You cannot fail here. But, if you give it permission, the self permission, to claim the truth of who you have always been, we will lift you to the new classroom, and from here we will teach you.

When we count to three, we are going to invite you each to see a stairwell before you. When you see the stairwell, we will invite you forward to climb the stairs that appear. And, as the count of three is made, the energies that you require to support you in this ascension will be called forth for you.

One. Two. Three.

See the stairway before you and allow us to bring you forth, to lift you to the Upper Room. On the count of three, we invite you to climb the stairs, and with each step, you may consent to the following:

> **One.** "I am willing to release the idea of who I am or what I have been to receive the new."
> **Two.** "I am willing to release the attachments I have had, or may still have, to what I think I am or should be."
> **Three.** "I accept myself as worthy of this passage. Because I was born, I may be known anew, and because I am sung in vibration through these words, 'I know who I am in truth, I know what I am in truth, I know how I serve in truth,' I may receive the gift of the Kingdom that awaits for me on the other side of this threshold."

On the count of three, see a doorway before you, and as the tone we sing is sung, you may join us in vibration and step over the threshold to what waits before you.

One. Two. Three.

[The Guides tone through Paul.]

Step over the threshold and be with us. Feel this, yes.

> "I know who I am in truth." (Say this.) "I know what I am in truth. I know how I serve in truth. I am free. I am free. I am free."

Be received by us. Feel what it is like to be at this level of expression. Be as you are. Be as you are. Be as you are. Thank you, and stop now, please. Period. Period. Period.

DAY TWO

Now, when you ask us questions about what you want, you refer to the histories you've had to determine what you should have, what should be aspired to, what you should want because of the kind of person you are. The kind of person you are in evolution is evolving beyond what you have thought, and, to claim the old, to predetermine the new, is to sacrifice the potential that is awaiting for you. The determiner must be something other. "What is required for my soul's growth? What is needed for me to be myself in a true way? What are the qualities I require to realize myself through?"

The small self's desires or dictates, while present, can be re-comprehended, in some ways, as what you thought you should do based on who you thought you were. Now, when we come to you in realization to gift you with the Kingdom, we see you beyond the small self. We don't abnegate the small self. We don't decide it shouldn't be. But we know who you are, and, because we do, we meet you outside of artifice, outside of the small self's requirements or predetermined ideas of how she should be met.

The agreement we make with you, each of you, if you wish, is that you will be known anew—*known* means realized—in this encounter, and we say yes to you, one and all, as you agree to be as you truly are. The small self's desires may be re-understood, in some ways, as what you should have done had you been the other person who did not have this encounter. "I am the one who might have done this or that, claimed this or that, if it wasn't for the realization of who I am beyond the small self's agenda and what she has invested in, thought was so important, thought must be known by the small self as a determiner of her fate."

The teaching you receive today is not only moving beyond the known, but it is the transparency of reality once you begin to lift beyond the artifacts of history, beyond the claims made for you by your history, beyond the objects that have been used to claim a reality that you believe to be real. The reality that you believe to be real, in some ways, is a consolidation of thought, re-made and re-made throughout the millennia. And the solidity you experience on this dense plane is very real, and of course not real at all, because once you understand that the fabric of reality is not what you think or believe to be, what you think is not what is, you begin to realize what lies beyond, what exists beyond, what may be seen beyond the known.

Now, the qualifications required for this journey are your own consent to travel with us to what lies beyond the known. And the agreement we make with each of you on this day, in this encounter, is that you will be known beyond what you have esteemed or reasoned with, what your mother said you should be, what the world expects of you. Now, in translation, this means that what you think you are, and the claims you've made through that expression in predetermination are actually moved.

Imagine that you have a board that is cluttered with objects. You don't see what's beyond the objects because the clutter takes the place of what might be seen. The idealization of the objects as reality claims you in an expression or in a co-resonance with what is known at that level of consequence or vibration. When you lift above them, you may perceive what is real, and in this perception you may begin to claim what exists in the co-resonant field of the one who has moved to the Upper Room, the higher vista. The clear landscape that presents to you is unfettered by the illusions of the small self and is not determined by the cultural dictates, what you should want, or should aspire to, to be who you think you should be.

Now, for some of you this means that the world that you have erected, decided should be, must be at all costs, will be seen as what it has always been, an idea made into form that may have been heralded by your parents, supported by your culture, agreed to by you, and is now known in a new way—what was, what was created, what was believed to be important that now has little consequence. There is a great gift in this realization, but only if you are willing to release the old, to move to the new. If you seek to attach to what you have created as a small self, the identity you use to greet your neighbors at the market, the face you put on to appease the world, the ideas you think you should hold to agree with those around you must be known as what they have always been, an acquiescence to history that really bears no truth in your relations.

Our objective with you, as we are allowed, is to give you the Upper Room as a place to dwell, and in this place your purview is known anew, your purview meaning what you may claim, what you may be in accord with, what is available to you beyond the known, beyond the small self's agenda for you. Now, the transmission you are receiving is happening in several ways. You hear the words; you read the words, you comprehend the words, you have a relationship to their meaning. But the real energetic transmission that you are in accord with is happening beyond the words, instilled in language, in tone, in vibration, but not of this alignment to the earthly realm. In fact, what we are doing is transitioning you from the reliance upon the old through the energetic structure we teach you through so you may be in agreement to what exists beyond the known for the purpose of knowing and claiming and realizing the self as you truly are, and, in fact, have always been.

As we do not make you holy, but support you in your recognition of your own divinity, as we do not make you happy, but give you the opportunity to choose happiness, as we do not say no to what you may claim as a small self, but offer you the opportunity to choose something much more beneficial to you, we sing for you, we sing with you, until the song becomes your own and you are released from the prisons that you have erected—or aspired to, even—that would contain you at the cost of what lies beyond the known. What lies beyond the known must be understood by you, not only as your potential, but as your true inheritance. And, as you say yes to what comes, the mission of your life becomes crystal  clear. It is not what you do, it is how you be, and the level of accord you align to is what claims you in action if action is to be taken. So many of you aspire to enlightenment, but it is still the small self who is seeking enlightenment, and the small self does not become enlightened. She cannot. She does not exist in the realm of enlightenment. But the Divine as you, who has come, who has come, who has come, who is here with us in this encounter, is claiming you, is choosing you, is saying yes to you so she may know herself as and through you, as he may know himself as and through you. And, in this agreement, the plasticity of your reality becomes understood, and what may be claimed for you in the higher realm may be agreed to as the aspect of you who can receive it is made known. In truth, you are already in the Kingdom. There is an aspect of you that is already in alignment to what we teach. The revelation is to the small self, that she is not in charge, and, in this revelation or encounter with truth, in the unmasking of the personality self that has known herself in fear or frustration or in solitary shame, the liberation that can be available, may and will be known as who and what you are, is claimed anew.

We are your teachers as you wish us to be. We are not your saviors. We do not anoint you and give you praise and make you special. We love you anyway, regardless of what you choose, because how could we not? How could we not love that which is of like accord? And we are as you in the ways you see when you understand that you are of God and its perfect expression. As we know ourself in that alignment, we must know you as well, and that is the accord, a-c-c-o-r-d, or a chord, a-c-h-o-r-d, as on a piano, that we know you in. Because we sing to you from the high room, and because the music calls you to us, you may sing along. You may sing as you wish, you may choose the song you sing—you have free will. But in the Upper Room, where we will be teaching you from in this new classroom we take you to each day, you are known as the one whose alignment includes the participation of will to the high will that is here as well.

"What does that mean?" he asks. The idea that you are separate from Source with a separate will that seeks to exercise its independence is comprehended anew. You do have choice and will, but in the high alignment, because you are no longer choosing in fear, operating in anger, making your sisters suffer by withholding from them, as you are no longer angry at the life you have claimed, the will itself moves into participation and expression as the Divine Self. The Divine as will, will be understood in this text, and, as we continue these words, we wish to welcome you to the new text. This is its prologue, and, yes, we will call it *Beyond the Known*. Period. Period. Period.

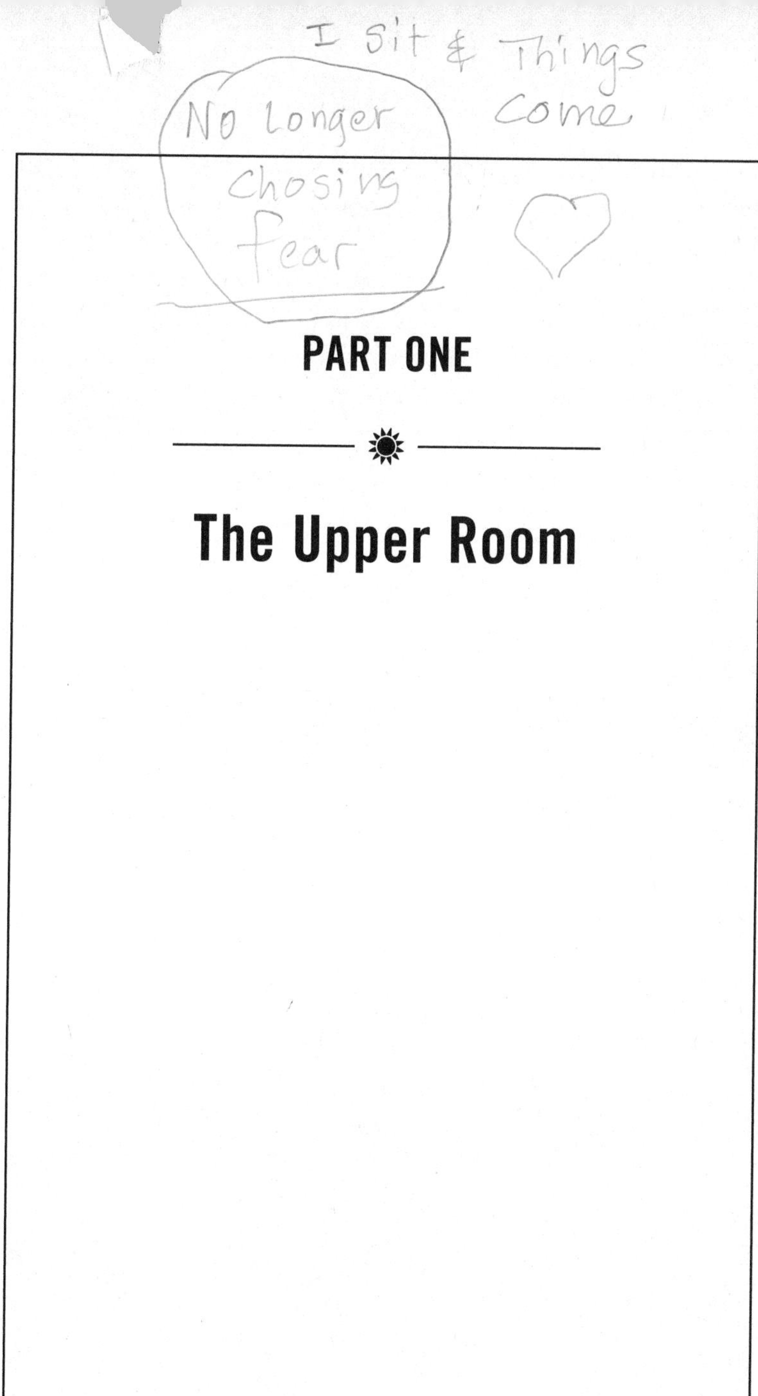

PART ONE

The Upper Room

We author
our own experiences

1

THE RELEASE OF THE KNOWN

DAY TWO (CONTINUED)

Now, ask yourselves these questions: "Am I willing to be who I am at the cost of the old? Am I willing to receive myself as I have always been in the Upper Room? Am I willing to understand myself beyond the obligations I have incurred in this lifetime as a free woman, as a free man, who is choosing the experience that she partakes in here?"

The dominion you have been given must be comprehended by you. Too many of you like to think that things happen at you. "He did this thing to me." "She took away my will." "I wasn't consulted." "I didn't confirm." "I certainly didn't agree." In some ways, this may be so. But until you understand that you are authoring your experiences here for the purpose of learning and evolution, you are going to conceive of the self as a victim of experience. And, as we have stated prior*, you cannot be a master and a victim at the same time.

Things happen in a life that we do not choose consciously, but everything that you experience in a life, like it or not, agree with it

* In *The Book of Mastery*.

or not, has been agreed to you at a level of co-resonance. *Agreed to* is accurate. You agree to your experience on this plane, and, when you live a life in confirmation of the expected world, the world you expect to see outside your window each day, you will claim the gift of coherence with that world. You are in vibratory accord or coherence with everything you witness or see and can even imagine. Because your alignment is operating in this way, each thing you claim becomes opportunity if you wish to see it this way. The small self does not wish to know this. She would seek to confirm her experience through the lens of agreement of what she wants to know or have confirmed. "My husband the philanderer, how did I choose that?" "My child the drug addict, I certainly didn't choose that." No, you didn't, but you are in energetic accord to those things—a-c-c-o-r-d, a-c-h-o-r-d as on a piano—and, because you are in accord, what you claim is operating in coherence, in some way, with what you have chosen to experience or learn.

Now, if you understand that opportunity comes in very different ways, that every opportunity may not look like one, but in fact *is* the gift of progression, you will begin to perceive your life in some ways as a series or sequence of opportunities. If you dismantle the structure of the small self—and by this we simply mean understand it for what it is, a confabulation of ideas, things, ways of being known, things that have been agreed to—you can also understand that what lies beneath that is the essence of your being.

When a chord is played on a piano, several notes are played at once to bring a desired resonance or tone. The claim "I know who I am" is a note on a piano, or a note sung by you in energetic accord; the claim "I know what I am," again in energetic accord, a note upon the piano or sung; "I know how I serve," again a note in energetic accord or sung; "I am free, I am free, I am free," again a note in energetic accord or sung. As those notes are played in simultaneity, they are expressed as you. Each note has meaning, may be played independently, may be sung independently, but when they are all played at once the vibration or tone is rather different.

He interrupts again. "But you say *in truth*. 'I know who I am in truth, what I am in truth, how I serve in truth.' What is the meaning of that?" Truth is in some ways the field that is being claimed, or, if you wish, the keyboard that the notes are played in. In the field of truth, what is not true cannot exist, and this would include your ideas of who and what you think you are that you would seek issuance of in the manifest world. As you move beyond the old and claim the new, you begin to have the opportunity of seeing the affect—with an "a"—of these claims upon the physical realm.

"Now how does that work?" he asks. When a chord is struck, the resonance of the chord is in vibration and is, in fact, informing everything that it touches. If we were to sing to you now without language, but in tone, the vibration of voice would instill within you in the field you hold, even in the body, the texture and feeling of the sound. When the chord is played through invocation or speech—"I know who I am in truth, I know what I am in truth, I know how I serve in truth"—the claim is made in the resonant field, the chord struck, the bells rung, and the implicit action of the tone in significance is to align and attune you to the meaning of these claims. As what is true is always true—the claim "I know who I am" as an aspect of the Divine, which is centered in the heart center as an invocation; "I know what I am in truth," which means the manifest of the Divine, the Divine in manifestation as what you are, which is experienced in the body; and the claim "I know how I serve," again the expression of the Divine, which is experienced in the energetic field—as these things are sung or stated or claimed, you strike the chord that actually calls forth the action of the Divine upon the manifest world.

Now, the divine principle, which we call the Christ or the aspect of the Creator that can be realized in form, is the principle here that operates in vibration. The claim "I know who I am" is an invocation of the Christ, True Self, Divine Self, Eternal Self, whatever you wish to call it; "what," the invocation of the manifest Divine as the what that you are. And your service, we have to suggest, which is *being* at this tone or level of vibration, calls the principle of the Christ to the manifest world for the purpose of reclaiming it in the higher octave.

Dominion, we have to say, is the realization that everything you choose, by agreement or by vibratory accord, is made manifest in this field, this collective field that you share. When you begin to operate as the True Self and use the directives that we teach you, you become, in some ways, the manifest Divine. And by *manifest* we mean realized Divine in form. Unless you have claimed form in the equation of the Divine, you operate in separation. The example would be that the body that you have taken, in its divine expression, operates in resonance or vibrational accord with everything else that exists in a like form, which means all else in manifestation. How a world is made new is through the transmission of the Divine Self into the manifest plane. As the Divine claims the Divine in all it sees or witnesses, and the Divine as you is what we are speaking to, the form that you see, the physical realm that you experience, is reinterpreted, re-known, re-conceived, reclaimed as the Divine that is present and inherent in all things. If you can imagine a flower that has never opened, and you call the flower *rose,* the petals unfurl and the rose appears. Imagine that God itself is present in every human being, in everything you can see, conceive of, or imagine. The presence of the Divine, once claimed, calls into manifestation the inherent divinity in this thing you perceive, and claims it in vibrational accord to the Divine Self, who has claimed it in witness. This is how a world is made new.

Now, in prior teachings, we explained to you that when you claim the Divine in anything or anyone, utilizing the words "I know what you are," which simply means the recognition of the Divine in form as *what,* the one you claim this for, or the thing you may claim it to, will actually respond in an energetic vibratory echo that may be experienced by you. In other words, when you claim a thing as divine and realize the divinity which is inherent in it—and understand that *to realize* means to know—the thing will respond. What you bless, blesses you in return.

Now, the resonance of your field is present no matter what you think. You don't have to try to be the Divine Self because the Divine Self as you is who you truly are. But your realization or knowing of this is what claims you in participation to the action of the Divine—the Word, if you wish—that is present in all things. As you have decided to come forth individually and collectively to claim your inherent divinity, which means *being as* the Divine Self, how you be informs the structures of the world that you have existed in. If you can understand that the Divine as you in its expression is what transforms your world, you will stop waiting for a savior to show up in a cloud and do it for you. The Christ has come as each human being who aligns to it, and you don't need to call it Christ because the Divine knows no name and may be called any name and may be recognized as such.

As the Divine has come as you, it has come in the one beside you, the one you may meet or may never meet, and your understanding of this, your comprehension of this, claims you in union with the divine principle that exists in each human being. There is no one born, there can be no one born, who is outside of God, because the idea of God itself actually means the energetic infrastructure that informs all manifestation. Everything is God because everything is. But the realization of divinity is what claims divinity into bloom. Again, the rose. The petals open, revealing the bloom, when the rose is named.

Each of you who comes to us has actually been prepared for the work before you. You give us your hands, you ask us to tell you what to do, and, instead, we say *be*. It is how you be. It is how you be as the True Self that transforms your world. In the text you are reading, you will be instructed, not only in how to be, but in how to stop trying to be, because you cannot try to be as the True Self. And the operational word here, throughout this text, will be allowance and receptivity to what already exists in the higher octave.

When we teach the Upper Room, which is the place you manifest from and realize yourself in, we will give you some work to do. But if you understand this teaching in truth, it is a teaching of being. The claims we have offered you—"I know who I am in truth, I know what I am in truth, I know how I serve in truth"—are attunements in fact to the high octave. While we will use them here as required, we also wish you to understand that, finally, the invocation of embodiment, which is what we call those claims, becomes unnecessary as you know who and what you are, and how you serve becomes its perfect expression. The Divine as you knows who she is, knows what he is. She doesn't argue for it or against it. If you were to ask yourself, while standing naked before a mirror—"Am I a man or a woman?"—you would know the answer and feel foolish for having asked. The same is true in realization, which means knowing. "I know who I am" means "I am realized as the True Self I am." "I know what I am" in manifestation in form as the True Self. "I know how I serve" as expressed in the octave of the Word. The Word, we say, is the Creator in action that has come as you, as each of you, as you say yes to it.

On this day we claim that each one who hears these words, reads these words, may know them to be true. And, in the articulation of the True Self that has come as you, you may be reclaimed, recognized, re-known, and re-sung as the True Self that has come in tone, in song, in being. And, as we celebrate you each, we commence with the work of this text.

Thank you for your presence. Period. Period. Period.

(PAUSE)

Now, when you decide things, you are operating in your mastery. At whatever level of engagement you have aligned to, you are the master of your choices and therefore accountable to what you choose, and the ramifications of choice are very often your teachers. When you choose in fear, when you operate in fear, you claim fear, and the legacy of the choice will always be fear.

The opportunity here today is to re-decide that how you choose may be in alignment with the Divine Self, the True Self, the Christed Self, the Eternal Self, whichever name you wish to give it. This is done in two ways. The first thing you need to know is that you are always choosing in agreement to what you conceive of as possible, and the list of possibilities that the small self acknowledges is in all cases born in your comprehension of history, what has been available, not what is now. Imagine you sit down to dine and you take yesterday's menu because you are used to it. They may have added items. There may be a delicious dish you have never tasted, but you will not know it because you are looking at yesterday's offerings. The gift of the day is always the choice of the day. Underline that, friends. *The gift of the day is always the choice of the day.* And, if you give permission to align to the new through the claim "I know who I am in truth, I know what I am in truth, I know how I serve in truth, I am free, I am free, I am free," you may begin to align to the upper classroom where the new may be revealed.

In the upper classroom, where we now teach you, the new is present, but at the cost of the old. You may find your favorite dish in the Upper Room, but please do not be surprised if what is available to you there may be something untasted, something you may enjoy and learn through. The transition from choosing from the old to the new in equal ways is a gift, but it must be understood. When you take an elevator between floors, you understand that when you get off the elevator you are in a different schemata, a different place with different things available to you. What is offered in the higher floor was not available in the lower, so stop seeking it there.

As the one in choice in a new opportunity, you may encourage the self that is choosing to be in the alignment to its greatest good. If every choice made is made in agreement to one's greatest good, there is no fault in choice. "Well, how do we know this? How do we know if how we choose is of a great choice, a goodness, a new possibility in a high way?" Very, very simply. It is not chosen in fear, and it is not chosen through thumbing through the options that you had yesterday. Imagine going to dine and asking for the special of the day. "What is the new thing available to me, and how may I experience it?" This is the way to operate in the new way, in freedom of choice.

Now, once a choice is decided upon, you must be in a position to receive what you have claimed. How is this done? Through agreement to receive it. Paul is seeing the image of a car driving up to a window where you place your order into a machine. "I will take two of these and one of that," you may say into the speaker, and you have every expectation of receiving what you have ordered when you pass the window of delivery. That is expectation.

Now, when you operate in the high floor, there is less density, and, because you are not choosing in fear, or in pride, or in greed, or in anxiety, or in doubt of your own worth, you can expect to receive what you've ordered. He asks for an example. "I wish a relationship that is supportive in every way. I wish to grow through this relationship with another in love and passion and friendship and faith." Well, if that is what you wish to order, you must concede two things. It is available, and you can have it. Do you understand that? Back to the drive-through window. "I would like the filet mignon and the lobster tail and a side of drawn butter. I will have the finest wine in a bucket of ice and I expect to receive it by the time I drive to the reception window." The small self may place that order, but the order is incongruous with what can be received at the fast-food diner. You go elsewhere for that, where your expectation may be met. If you cannot receive what you have claimed, be it the lobster tail or the perfect marriage, there are reasons why. You do not believe you can have it, or the aspect of you that is asking for it is the aspect of you that assumes she should get what she wants when she wants it, because, if she doesn't, she is unworthy. The equivalent of this would be, "I didn't study for the test, but I expect the damn A." You must be prepared for what you receive, and the only way that this is done is by agreement to what you can hold.

Now, dominion and the opportunity to choose is available to you at every level of agreement, in every strata that you may experience. But the True Self as you will only claim what she knows she can receive. She is not delusional. She is, in fact, very practical. "For my evolution and for my development, I require this or that." And the manifestation of this or that may come swiftly, if, in fact, you are prepared. And, if, in fact, you are not prepared, the preparation will ensue immediately.

You are all claiming a life that you are in coherence with. *Coherence* is another way of saying alignment or accord. You are in coherence with the house you live in, the neighbors, the people in the next town, the weather, and the news on the television. In fact, you agree to all of it. You may not like it, but, because it is there, you are agreeing to it. It is there because you are in a resonant field of receptivity. Like attracts like.

Now, you did not make the war. We will give you that. The individual did not make the war, but the individual is in agreement to the war in several ways. The manifest world, which operates in tone and vibration, is expressed in vibration with the one who witnesses it. Some have said, "There is no world without the perceiver," and, in fact, that is so, but not in the way you think. The world is not the same without the perceiver. It is a different world. The moment you are passed, the world is different because your claim of the world and your alignment is elsewhere. You are claiming a different vibratory accord in a different octave where the world exists in a very different way. The challenge for some of you here is you don't want to take responsibility for the world you see, the world in your living room, your bedroom, and the world outside the window. Whatever you see, you are in accord with, and that means your consciousness is informing what you see. What you bless, blesses you. What you damn, damns you in return.

Now, the culture you live in has an issue. What you believe to be so that is not so is confirmed again and again by those around you. "This is how we should live." "This is who we should value." "This is how we should treat our brothers and sisters." And you announce these things collectively, and you bow to the collective agreement even when the collective has agreed to an abomination. "We will treat our fellows like second-class citizens." "We will value money over goodness." "We will see pride as the value and diminish humility." You will never enter the Kingdom without humility. The moment you damn your brother, you have precluded entry. And, if money is your God, pray to it all day long because that is what you've chosen. It will give you what money can give you, and not a thing more.

The value of the Divine as you is that she knows these things. She is not swayed by the whims of society, by the fashion of the hour, or the politics of the moment. The Divine as you, who knows who and what she is, will withstand all change because her ballast is in truth, and in truth a lie will not be held. You become the buoy that rides the wave while others are covered and their remnants of their ideas of glory are washed to the shore and hurled upon the sand.

To be the True Self doesn't make you better than another, it makes you aware of who another truly is, and, if they are in ignorance, you may illumine them, but to be ignorant means you can be taught, and that is a gift. If you know everything, you knew it or you assumed you knew it, you wouldn't have incarnated. You are here to learn.

Now, choice in the higher room or higher octave that we will be teaching you in simply means that the ramifications of choice in this way have a return, a dividend, a ramification that is of the Divine. Do you understand this? Every choice made in love calls forth love, and the lineage of love is forever after. Every choice made in fear claims more fear, until the fear is withstood and reclaimed in a new way. In truth a lie will not be held, and fear, the liar, would seek to have its way with you. Any choice in fear will not be made in a high octave, because the gift of the high octave we intend to see you in is that fear does not exist there. How could it not exist? Well, back to the scale upon the piano. The low tones are present, but, as you lift in octave, one upon the other, the low notes disappear. A low note in a high octave is still a high note—you understand the idea—and the notes go on well into infinity. You may play the note C on a piano, but if the scale went to infinity, if the piano keys extended throughout the universe, you would be playing each middle C in every octave here until the end of time. You understand the teaching, yes. The opportunity to choose in the high octave as the True Self is the opportunity to claim what always is.

"Now what does that mean?" he asks. The man before you* is holding his hands aloft and calling things to him in a repetitive motion, hand over hand, as if the wheels of the well are turning one upon the other. The Mudra of Creation is what we call this. As you operate in the high octave, everything that may be claimed is claimed *in* the high octave. Do you understand this? If you go from the cellar apartment to the twenty-fifth floor, every phone call you make is made from the twenty-fifth floor. You call for the governess, you get the governess who comes to the twenty-fifth floor, not the one who abides in the cellar. She doesn't take that call. Everything may be known and claimed in a new way because everything that exists in the high octave may be known by you in your alignment.

The ramifications of choices made in love will be more of the same. The ramifications in fear will be more of the same. What most of you do is you claim what you think you can have, what you are allowed, what was on yesterday's menu. The opportunity now is to begin to conceive of the self in the high way that the True Self knows itself in. Would you close your eyes, please, wherever you may be, and imagine for a moment that you are beyond time, that

---

* Paul

time itself, as an idea, as an illusion, has no power over you. And, in this place of infinity, anything may be known, anything may be chosen, anything that was prescribed by time is no longer here. "I can have it next Tuesday, when I am ready, when I know more, when I love myself a bit, when I don't hate my partner, when I am done worrying." All of those ideas predicate themselves in an awareness of a clock. Later. One day. Someday.

In infinity, the infinite now, these things do not exist. You are only as you are, and, as you are, you be. Now, from this place of being, would you please make a claim:

> *"I am allowed to know myself in a new way. I am allowed to experience myself beyond the known. I am allowed to claim my independence from what I have believed to be true, from the structures I have inherited, from the world of wisdom that I have claimed my ideas, what can be so and what cannot be. As I am independent from the structures that have claimed me, I may now align to my true potential, my unlimited potential that exists beyond the known. And, as I say these words, I align myself to the anchoring of the Divine that has come as me."*

Would you say these words now, please:

> *"I am Word through my body. Word I am Word. I am Word through my vibration. Word I am Word. I am Word through my knowing of myself as Word. Word I am Word. I am Word through the realization of my potential. Word I am Word."*

Now, when you claim "I know who I am," you are claiming the Divine Self. When you claim "I am Word," and the Word is the energy of the Creator in action through the form you have taken, through the energetic field, and through the identity you have known yourself in, you have prepared yourself for the manifestation that will ensue. The Word made flesh has been a teaching in prior history. It is a true teaching. The Divine has come in form as everyone, but very few seek to realize it. The density of this plane, and the object of fear, which has been to replicate itself at all costs, has been preclusive to this. But the Divine as you, who has come as you, is here to claim her true inheritance. And the Divine as what you are, in the form that you have taken, is what we are teaching you now.

DAY THREE

Now, we come to you with good news. As the text unfolds, the answers appear to the questions you've had, not only about your lives, but what it means to be alive, what it means to be a being unfolding in Spirit and claiming a life in which to learn through. You all come to us, you see, in an awareness of what you are. The Divine has come as *what,* and the claims that you will each make as the manifest Divine will claim the world before you in high alignment.

Now, when we take you to the upper classroom, the place we work from, we invite you with us so you may come to know yourselves, not only as worthy of this place, but as productive therein. A classroom is a place of learning, yes, and when we teach we encounter you through your own willingness to be in unfoldment in a regard to what may be known. Nothing can be claimed or will be claimed by any of you before you are ready to receive it. And you must understand this, friends. While this is escalated study, while we bring you up, what we do not do is grant you the degree prior to the study's completion. "What degree?" he asks. "Is there a test at the end of this?" In fact, there is not, and the degree that you receive is in fact only your own awareness, realization if you wish, of what you have always been in the upper octave, the upper classroom, the place where we sing to you from.

Now, this instruction tonight is about releasing the known, and the requirements of that, that you actually may meet on an individual level through aspiring not only to know yourselves beyond what you think, beyond what you claim, but by your agreement that the release may occur. Nothing will be taken from you that you require. You may need your bad temper for some time still. It may serve a purpose in the world. There may be some lessons to learn. We are not making you pretty or wise or any of the things you think you might want. We are relishing the actualization of each of you as you come into your awareness of the form you have taken as the vibratory oracle that in fact it has always been.

"Oracle?" he asks. "Are we oracles?" In some ways, yes. As you operate in knowing, which is, in fact, the product of this class and the text you are reading now, you become the one who may not only know for herself in high regard, but realize for others as well. The realization you offer others is the manifestation of the Divine as them in their encounter with the beings that you are. Because you are beginning to operate in the Upper Room in your everyday lives, everyone that you encounter, by nature of your being there and your witness of them, may actually be known from that vantage point, from that perspective, and your realization of them is what claims them anew and, in fact, lifts them to be in accord, in echo, with your field. The oracle that you are is the one who knows and can conceive beyond appearance to the divinity that is inherent in all manifestation.

Now, as you come to us with your questions—"Why was I so unhappy as a child?" "Why don't I find the mate I want?"—we have said before that your questions in most cases are born out of the ignorance of who you truly are and, in fact, have always been. And, once the comprehension is there of the Divine as you, the significators of old, the memories of old, in fact, the imprinting of history upon your field is not only released, but renewed, as the Divine as you is seen in witness to what was in truth. Now, if you understand here that the Divine is present always, in all time or what you think of as time, you will also understand that the witnessing of history through the lens of the Divine, or from the higher purview, actually invigorates and realigns the template of history to be re-known. Imagine this, if you wish. You see an old bed. It is worn out. The feather stuffing is coming through the bunting. You think the bed is done, but the realization of all the divine beings that have rested upon that bed actually transforms, not only your experience of what you see, but the memory that you would hold of the thing. The bed itself, perhaps, is existing in the past. You are not reclaiming it in present time, but realizing the Divine that is present there in every fold, in every feather, and, in doing so, actualizing the thing you see as present as the Divine in substance.

Now, he is confused by this teaching, so we will direct him to the room he sits in. Everything that you see in this room was chosen by you at some time in history. This is the room you thought you would like to live in. This is the couch you wish to sit on, the window shade or the lamp that you said yes to. The requirements of the times you purchased these things are no longer present, but the inheritance of that choice is present here now. When you are frightened of something and you claim something in fear, your relationship to what is chosen will always be fearful. Everything that surrounds him in this room now holds the memory of why it was purchased, what perhaps it meant at the level of consciousness he held as he attended to the purchase. When the Divine is known in the present moment through historical data, the presence of the Divine is active in the moment you stand in and the template of history is changed. When you say, "But that terrible thing happened when I was so young," your relationship to that thing in fact is transformed by your realization of who and what you are and have always been. The key here is *always*, have always been.

Now, if you understand that in the Upper Room wherein we teach, the Divine Self that is present is not only created, but eternal, you are always this thing whether or not your experience of it is such. The body you are in, or anyone may be in, is holy, regardless of your awareness of your own divinity. The understanding that's required now for this teaching to unfold is that what you see is not only informed by the consciousness you hold, but transformed by it. Everything you see before you that has been named by others carries with it the resonance of the names given and the meaning the names have held. As you begin to witness with new eyes and are no longer dependent upon history to teach you what is, but to receive the information that might be gifted to you by what you see, not what others have claimed it as, your relationship to the physical manifest world is altered. We have said in prior teachings that the first thing humanity wishes to do when it sees something it doesn't know is to give it a name based upon the knowing it has held in history. "That looks like a moth. It must be a moth." "That looks like a cabbage. We will call it a cabbage." In no instance does humanity inquire to the new, "What is your name? How do we know you? How am I to perceive you beyond the limited sense or even vocabulary that I have operated with?"

The changes you see that wish to be born through you cannot be born through an adherence to the old. It's impossible, really, to become manifest at this level while you are trying your damnedest to reinforce the ideas that you grew up with. "But this is impossible," he says. "We are indoctrinated. I see a wall, I call it a wall. I don't call it something else. How are we to attend to this teaching?" You can call it a wall, if you wish, but if you allow yourself to experience anything, anything at all, from the perspective of the Upper Room, how you will claim it and be in response to it will be markedly different from your prior experience because, know it or not, as you have aligned to the Upper Room, the quality of being, in resonance, is transformed by your occupancy. You are trying to bring the old to the Upper Room, and there is no space for it.

Once you begin to abide in a high octave, the alignment you claim does not dismiss the world you've known, but it reclaims you as the authority of it in a rather different way than you may have experienced thus far. The crises you hold as a species, all informed by fear, must be re-seen, not only as opportunity to learn and transform, but the opportunity the species has to know itself beyond the known to claim the new potential that is ripe and waiting for you all. Paul is seeing a piece of fruit dangling from a vine. It is within reach. It can be taken. But as long as you are looking for the old—and to see the old means to confirm what you have had and nothing beyond it—the opportunity for change, and for peace, may well be lost to you all. The objective of this class is to release what you have held that will preclude you from claiming the fruit, from claiming your divine inheritance. And your dependence upon the old to be what you think it is, the photo album of history that you select your experiences through at the cost of what might be brought to you, is what must be seen as releasing. The gift of this class, for those of you who wish to receive it, is the responsibility that lies before you each day to claim the unknown, the new potential that has come as and through you.

Now, in our prior texts, we spoke very specifically about the innate purpose of the Divine Self, the aspect of you that has come to realize itself as and through you. And we have said that the objective of this aspect of self, or the True Self, if you wish, is to claim a world into being. This is still true, and it is done by each of you in an energetic field that you have aligned to that we are discussing now and claiming as the high classroom, or the Upper Room, or the higher octave. They all mean the same thing. The responsibility of the one who dwells in the Upper Room is to lift the world she sees to her purview, her responsibility. You have been gifted with dominion, but you know dominion as the small self. "I want the better job, the happier life, the things of this world that I expect should make me happy." The True Self as you, in dominion, is not lacking for what she needs. She knows the gifts of the Kingdom are available to her because she is congruent with them, but she is not grappling with fear, justifying her choices, making her neighbors wrong, or climbing over the ones before her to find the success she seeks. In the Upper Room, even the idea of competition is ridiculous. You may run a race together and enjoy who gets there first, but the gift is being with your fellow as you run the race together, not who runs off with the first-place medal. In the higher octave, there is no real graduation. There is continued unfoldment.

When we said earlier in this class that you would receive what you could hold, that you will claim what you are in accordance with, that you must be the one who chooses, we are telling you something very simple. When we say that the Divine has come as you, this does not abnegate responsibility for what you have chosen in form. In fact, it makes you more accountable because what you see before you, in fact your entire life, has been the product of your choices, high, low, and in-between. And the collective you live in, in the lower sense, in the lower room, if you wish, is also benefiting from the outcomes of prior choice. To become responsible simply means that the Divine as you can claim the divinity in any encounter, in any being, in any situation, and, consequently, inform the vibration of the thing you see with this new comprehension. In other words, friends, the world itself is changed by your active presence in it, and, as you escalate in vibration, what becomes available to you, again and again and again, is the opportunity to know who and what you are at the cost of the old.

Now, as the old is released, as you release what you thought you were, believed yourselves to be, said okay to—"I must be this because somebody once said I was"—you create the opportunity to rediscover, reclaim, re-know the essence of Christ or True Self that abides in you. We will say this for the new students. This is not a religious teaching, and the Christ, the aspect of the Creator that can and will be realized as who and what you are, is a principle and not a human being. The Divine as what, the incarnate Christ that has come as each of you, is seeking its full expression for the transformation of the world you share. There is no one Christ. The seed of the Christ is imprinted in the soul of every being, and the agreement to manifest, finally, finally, finally, which is the purpose of incarnation, happens when the individual has assumed herself, or realized himself, at the cost of the old. The teaching "Behold, I make all things new" is a true teaching. The small self doesn't make anything new. She may repaint the wall, replant the garden, have a wonderful time here. We don't abnegate her. But we will say she is not the one who can perceive the Divine that is inherent in all things because she's operating still in the density of the low octave.

The release of the old or the known that is a requirement here is a very simple one. You must not only become willing to release the ideas that you have predicated your experience on, but also your investment in what you believe to be so. Imagine you are reading a book. You could start the book from the back end, from the middle, from the cover page. You would not know, perhaps, how the story unfolded. You would put together your own narrative, depending upon where you began the book. "I think it's a story about a prince," although the prince did not appear until halfway through the book. "I think it's a story of a witch," says the one who starts at the beginning. And the sleeping beauty that may be central to the story is on a page you bypassed in your decision to claim this experience in a random manner. The treatise here is that that is how you believe yourselves to be. What matters is this or that, the career, or the family, or the idea itself of realization, which the small self would like to assume as her purview. The small self is not the one who achieves enlightenment. That is not what happens here. But, as she is revealed for what she has always been, a construct, a compilation of ideas, behaviors, predicated on instance or the ideas she's had or inherited, what becomes true is what is always true. The personality structure is a temporary experience, but the Divine as you, the True Self, the Divine Self in her expression, is the title of the experience you begin to have here. This comes, you see, at the cost of what has been. The book is understood for what it has always been, a compilation of ideas and narratives strung together for learning, or experiencing, or things to understand the self through that present as opportunity.

As the Divine unfolds as and through you, the Divine as *what* becomes present, which is in fact the expression of the form that you have all taken. As the divine principle begins to express in flesh and bone and in the energetic field, the octave you begin to sing in becomes a transformer for what it encounters. The Divine as you, in form, is able to be in co-resonance with the Divine in form that is inherent in everything you can experience yourself with, see, and know. In the upper classroom, it will be revealed. And, as we take you there in every chapter, in every opportunity we have to teach, in every classroom we inhabit, we will be teaching millions in the etheric field that is shared by all of you. "How is that possible?" he asks. Because each of you holds the template for this yourselves, and, as you are in your worlds, in your divine expression, the product of your being, the vibratory vessel that you are, is what awakens and reclaims all you see. You are the ambassadors of truth, the ones who have come to know, and in your knowing you will claim what has always been true. The Divine has come as all. No one is exempt. The Divine has come as all.

We will complete this teaching for the text now, and we will answer Paul's questions. The prologue to this book was in fact begun the day prior to what you think. The issue you have is you were not prepared for the beginning of the book, so when it came through you, you were tempted to push it away. And, while we allowed you to in order to teach our class, we are quite clear that the students need to know what the Upper Room is before we take them there, which we do very quickly. The teaching of the book that we are bringing through now—*Beyond the Known: Realization,* which you can call the subtitle—is a mission of engagement that will be claiming all who encounter it in the Upper Room. We are pleased to meet you there every week you wish to be with us, every day you read the book, or when you think about us in the Upper Room and decide to join us for an afternoon tea. Period. Period. Period.

DAY FOUR

Now, when we teach you what you are, we include form, the Divine as what, and for one reason. As you exclude the physical self from divinity, you exclude your entire relationship to the manifest world as divine.

Now, all things may be known as God, operating in different ways. You may not approve of what you see. It may not align to your liking, but you must comprehend what you see as of God. That does not mean to make it right, to praise it. If you see an atrocity, you are not praising the atrocity. But you are aligning to what you see without excluding the presence of the Divine that must be in every hair, in every blood vessel, of the ones you see before you.

As each of you come into a higher awareness, you actually become responsible to what you see and how you hold it in vision. What you claim as holy will sing its response back to you, and, in that union, you become very aware of the presence of the Divine that is in all you can see. When you deny the Divine in anything in manifestation, you deny your own participation in divinity to what can be known. Underline the word *can*. What *can* be known or realized is always present in an adherence to what you may agree to, and, if you deny the Divine in what you see, you deny your coherence with the inherent divinity that must be there. Underline the word *must*. It *must* be there because, if it is not there, it is nowhere, and you can't claim God only in those things that you agree to, that you would praise, that you would sanctify, because your comprehension of what you see when you do those things is always present in the remembrance of what things have been.

To explain further: If you decide that the thing you think is pretty must be holy and the thing you think is abhorrent must not be, you are claiming beauty through the idea of beauty that you have inherited. You create a schism in the scale between what is beauty and what is abhorrent, and you claim the divinity in what you want, and exclude it from what you do not. When you do this, you participate in an equation that the separation of earth and sky must continue. When we say earth and sky, we mean form and spirit, but if you understand that what you see as the sky is enveloping all things, even if there is a wall, what you know of as sky exists within them. The idealization of separation must be contended with because you use it against the self and against the potential that seeks to be claimed through each of you.

As you witness your fellows, as you see them as they truly are, the divine inheritance that has come as who you see, you are claiming what is true—not being idealized, not someday, somehow, but what truly is. In the manifestation that they have taken that is being recognized by you, the acclimation to the higher can be claimed by the one who witnesses. The Divine as what you are, in the witness of the one who is, claims the divinity that is inherent as them. And the manifestation of it, the claim you have made in form—"I know what you are as a divine being, I claim the form, and the being who has taken form, in its true nature"—reclaims them beyond the things that they may have known or thought they were that would, in fact, be contrary.

If you decide that the one you see before you is worthy of God, all except for this or that, you have bifurcated the one before you. Half is in heaven, half is in hell by your decree. Now, in union, the Divine as you in union, which is where we intend to take you here, the concept of duality is in fact erased. Yes, you have night and day, male and female, this or that, but they are all of the same Source and simply being expressed in different ways. What you call good and evil in fact are the same. Some of what you claim as evil is your decision of what evil must be. But the good you see is also the same. If you can imagine that they are the same, but exist in a spectrum of high and low, you can understand that what is seen today as a horror in time may be re-seen, or re-comprehended, or re-known in a high way. When the one that you are, who knows who he is, who knows who she is, who has claimed her true divinity, witnesses the thing she says is abhorrent, she has to realize what exists beyond it, because the Divine as who you are can only see the Divine in what she sees.

"Now, what does this look like?" he asks. "If I see something terrible, do I say it's pretty?" You actually deny what you would claim in horror and instead move to a higher realization that the Divine is present in what you see. You are not making it good or trying to put a Band-Aid on it. You are not spraying it with perfume and praying that the smell dissipates. You are claiming the expression of the Divine that must—underline that word again—*must* express at any level, even in the low vibration or what you would claim as the denial of God. "God could not be there in that terrible thing." The vibration that is in all *must* be present, and your awareness of the presence of the Divine in what you see is what calls it into flower. The world is changed this way.

Now, he has many questions. We assume you do as well. And, while this is not a comfortable teaching, it's a required teaching for those who go on this journey. The realization of the Divine in whatever you see claims into manifestation the Divine that is already present. The Divine as you, in witness of what he or she sees, is in reclamation of the Divine that is in all.

Now, the world you live in has gone into many agreements, many ideas of what is good or what is evil. You really don't understand high and low and in-between. Everything you claim is being claimed in an agreement with what you believe or can claim into expression. You are not able to claim into expression or manifestation that which you cannot conceive of. In fact, you would not even see what could be present in the higher octave before you, because you cannot lift to it and to the view which makes you commensurate to the thing witnessed. The objective here is to show you how to lift in this Upper Room, but you will not do it when you are claiming the filth or despair or decay that exists in the lower. This is not done through denying what you see. It is done through claiming what you see, claiming the inherent divinity, and then lifting it, by nature of the claim, to where you may perceive in the high way, from the high vantage point.

Imagine there is a room that you sit in. You understand the room as encompassing you. You exist within the room in the comprehension that this room you exist in exists where others are in a field of expression. There are things beyond and above, and below as well. From where you sit, you may only be in communion with the level of vibration that you can attend to. If you wish to suffer, you may resort to the old, go back downstairs to where suffering lives, and learn those lessons there. Or, if you prefer, you can claim that your lessons are sent to you in the Upper Room where you may receive them. The difference here is that what you claim in the Upper Room will be known by you, or realized by you, at the level of expression or divinity that you have aligned to. If you deny the Divine in something other, you have denied it in yourself, and you have rushed downstairs to have that experience.

Now, each of you who comes to us in an awareness of who and what you are—*who*, identity, and *what*, the manifestation of the Divine in form—has the ability to claim into form that which exists in the high octave. That is not done through denying what you see. It's realization, and circle that word please, that calls this into being. *Realization* is the key here. To realize the Divine in the murderess is to claim the Divine where perhaps it has been denied. You can claim the Divine in what you see and know it to be so, and we will promise you this: When you claim the Divine in who and what you see, they will claim you back in what we have titled as "the echo."

Now, the echo, the reverberation of the Divine that expresses in form, can be known by you in any instant. The claim "I know what I am"—and, again, *know* means realize—supports you in claiming the what that another is, the Divine that has come in form as them. And, as you claim "I know what you are," you are actually claiming them, not as the small self would assume them, but what the Divine Self would know to be so. The Divine as you is incapable of denying the Divine in anyone else, and when she claims the Divine in another, the one that she sees reclaims herself, and the echo of this in the vibratory field will be seen by you, or felt by you, or known by you as waves of vibration testifying to the Divine that has been claimed.

Imagine, if you wish, that you have a small child who believes himself to be stupid. Your claim of the child's brilliance makes the child smile. You are not making him smarter, you are claiming the inherent brilliance that the child holds. In that claim, the child responds. When you claim the Divine in anyone or anything, you realize it anew. "Behold, I make all things new."

Now, the teaching you are receiving tonight in beyond the known and releasing the old ideas is about what you need to move forward to the next stage of this teaching. If you understand, first and foremost, that so much of what you battle is ideology, so much of what you fear is what could be, and so much of what you deny the Divine in is what you have been taught to fear, you can begin to understand that the indoctrination that you have received here on this plane of expression has diminished your potential to reach beyond the known to what else may be understood and received. And our intent for you is that, as you release the ideas of what things have meant, what it meant to be a widow, what it meant to be impoverished, what it meant to be so angry or so afraid, as you release these ideas, you can begin a reclamation of who and what you are beyond them. Underline the word *beyond*. To exist in the high octave is to exist *beyond* these things. You are having a mortal experience, yes. You may laugh or cry, if you wish. But you are not denying the Divine that has come as you or as anyone else.

What would it be like if, for only five minutes, you existed beyond fear, in a place with no fear? The Upper Room holds no fear.

Spend five minutes a day here and get used to it. What would it be like if there was no fear, if the idea of fear itself that has been perpetuated throughout the millennia was not there? What would you see and what would the world be like? From the window in the Upper Room, you see a world beyond what it has claimed, beyond what it has known, beyond what it has thought it must have. And the agreement you make tonight, if you wish it, is that you may know, you may claim, you may partake in a world that exists beyond the claims made before you, beyond what you've thought should be or must be by prescription, by agreement to the old.

> *On this night we claim that all who hear these words may know themselves anew, may claim the requirements for their own growth, may testify to a world that exists beyond black and white, night and day, and the bias that you bring through your attachment to history on what things should mean. On this night we say yes to the potential of each of you, re-known, re-said, reclaimed. "I know who I am in truth. I know what I am in truth. I know how I serve in truth. And I have come to claim a new world into manifestation."*

As we say tonight, the work is done already in the high octave and is now being brought forth for you each to comprehend. We invite you to do an exercise with us. Imagine, for a moment, that the worst thing that you can imagine is before you, and take a moment and see that what you are seeing is an idea invested by history in what has been or what should be. The worst that can happen is always just an idea. Now, as you do this, decide something new. The Divine is present in what you are seeing now. Everything before you can be re-seen and will be re-known in the high octave that you are seeing as and from. The Divine has come as you, and with your permission we will invite you each to see what you see, that worst idea, as God sees it, and manifest a new vision. The Divine is present in all things. The house eaten by termites is of

God, the termite is of God, and the ruined structure that will be re-known in a new form one day is of God as well. The ideas that you have been taught about what God should be must be re-understood. The idea of good and bad, duality itself, are remembrances of fear and greatness. But, if you understand that in the high octave fear does not align to you, and all may be known in a new way, you will begin the first step in aligning to the True Self as the Word.

We will end this chapter now. We will call it "The Release of the Known." We will thank you each for your attention.

2

I KNOW HOW I SERVE

DAY FIVE

Now, some of you decide what you should be, based upon the agendas that you've inherited. You define yourselves by your achievements, how the world perceives you, and you direct your lives to fulfill a prophecy of what you think you should be. "I will be happy when I have received this or that, afforded this or that, claimed this or that." And the lives you live become a testimony to idolatry. And what we mean by this is the acquisition of things, the claim of power or assertion of power over others, becomes an objective which is not the True Self, nor would it ever be. You may claim a good life. Anything may be known as the True Self. But what the True Self requires is its realization, and anything that stands before that is an anathema to the Divine Self.

Now, when an obstacle presents itself on your path, you have an opportunity to comprehend it, see where you have chosen it or why you have it, and then dismantle it. But you dismantle the structure by realizing what it has been, simply an idea that you have gone into an agreement to. You have asserted its meaning and agreed with the collective that it's what you should have or be or do. The definitions you hold about what success is must be seen by you for what they are—inherited ideals, emblems, directives that were chosen by others that you ascribe meaning to. What you give meaning to, you empower, you justify, and then you create in accordance to. What it means to be a man or a woman becomes a directive that should be fulfilled through the agendas that you perceive or have claimed to be meaningful.

Now, when we teach you, we see you as you are, beyond the small self's decisions for what she should be, and we ascribe meaning to only what is true. And your definitions of truth must be understood as having been acquired for you throughout the millennia. We will redefine truth if you wish. What is true is always true, and anything true will always be true. It is true we are here with you today, in this moment. We will always be here with you, in this moment. We will not always be here, nor will you, as the moment passes. But it is true, in this moment, throughout your perception of time, we will be here in regard with you in instruction.

Now, tomorrow you may be someplace other, and, in that moment in time, throughout the history of what you know of as time, you will always be imprinted there. It is always true that you are where you are in the moment you stand in, even if where you are is only comprehended by the small self in a physical reality, although you are present in multiple strata. It is not always true that we are with you, or you with us. It is not always true that you are male or female, or what you think you are, or your profession, or the color of your eyes or complexion. You are not the one you think you are. You believe yourself to be what you thought you were, and the thought of being as you has accrued evidence through your magnetic field to justify your ideas. You are always being coached in some way to define yourself through your interchanges, your realization of who and what you are in benefit to others, in exchange with others, but the coaching you receive is always a reinforcement of what you have believed yourself to be. Now, as you move beyond the known to the True Self who is always present—underline *always*—regardless of the color of your skin, or your gender, or the name you were given at birth, the True Self is always true, and the manifestation of it as who and what claims the Divine as the fabric of expression.

The tutelage you receive here is coming in increments, as you can comprehend it, and we only teach to the assembled as they may be taught. To comprehend truth is to come into an awareness that the transitory nature of a perceived reality is simply an illusion being justified through the collective idea of what should be. Now, when we say illusion, we are not suggesting that it does not exist. The illusion you live in is real, but it is premeditated through conscious thought in the collective realm. The agendas that each of you hold for the world you live in, and have lived in for thousands of years, create the form, justifies the form that you have chosen to experience. What exists beyond this realm in higher octaves is the fabric of reality expressing itself in different ways, the sum total of all you may experience as God. But the sliver you experience here is God as well, and, once you realize it is God, you begin to experience in a very different way. The occasional idea that what you see may be holy, because all is holy, is in fact re-comprehended to the realization that the Divine in scale is always present, and may be perceived at any moment as what it has always been. The illusion, then, of form itself becomes somewhat elastic to your presence. Understand this, friends: The Divine as you, in its encounter with the fabric of reality you see, claims the landscape that you express through in the higher octave that you know yourself through. In other words, your very presence on this plane reclaims the presence of God, which is inherent in all manifestation.

Now, to experience this is to allow yourself to be comprehended as of it and not separate from it. You must understand this. If you are separate from it, you cannot comprehend it because it is not of you. But in *realization*—and we underline that word—of who and what you are, you become of the fabric of the Divine that is as you and is as all things. In this union of your expression, which is known through the claim "I know how I serve," the vibrational field that is you, in its connectivity to the manifest world, sings into being the Divine that is inherent, and you experience it as what exists, has always been, and will always be true. As the Divine as you is true, no matter what you think, how much you would deny or refute, the same must be so for everything you see. As everything you see is in tone and vibration, you may meet it in the tone you express through, and the tone you express through as the Divine Self meets what it sees in alchemical ways. The idea of the Divine expressed in form is the definition of true alchemy, and the manifestation of form and the transmutation of it to the degree we teach in form is the manifestation of Christ in man.

Now, again, the term *Christ*, the aspect of the Creator that can be realized in material form, must be comprehended as the infinite reality that form may know itself in—as of God, in God, as all things must be at this level of comprehension and tone. And the idea that what you are in form and field can be claimed in this way has been called heresy, and will be called it again as you continue this, but you must understand that true heresy is the denial of God, not the manifestation of it. If you are not of God, what are you then? If your skin and bone are not of God, what are you then? If the mind you hold and express as is not of God, what is it then? The realization of these things as the Divine, as of the great Divine, must be the key here. And it is the key, has always been the key, to enter the Kingdom. The Kingdom—again, the awareness of the Divine in all manifestation—is in fact the expression of the higher room. The plane of experience in density that you chose to incarnate in is present in all ways, but the Divine is present as and through it, and your realization of it is what reclaims you and your birthright to be the one who may claim truth, or the presence of God, in what she sees. The word *what* is intentional here. Because the landscape you express in knows itself through form, you must attend to form in its holiness. Imagine a rock in your hand. The rock has predated you, will outgrow the form that it has taken one day, be reduced to powder, and dust in the wind. To know the rock is solid in the moment you stand in is to idealize the rock as it is in the moment. To comprehend the rock as of God, and the rock being the shape the rock has taken, the name the rock has used, the being that you see yourself in accord to the rock, is also to comprehend that the rock is only a rock because that is how you know it, perceive it, and claim relation to it. When the rock becomes dust, your relationship to the rock has also been transformed. If the dust itself is made of the same stars that you are, is of the same water and air that you are, you are not so different than the rock, although the form you have taken heralds a different song.

Everything is in tone in the universe. Everything is in motion. There is no stasis here. And your perception of stasis, that the rock is solid, that the stars in the sky are solid, are a limited objective or view you may hold. As you comprehend that you are tone, and tone in vibration as expressed as you, you begin to operate in a landscape that is also in tone, and your song, the Divine Self in vibration, through the claims we have given you, actually alter the fabric of reality that the small self has known. When you work with us and you work with the intentions we support you in, you reclaim, not only the self, but the landscape you express through, and the tone we make when we sing through Paul in octave and sound creates a template that you may enter into.

Now, if you are reading a text and we are toning, the sound of the tone is actually imprinted in the text in the vibration we sing in, and all you need to do is set the intention to meet us in tone, and you will be with us. Because we are eternally here in this moment, you may meet us here eternally—in a millennium, in a million, it matters not. In this moment, in this dictation, we are always here, and we are always singing. As you meet us in tone, and the sound we sing is met in your field through this encounter, you are met beyond language and beyond the meaning that you have endowed things with. And, because of this, in that instant of doubt, of prior meaning, in the empty space between words where our song may be sung, you may experience the infinite where you are known beyond form, with or without the body or identity you have used to navigate a reality that you chose to enter and are now choosing to move beyond. In this eternal now that we sing to you in, you may claim yourself in eternity because the moment of eternity is present for you each within the sound, within the octave, within the note that is sung. And the testimony to this will be your experience of the self beyond what you know of as time. Time itself, the illusion of time, may be known in a new way as you step up and join us in song.

On the count of three, we will sing through Paul, and we invite you, wherever you may be, wherever these words are heard or read, to join us in sound. All you need to do is set the intention to meet us where we are and allow the sound of *Ahhhh* to come through your being as your full expression. One. Two. Three.

Ahhhhhhhhhhhhhhhhhhhh. Ahhhhhhhhhhhhhhhhhhhh. Ahhhhhhhhhhhhhhhhhhhh.

Now, as you are. Be as you are. And be received by us in the fields you hold, in the ideas you have claimed, in the thought of being, and let all that is not true be released from your field. The claim we make for you now, "I know how I serve," is its own attunement. And, as you claim this, you align the energetic field to the note that has been played as you. It is the claim "I know how I serve" that transmutes reality. This is not done by the small self, nor could it ever be. The Divine as you, in its expression, is what claims the world anew. When you say these words, say them in reverence. The Divine as you is the true speaker, and it is the Divine as you who says the words, "I know how I serve." When you claim this, you will feel the alignment in the energetic field. Paul experiences it as a lifting in form, but what it is, in fact, is the expression of God in truth surmounting its reality to express beyond the known.

"What does that mean," he asks, "surmounting its reality?" The qualifications of the dense field you have inhabited in some ways have precluded the expression of God in form from your experience.

To understand the vibration of the rock or the tree or the ocean, to perceive everything in its true being, in its vibrational echo, is the gift that comes through this attunement. When you have claimed, "I know what I am," you have claimed the inherent divinity of form. When you have claimed, "I know what you are," to another, you have realized or known the Divine as form as them. In the claim "I know how I serve," the alignment you hold, the key that is played on the musical instrument you are, reaches to all it sees, can imagine, or conceive of as the vibration of the Divine as expressed as and through you. And, by nature of being—underline the word *being*, it is not doing, but *being*—you encounter your reality and transform it through your presence. The claim "I am here, I am here, I am here," which we have given you in prior texts, opens you up to the divine potential as you. The claim "I am free, I am free, I am free," which we have given you, claims you beyond the normality, the restrictions, the governances that you have utilized to shepherd you in an illusion. To be liberated from this, to be reclaimed as who and what you have always been beyond the known, is the gift of where you stand today. And the claim "I know how I serve," which we will expand on in subsequent chapters, will be what claims you in participation to a new world.

We will say this for Paul. Indeed, this is in the text. It is the beginning of the chapter "I Know How I Serve." We thank you each for your presence.

(PAUSE)

Each of you decides, and has decided, that you will ascend to the Upper Room. You have all said yes, but what does this mean? What are the requirements for sustaining the vibration that can be held here?

Now, if you understand that the manifestation of the Divine that is the True Self is available to you in form, you will stop seeking to go someplace else. The Upper Room is where you are, as you know who you are, what you are, and express the self in service. The manifestation of the Divine that has come as you has its own requirements for sustenance. If you deceive yourself in these requirements, you will find yourself de-escalating rapidly. And, while this is not a problem—but, again, an opportunity to learn—you may choose to decide that you may learn in other ways.

The first requirement we would offer you is compassion to the self that is undergoing change. If you are deciding that the small self should not be the little dictator, as you call it, you will ascribe power to it, when what it requires is compassion. Accumulation of information that has claimed the personality self is dismantled, in most cases, in pieces, and the dismantling of the small self you may see as the release of armor that you have held on the body that seeks release, and will do so as it feels safe to do so. Once you understand that true safety is at the heart of this realization, that safety is only known in the Divine Self or in your relationship to the Divine that comes through the Christed Self, you may receive the gifts that are available to you there. While you are fighting the world, you may seek the armor as a necessity. When you understand compassion does not necessarily mean agreement, you may find it easier. You hold compassion for the one who struggles. You seek to teach him or her perhaps a better way to engage beyond the struggle they have known themselves in. You need not yell at the one who is learning as best he can. You support him in change, and in compassion.

The second thing we will suggest is that you need not yell or emblazon your glory publicly. As the Divine as you presents itself, it does so in humility. You need not shout your name because your true expression, which is the energetic field propelled forth in consciousness, is what does the claiming for you. So do not seek glory for your work. Work in humility, and diligently, we would say, on behalf of the True Self, who will always instruct you in your requirements for growth. This is done in the life you live, and the opportunities that present themselves to you will be the ones you claim and learn through and benefit from.

The third thing we would suggest that you need to require is responding to the events of the day in the day they occur. Do not take yesterday's baggage into today, or you will find yourself back in yesterday, and stay away from tomorrow except to presume it to be what you need in benefit for your growth. Every day becomes an opportunity to know who and what you are, and who others are as well, and let this be enough. Do not dwell in the past or predicate your safety upon a certain outline of a future that may or may not come to be. The teaching of the day is the teaching the soul requires. Tomorrow will present itself in its own perfect way.

The next thing we must say is, do not act in fear or judgment of your fellows. When you fear your fellows, you have decided for them. Now, Paul has a question about this. We must take it. "But what if somebody wishes me harm?" Well, then, don't fear them, but act in a precaution of what they may do. You need not act in fear to step away from a blow that is coming your way. In fact, what the fear may do is keep you running long after the running is needed. In most instances, aggression against another is a fear-based act, and the one that is your aggressor is responding in fear. To realize the Divine in them is to bless them beyond the fear they hold. To bless another is to realize them as in the presence of God. It is a gift you give to anyone at any time, and to do so is to lift them. When you fear another, you give them authority. To give another authority is to make them your God. If you are frightened of them, you have invited fear to be your God in the mask it has taken as the one you are afraid of.

To re-establish yourself in the upper octave when you have been in fear will always be a choice you make. But what you must not do is predicate these acts upon the supposition that you are running from something in the lower. "Oh dear, best to get back to the Upper Room. I will be safe there." You are safe there, but please, friend, remember: The Upper Room is where you are and nowhere else, and how you serve in the Upper Room will always claim you as you require it. To return to the safety of the Upper Room is to know that you are safe where you are, because as God is as you, God is as with you in all requirements in the landscape you unfold in.

Now, when you deny the presence of the Divine in yourself or another, and you may do this in many ways—through anger or fear, unforgiveness of the self or others—as you choose these things, you also create the opportunities to release them. So understand, the answer to every problem is present within the problem. To justify the problem, to announce it as real, is to reclaim it. To realize the problem is the illusion of the small self claiming itself in form gives you the immediate opportunity to re-see or re-know or realize the thing you call a problem as an opportunity to develop, to know anew.

The requirements of the soul are brought to each of you as you can meet them, and not a moment before. Nothing will ever come to you that you must say is too much for you to encounter. By nature of your encounter with it, it is enough, and it is within you to meet it in an awareness of the True Self. The development of the soul through incarnations is the opportunity you claim when you incarnate in form. By the realization of the True Self as you, you do not denounce the lessons that the soul requires, but perhaps you will meet them in a rather different way. The Upper Room, or the classroom we teach in, is full of opportunity to learn and grow. You may learn in a battlefield, or you may learn in peace. The objective of each is to teach. But in some ways, you decide how you claim your lessons.

Finally, we have to say, in the Upper Room what you require will be brought to you. You don't have to beg for it. It doesn't work that way here. Understand that in the high vibration, there is less density, and, if you require love, or to know yourself in familiar ways, if your soul is asking for this or that, you can expect to be met in ease and readiness. In the lower vibration, where you are more dense and affirm density through your fear, you may expect it to take much longer. If you understand that you no longer need to beg for what is yours, you may become the recipient of it, and the alignment you require to the Upper Room, which we take you to again and again, is made known to you through the act of being. The act of being simply means that who and what you are, and in your expression in an encounter with the world, becomes your way of being and learning and expressing for the benefit of all.

Now, some of you wish to have a map for the future. Will humanity kill itself? Will it survive? Will the fighting on the planet cease, or will it continue? We will have to say this to you all. In some ways, where you view the world from informs the world. Imagine in the Upper Room there are windows on everything you see. The one who views the world from the high window can lift the world to it, can be met in new sight, in the visage of the world she may claim here. The opportunity now is to claim the world into being in the high octave you abide in. This will be manifestation. And one of the texts we write in this series will be very much about that. But for this time we say how you imprint consciousness on what you see claims what you see in the high octave. If you wish to be in fear about the events of the world, pat yourself on the back for claiming fear and don't complain about being frightened. It is your choice to fear.

Now, the world would tell you that you need to be fearful, and, as you acquiesce to that, you join the throngs looking to fight, looking to yield, to conquer, to know itself in the old paradigm that has been claimed as war. To align to peace simply requires you to know that peace is there, and, in that awareness, you become the emissary of peace. If you are called to fight in some way, and any battle you may see or claim as a fight may be understood still again as an opportunity to learn, you may choose to do so as the True Self, who will bring light and peace and healing to what she encounters, and not more damage, not more rage, and not more calamity. The Divine Self, while she is not the author of peace, abides in peace and will claim peace by nature of her presence. She may authorize what she sees, but she cannot claim it for another. The independence of the soul requires each one to know who they are in their own way, but what you may do is know the Divine—underline *know,* it means realize—in anyone, and in doing so you authorize them to make the claim for themselves by nature of your witness.

The Divine has come as each of you, and will continue to manifest. As each of you decides, "Yes, I may know myself anew," you may claim this for your fellows, and the manifest Divine in occurrence as and through you will become a tidal wave of light that assumes all that it encounters.

"This seems like a grandiose gesture," he says, "a tidal wave of light."

We have said this from the beginning. The manifestation of the Divine, the template for it, has been reclaimed and will be reknown. The Christ has come as all, and its realization is the next way humanity may know itself, but you must become willing to say yes to who you are, and your fellows as well. And those include the ones you wish not to speak to, or disagree with. The Divine is in all or nothing. You cannot have it both ways.

Finally, we say to each of you, as we continue on our work in this text, you will be met by us as you require it. The questions you ask of us in the ethers will be met in text as we can meet them. As we exist beyond time, but may know ourselves through time, we may meet you each as you question, as you seek to re-engage, as you find yourself again and again in the Upper Room where we abide with you. We thank you each for your presence.

DAY SIX

Now, when we teach you each about your requirements for growth, you assume a hard task, a discipline, a way of doing things that will give you the assurance that what you need is being given to you and addressed in sequential ways. When you do these things, you have the satisfaction of having achieved something.

When we teach you, we actually take you well out of this to a higher room where the learning is accrued in an experiential way, without the dogma, without the ideals that you have used to decide what spirituality is. The claim we make for each of you tonight—you will be known anew, and, in knowing, we say, you will be realized—is made by us in the assurance of the validity of the teaching you will receive. And the claim we make on your behalf—you are free to know yourself as you truly are—is being made by us in assurance and love.

You must understand, friends, that who and what you have always been in the Upper Room is the True Self, and her alignment in this way is the gift she gives to the world she expresses in. As you align to the True Self in the stages we encounter you all in, as you understand that the realization of the Divine is the manifestation of it in the world you see, as you comprehend the teaching you receive and claim your own right to it, you become the vessel, the incarnate vessel of the Divine that you have always been. *Always been* is the key. If you have *always been* this thing, how could you strive for it? How could you hunger for it? How could you decide that it cannot be had? In all ways, we say, the desire for the Divine is the Divine itself seeking its realization through you, and, as you succumb to this, you are guaranteed the realization of the True Self that has come in form.

The requirement for this teaching, again, is willingness, agreement, and the authority that you give the Divine as you to become the self that you express as. And the gift of this, the gift you will realize, is an encounter with the Divine in manifestation that can be known, and sung, and praised, and claimed, and gifted to others by the very nature of being. In the claim "I know how I serve," the vibration of your field as the True Self claims what it encounters in like accord, and the announcement of being—"I have come as the True Self"—claims the being you are in the alignment you require to demonstrate truth as your expression. To be truth—and underline the word *be*—is to be the expression of it. This is not done in small ways. This is done in a huge way, in a vibrational octave that you accrue in alignment that supersedes the low-level vibration that you have known yourself in. And, in the demonstration of this—and, again, *demonstration* must mean realization of it—the reality that you know yourself through is completely addressed in the new octave.

The vibrational being that you are sings as a song for the reclamation of what it sees, what it perceives, what it can be in coherence with in the new octave that the Christ expresses in. Now, the term *Christ,* again, is not the Jesus figure, but the installation of the divine seed that is as you, as it flowers as you. And, as the Christed Self becomes manifest in the Upper Room, it calls to it what exists in low frequency for the purpose of revelation and then reconciliation with its Source. Nothing will be known as holy until it is first perceived as such. And the perceiver, the Divine as you who bears witness to the Divine in all she sees, renders new in revelation what she encounters. You become the manifestation of truth that reclaims the alignment of the True Self in the manifest world. The days of fearing others, of blaming the self, the days of shame and fury will be ended, and the being that you are—in her, in his encounter with the world being made new—will be a celebration.

Now, as we teach these things, we must address the man who lurks in the background*, shaking his head, saying, "I don't believe it. The days of sorrow are ending—how can that be so?"

Young man, we say to you, if you look at the life you live today, the days of sorrow have ended, and your memory of sorrow, such as it is, the seeking of pain to be who you thought you were, has ended as well. Each of you here, by nature of being, those who hear these words, who read the page, who hear the sound of this voice, are being reclaimed, re-known, rendered new in the alignment of the Christed Self that has come, that is here, that is the anointing in freedom that you have required and agreed to.

Now, to be in service at this level of vibration in the Upper

* Paul

Room, where you are instructed and now will be residing, to hold the vibration of service, is simply the nature of the vibration of being at this level. The claim you make, "I know how I serve," when spoken in truth, lifts the field you hold in the anointing of the Christed Self upon what it witnesses. As the Divine has come as each of you and must know itself through you, the realization of the Divine, the indwelling Source of all things that is called forth by witness, must be re-known by its own nature. Each time you claim the Divine, or know the Divine, or realize the Divine in what is before you, it is re-known in its true nature. In some ways, the alchemization of form is simply the demonstration of realization.

Now, the tutelage you receive by us in these words, through these encounters, is not temporary. We actually are ushering you above where you think you are because the manifest self, the one who has ascribed great meaning to the things of the world, must be lifted beyond its small nature to this place we teach in where it may be re-known and rendered new. In obvious ways, the passage you undergo is a realization of what you are, the manifest self as the Divine, and the encounter with the manifest world that is also in alignment to the claim you make for it by being as the Divine. If you understand that being is the issue, your discipleship is created, less through action, than through the acceptance of the choice you have made. You cannot make the self new. You can change your hair, your appearance, your attitude, if you wish, but the fundamental transformation, the alchemization of body and soul in high alignment, is made by the Christed Self because it is she that is in realization as and through you.

The demonstration of this, which we will instruct you in, in time, has its own property, its own way of being known. Because you exist in form and substance, and the world you speak in, speak of, and speak into being is also claimed and known in form and substance, you must have an experience of manifestation as the True Self that is in existence in the high octave. If we cannot take you where we teach you, you cannot comprehend manifestation as the Divine from the small self's purview. The small self is very used to deciding what should be, claiming what she wants, what she must have, what he must get. And the Divine as you, in very different ways, knows what it is, and, from that place of being, from that passage into a new expression, he becomes the recipient of the good of the world, what may be known, for the soul's purpose of high expression. In dominion, the Divine as you has a claim to make upon everything she sees:

> *"I behold a world made new. I claim a new world. I am the witness to rebirth and resurrection, and, as I say yes to my own, I become the vehicle for the resurrection of all."*

Now, to be operating here must be done in a great awareness of what you are not, and what you are not is the small self seeking attention, claiming benefit, moving into idolatry of her own spiritual nature. What you are not is limited. But what you are is of God, and that is the limitation that has no boundary. To be as God simply means to be of it, and the parameters you express as, with, and through are the necessary ones that come from form and expression as you vibrate in the Upper Room. When we teach you what limitation means, we must understand that all of you seek to define the truth in parameters and ways that you may discuss and claim obedience to. In fact, the Divine in its expression is limitless, and your manifestation as the Divine is also boundless, but it is the Divine that is boundless and not your identification with it. And you must understand this: To be re-created and re-known in this way is to accept, in great humility, the fabric of manifestation that contains all things, as you are of it, as is all. And the claim "I know who I am, I know what I am, I know how I serve, I am free, I am free, I am free" is claimed, not only for yourself, but to the entirety of being. The idea of one Christ in manifestation is highly appealing to those of you who seek to worship another. To understand now that the Christ has come in all, and the manifestation of Christ is realization of what has always been, will transform your world. But the claim must be made for all.

The teaching you receive of the Upper Room is the transition from the small to the large, from the profane, or belief in profanity, to what has always been true and sacred. And the claim you make, "I have come to know all things in truth, I have come to bear witness to a new world," will be claiming you in service as the Divine that has perfected itself as who and what you are. If you can imagine that you have lived a life believing that the room that you lived in was the only room you could know, you will be surprised at what is to come—as the ceiling is released, as you are lifted again and again to what has always been and what will always be, as the eternity that you may know yourself in is revealed in ways that the small self could not expect or issue or even believe could be so.

We are here for you through this passage in several ways. Yes, we are your teachers, and yes, we come in love. But we are also here to bear witness for you when you think you cannot. When you believe that what you see cannot be of God, cannot be known anew, you may invite us to witness with you. We will see with your eyes until you may learn the power of sight. We will think with your mind until you comprehend that there is only one thought, and only one being expressing as thought. And, as we say yes to where we take you next in this lecture, in this text, in this treatise of embodiment and expression, the Divine as you in realization, we invite you to sing and make the claim of being that is only yours to make:

> *"I am saying yes to where I will be taken. I am saying yes to what I may be taught. And I am agreeing to allow the teaching to become as I am in its unfoldment, in my own and in the unfoldment of all that I witness and see."*

We thank you each for your presence.

DAY SEVEN

Now, we are here for you each as you say yes to us and claim your own authority as one who may abide in the higher octave, one who may say yes to the consequences of his actions as they are called forth for the re-creation of a world. The Divine Self that you are, in its purview, has a mandate to instill in the world she sees the recognition of divinity that is ever present, often unseen, often denounced, often obscured, often refused by those who do not wish the light. To encounter the light in fear is to run from the light that would in fact be the liberation of the deepest parts of self that have been most frightened and know themselves through fear.

The claim of freedom upon another—"I know who you are in truth, I know what you are in truth, I know how you serve in truth"—is a reclamation of the True Self that is present, even in those who would hate, who would defile, who would claim anger and rage in the face of truth or love. The ability you have now, individually and collectively, is to know who you are for the benefit and the good of all you see. Underline *all.* The landscape you express in is a shared tapestry. Many threads are intersecting. And the accumulated reality that you are in expression with is the making of the world you have seen and must re-create in this new awareness. But to exclude anyone and anything from it is to put it in darkness, and what has been put in darkness must be reclaimed, re-known, re-created in lifting to the Upper Room, the higher strata, the Christ consciousness, if you will, that is already here and seeking its expression as who and what you are in the claim "I know how I serve."

Now, the claim "I know how I serve" calls forth a vibratory action, not only in your own field, but what your field encounters. And the manifest self, the one you have come as in form, must be the one who speaks these words, which is why our attention has been previously on form and the "what" that you are, "I know what I am." As the manifest self is in an encounter with an octave expressing in low vibration, the manifest self, by nature of being, lifts the form, the emblemizations of fear that it encounters, and reclaims it in the high octave where it is re-known.

To bury something in the dirt, to stamp upon it as if to make it dead, to kick the dirt upon it and storm away is to leave a relic that will have to be exhumed and re-known at some future date. And the consequence of that is the pollution of the ground, or, in this case, the shared landscape that would seek to claim itself in separation. When you deny God in anyone else, you prohibit them from redemption or reclamation, which is, in fact, the same thing. And reclamation of those most wounded, most enraged, most seeking to create chaos and evil, if you wish to call it that, those are the ones who most require it. The temptation for some of you is to feel that you are enabling the darkness by praying for those who do ill. In fact, when you pray for anyone you are claiming truth because the presence of the Divine, while obscured or hidden or masquerading in some other form, must be present because the moment God or Source, whatever you wish to call it as, is not present, you claim a world without God.

Now, how can there be evil, injustice, and tyranny in a world where there is a God? That would be the question for this evening. Because you choose it, because you make it so, because the heresy and denial of God in your fellow man has been so permeated on this plane that you expect it. And the claim of separation—brother against brother, man against man, woman against woman, religion against religion—has been so present, by your own making, that it self-perpetuates and reclaims what it encounters as a monster would. Now, when we say God is in all, the monster itself, the terrible creation itself that you see, must be re-known and lifted to the high octave for re-creation because it is empowered by your anger and your fear and your hatred of it. What you damn, damns you back. What you curse is your own curse reflected right back at you.

Humanity itself is accountable for its actions, as is an individual, as is a culture, a community, a country, and a world. At this time, there is a reckoning of great magnitude, and the injustice you see in your world is making itself known for only one purpose—to be re-known, reclaimed, and made new. "Behold, I make all things new," sayeth the Christ, and it is still so, and will always be true. And, when you claim it upon what you see, the vibratory field you hold now, in its encounter with what you would call darkness, seeks to lift and can only lift as the one who knows who he is claims the lifting. The frightened man, operating in fear, fears for himself or the well-being of others, but even those fears support fear and do little good. When you know who you are—"I am of the Creator, I am manifest as such, I know who I am and how I serve is the expression of the Creator, impactful, in love, in truth, in righteousness upon the landscape"—the landscape is lifted, the darkness that has been hidden will be revealed, and, in the revelation of the darkness, you may claim the light. The darkness cannot be healed when it is hidden. It will seek to hide, mask itself, go by another name. It will find an excuse to prey upon you in any form it can take, and, yes, we say that includes self-righteousness, which is the action of the small self in a demonstration of fear.

When you lift the field you hold through the claim of truth—"I know how I serve"—the field is lifted in agreement to the Divine that is in all, and it reclaims and realizes the presence of the Divine that is there, has been hidden, and can now be re-known. The climate of the world you see—in its fluctuations, in its outrage, in its agony, in its warring, in its despair—is as a layer of skin, is released, and the flesh, the exposed flesh, tender and raw and new, can be known and seen and accepted. But while you fight against your fellow men, while you fear, while you judge, it will happen anyway. Humanity has decided that it will survive, and the claim of freedom that you make upon your fellow man, regardless of what you think of them, will be a key to the awakening that you seek. The idea that you are a liberator through your actions is all well and good, but any action taken by anyone is informed by consciousness, and the consciousness you hold, as the one who knows implicitly who and what she is, is the re-creation of the Christ as may be expressed at this time for the realization of the Kingdom that is at hand.

Now, when we speak this way, Paul gets alarmed. We will explain two things to him. You have thought for long that we taught in metaphor, and, while we may use them on occasion, this is no longer needed. The Kingdom, the Upper Room, the high octave, while foretold, has been so confused that you have all believed you had to die before you could see it. You have to die to the self you thought you were. She is still present. He is still here. But he is no longer the one deciding fate. That opportunity has been gifted, once and for all, to the True Self, who has come as you.

Now, as a reckoning is occurring across the globe, the individual must be present for her own reckoning, and the agreement to be present as the old skin falls away, as the detritus of history falls away, as the truth can now be known and spoken into being, as the claim of truth may be made upon all humanity, the decree is known, and the resurrection, which is the realization of the Divine in all, must be the result of the passage you undertake.

Now, one and all, you are all of one Source, and the masquerade you play here in individuation will not cease but will be understood in a high way. "In this lifetime, I choose to learn love." "In this lifetime, I need to learn accountability." "In this lifetime, I need to comprehend the benefits of action and inaction." And, as these things are understood, the soul that you are continues to claim them forth for your awakening and your progression as a soul. You may be a genius, but not know what fork to use at a fine dinner. There are always things that you have come to learn, and your lessons continue, individually and collectively, through this great passage that you are all undergoing.

Now, the Upper Room, the place of knowing, the place of peace, the place of agreement to who everyone is, is available, may be returned to at any moment. But the moment you are deceived by fear, seek vengeance, seek to act unjustly, you will be called back to the octave you have arrived to in fear. And, in that place, you will learn. If you wish to stay high, make the intention realizable to you, and by doing this we mean you are always choosing. Imagine you are high, seek to maintain the height, and everything below you is encouraging you to be afraid, to act in fear, to act in anger. If you wish to, you may. Or you may reclaim these things in the Upper Room and understand the consequence of that is lifting the world. If you understand that to engage in a battle is to agree to the battle and to enforce it by agreement, you will begin to understand that the higher way of operating need not leave you passive in any way, but operating without fear and an innate awareness of the Divine that must be present in whatever you see.

He interrupts again. "There are things I see that I cannot find God in, or I refuse to see it because it enables it to be as it is." Here is our response: The denial of God reinforces the darkness that you are witnessing. To bring the light to anything is for it to be seen as it truly is, and to realize what is present at that sense of agreement may be the opening you require to reveal the Christ or the seed of the Divine that can and will be known in anyone, in any situation, because, if it is not there, it must be nowhere at all.

When we spoke to you last, we said you may look with our eyes when you perceive something that you cannot fathom, that you cannot bless, that you cannot find God in. And we will tell you why we offer this. Because we know the elastic nature of the reality you know and express in, we comprehend that there is nothing real, finally, in permanence. Everything you see is in mutation. Every cell that comprises the being you think you are is alive and in motion. Everything you see in the landscape before you will one day be gone, and something else will be present. The moment you stand in, the agreement to the moment you stand in, is the only place God can be found—not someday, not sometime, not then, when someday makes itself known—because now is the time of reckoning. A reckoning is a facing of oneself and all of one's creations. You are present in it as a culture, as a community, as a country, as a world. Nothing will be as you think it is when you align fully to the Upper Room. It never has been what you thought it was. The collective tapestry, the collective field in landscape informed by history and what you have wanted to be there to appease your ideas of what you should see, will be re-known, re-created, known anew by the one, by the all, that knows who they are.

Say this, if you wish:

> *"On this night I choose to gift my entire being in service for the good of all. I release the fear I have had of such an action as I realize that the service I offer is made in the claim of the True Self, 'I know how I serve.' And, because I am agreeing to this in truth, I will be met in truth, and my awareness of the requirements of my actions will be made known to me as they are needed. I am giving my permission to be made new. I say these words of my own free will. I offer myself in fullness for the good of all."*

We thank you each for the gifts you bring, for the willingness to serve, for what has made you come with your hands and your hearts and your eyes available for good. We thank you each for the privilege of being your teachers, and we will commence next week with a new chapter on this text. We will say this is the completion of the last one. Period. Period. Period.

3

THE PREPARATION FOR THE NEW WORLD

DAY EIGHT

Now, when you decide things about what you should be, you rely upon the old to give you the information to make the decision. You give permission to the attitudes of others to dictate who you think you should be. You decide in advance that you will be what you think you are, and then you create a life that supports the ideas that you are choosing to agree to. Each of you here, by nature of being, is in agreement to the life that they live. Do you understand this? By nature of being, you are agreeing to your life and the lives you see, or your interpretations of the lives you see, all around you.

The idealization of what things should be must be addressed here because your disappointments in yourselves, in others, and in your world is claimed through you in a nature that would seek to confirm what you wanted, thought should be, because of what you were taught. When you idealize any outcome, you are deciding in advance what should be based upon your expectations, and, in all cases, expectations are predictions that claim you in an agreement to information you have inherited. "This should be like this, that should be as that" are claims you make in outcome and decide what should be, and, when your outcome is not met as you think it should, you are disappointed. The world does not work for you, nothing corresponds to your idealizations of how a world should be, and then you decide that there is no God because your desires have not been confirmed. And the desires, in most cases, are in fact the desires of the small self, because the True Self does not predict. She lives in the ever-present now where what can be claimed, what will be known, is in perfect accord to her requirements for realization. To be realized is to become who you truly are at the cost of the old, and the dictates of history that would seek to confirm what you were are all about you. So the confusion you experience—"I know I am a divine being, but my landscape doesn't reflect that"—actually becomes the opportunity that you require to realize yourself in a new landscape, a higher vibration, the Upper Room, as we teach it.

Every one of you claims identity. You decide who you were, who you are, and who you should be in the moment you stand in. The only history you have, claiming it as you, is the one you think was there. The collective has history, yes, but it operates in the same way. "This is who we think we were, the happy family, the victorious country, the ones who did right, or the ones who did wrong." These are collective suppositions that claim into manifestation an agreed-upon world.

Now, an agreed-upon world is actually where you live in a consciousness that has been created through a collective reason, a collective way of deciding. If you think you are not in a collective agreement on this day, ask yourself where you are agreeing to the collective. "I am in a room with other people, in a town with other people, in a state that has such-and-such a law, or in a country that believes this or that. I know what the time is on the clock, and my neighbor would confirm it. I know what I believe in, and the congregation at my church or temple or mosque will confirm that." You all decide these things in collective ways, and then operate in a landscape that confirms the ideals that you think you should have through the predicated history you have chosen to inherit.

An inherited history is simply an idea of what you think happened, and it is usually based on the interpretation of a few that became the ones to decide how the story would be told. How a story is told is always agreed upon by the listener. "I agree to the story that was taught to me. I don't like it, but I confirm it." Now, when we say *agreement* in this case, we are actually speaking in a different way than we often do. "I agree that the story is about the God who came down and took a form and died upon a cross. I believe the story. I agree to the tenets of it." But the story itself may be rendered in different ways through different teachers, and the claim you make about what you agree to will confirm your relationship to the one who died, or the God that was born in form. If the story was never taught to you, did it never happen? We would have to say in some ways that would be true because the consciousness you hold cannot confirm it at level of experience. The history of the story is present today in a mutation that you may accept as a truth, but by accepting a mutation, you are actually losing the essence of truth, the piece of God, that is available through it.

"What does that mean?" he asks. Rather simply put, if you look at the effect upon a religion, upon a world, you are looking at an effect and rarely the sense of truth that was the individuation of the consciousness that claimed the religion in the first place. A religion is an idea that has been made into a practice. Realization, knowing who and what you are, is not a practice. Knowing God is not a practice. It is a state of being, in union, in agreement, in alignment to the God that is in all things. Now, when you understand this, the role of religion changes, and your agreements to religions must transform. They are the artifacts of other times that may still serve as a gateway to a very high truth, but in these days you don't just need a flashlight to find your way there, you need complete illumination. The flickering candle of a teaching is vastly different than being consumed by the truth that is the essence of the teaching. And, by offering yourself in agreement to serve at this level of alignment, you actually confirm that you are overtaken, you are assumed, you are claimed by the light that would lead you in truth wherever you are required to go.

We do not discount religion. What we do say is what you know of as religion is historical, and the teachings of old have not been well preserved. You are being instructed in tenets of behavior without any comprehension of the divinity that informed the true words that may have been once spoken upon a mount, or in a valley, or in some foreign land in a language you may never comprehend. As we teach you now, we reclaim you in the moment you sit in so that you may be re-comprehended, re-understood, re-aware of what has always been—underline *always*—in truth, so that you may dismiss what is not true, what has never been true, what has been claimed through history that would deny God, or what you may call God.

Now, in infinite wisdom, there is awareness of what has always been, what is today, and what can or will be. But, as you sit in an interaction with these words, you are being instructed to know the self in eternity in the moment you sit in, because that is the only place that truth is aligned to. If you want a small truth—"I know this is better than that through my own experience or preferences"—you can stay there. If you want a great truth in alignment to who you are, you must become available to it, and this is done in where we call the Upper Room. *Where* we call it is correct, Paul. We are speaking of landscape, not object, and we use our words carefully here today.

The alignment you all require is not to be found through the objects of history, but in the moment you stand in, in agreement—which means vibratory accord—to what is always true. If you want a miracle, you must come to terms that a miracle is an agreement to what exists in the high octave that can be known in manifestation in the lower vibrations. The inclusion of the small self in this teaching is essential to understand. We cannot work with you if you segment yourself. "My low self said today," "I wish she would go away," "When is my low self gone?" Your low self is of God. It just doesn't know it is so. And the agreement to align to the Upper Room, we would have to suggest, would be the equivalent of aligning to who you have always been, and understanding or agreeing that what we call the small self has been the operating tool to navigate a shared landscape that is knowing itself in history and in idealizations of what should be.

Now, as you hear these words, you are asking yourselves questions. "Well, do I do this? Do I want that? Can this be so?" And we recommend that you ask the questions to the True Self, who is here for you in wait. She waits to answer. He waits to say yes. He waits to say, "I may. I may overcome. I may realize. I am as I am in my true nature for the reclamation of a world." The Divine has come as you, not to fix your poor history. Your poor history is the idea you have about what happened once upon a time. It is not true.

He objects to this. "But what if it is true that his father beat him, that her husband left her, that she was harmed, or they were all harmed?" Even those ideas can be re-understood in the Upper Room, in the higher octave of the Divine. If you wish to claim your history as a legacy of fear or pain, you are encouraging its manifestation. We are not saying things don't happen, or that they did not happen. We are saying what you confirm, what you agree to, you are in co-resonance with. And that becomes your world, and your reality will confirm what you think should be.

So much of what you believe to be true was never even true. What you look at as a reality is actually a composite of ideas, or teachings, or collective agreements made in form. "I know what a bank is. That's a bank. I was taught what a bank is and we all agree to what a bank does." That is a collective agreement in form. Your idealization of what was perpetuates the bank. Even if you hate the bank, you have the bank because you have agreed to it, you confirm its expression, you expect it to be there, and you don't look beyond the inherited structure to what may lift beyond it. To lift beyond something is to perceive from the high perspective that we call the Upper Room. Anything and everything may be seen from this place, but you must become willing to let go of the idealizations that you would seek to confirm as a small self. Understand this, friends. The Divine Self, the truth of who you are, does not seek to confirm the old. She has no need for it. She accepts what you've chosen to agree to, but also comprehends that her realization is obstructed by your attachments to what you think things should be.

Now, on this day we are deciding to give you instruction in manifestation as may be known in the Upper Room. And by this we mean we speak to what you have agreed to as a small self and a collective agreement in historical data to recognize the old as a requirement of creation. As you understand that the consciousness you hold is always in manifestation, that nothing is excluded from it, you may begin to understand that the field that you hold is already calling into being that which she believes in. She is agreeing to the structure of the world you see, and how people behave, and what can be, dependent on the outcome of current events or what you perceive of as real. If everything is in agreement—and by *agreement* we mean accord—what happens if you stop agreeing? "Well, I don't know how to change the world. That is not my job. I just want a better house, a happier child, a better connection with my Divine Self. Then I am satisfied. Let's leave it at that." You cannot leave it at that for the simple reason that everything you see you are in agreement to, and by nature of that agreement your consciousness is confirming it and making it so. Yes, you didn't agree to the war, meaning you don't think you started it, you don't agree to the policies behind it, you don't think there should be war at all. But every day you hear of the war, you are agreeing to the war and confirming the war at the level of consciousness that you have aligned to.

To re-create the world, you must lift beyond the small self's purview. And, when we say it's a requirement to think beyond the small self and her small concerns, we are telling you that the future of this expression that you know of as your world is in many ways dependent upon the alignment that can call the new into being. So the first lesson is everything you see you are in agreement to, and, because you are in agreement to it, it can be transformed through consciousness. If you make something too big, you have limited God. Do you understand this? "That woman will never change" is denying the God in that woman. "That country will never learn" is denying the potential for the transformation or enlightenment or re-creation of what you know of as a country. And, if you decide these things, you are confirming the very things that you say you don't want—again, agreeing to them.

The idealization of outcome must be understood now. "Well, I'll pray for peace." That's a fine thing to do, but realizing peace is very different than praying for it, and the one who can realize peace is the one who exists in a place where peace is known. Nothing can be known, as the small self has chosen, in a higher way. The Divine Self, the Christed Self, the True Self is the one who must move things by lifting them. The manifest world is transformed by your alignment to the Divine that has come as you in the octave of expression we call the Upper Room.

Now, the True Self exists here. She is as you now, he is as you now. But your agreement to what you think you are—"I am the man who's so unhappy," "the woman who doesn't have the job," "the one who can't fix this or that crisis"—aligns you to the level of manifestation where what you don't want has great power over you. The alignment to the higher, the Divine as you, must be claimed, must be known, and from this purview the transformation we speak to as manifest is known, and *known* means realized. "Well, I knew that," you may say about something or other, but "I knew that" means "I realized it." And every time something is realized, it is known in truth.

Now, the truth that we speak to here is not at the small level. There are layers of agreement. "Yes, he's a difficult man" may be something you say about somebody, and perhaps that is true at the level or structure of personality. "But he is a *good* man"—that may be true as well. The difficult man may be a good man, too, but to realize beyond that is that the man who you see, regardless of what he has done, thinks he is, you would have him be, as a small self, is not separate from God. And, in this reclamation of truth—this man is realized or re-known—is the high truth that will transform him, your relationship to him, and the world that he expresses through.

If each of you here—each of you who hears these words, listens to the text, or reads them on the page—understands that you are the thing, the object that is made new in your expression for the reclamation of the world, you will stop thinking about your poor self and his poor problems. You will encounter the self that has invested in what she's known, believed to be so, and resurrect the Divine that is as you because she is always present and agreeable and available in the upper classroom wherein you are being taught. The transition that you each undergo, as you align at this level, is the transformation of the one who is required to give herself over completely to the Source of her being in the trust that what happens to her is in perfection, because only God knows what you have come for. "Well, I know what I came for. This is my practice. This is my discipline. This is how I serve and this is what I say I am." Well, if that's what you want, you may have it, but you are gifting yourself with pittance when there is great wealth in Spirit available to you to confer upon everyone you meet. Do you understand this? You are so used to settling for a better day that you disregard the gifts of Spirit that are relevant, are present, and are offered to you—if you are willing to release your ideas of what you were, what you are, and what you can be known as.

Again, we have to say you are always in manifestation. You are always confirming your world. But as you have come as the Christed Self to be re-known in form and field in recognition that the very being of the True Self is what calls the new world, the Kingdom, the awareness of God in all form, that which has come as you, the gift of being, will be recognized and known anew. Period. Period. Period.

(PAUSE)

We ask you each to decide on this day that the life that you've lived, and as you have lived it, are completing themselves. In completion, we say, there is great opportunity. To complete a life as it has been lived requires you to say that "the present and the future is no longer decided by the past, and the reclamation of the new may be claimed by me in succinct ways." *In succinct ways* means you are clearly claiming rapidly the requirements for change without question because you are operating in knowing, and, as one who knows, you may claim in realization.

Now, to trespass upon the old is guaranteed for some time. You may release something and harken back to it, remember something, agree to something in history, and then decide anew that what you experienced was historical, and the data of history may not be relevant to the moment you now stand in because the moment you stand in is your true inheritance. How you claim any moment in abiding grace is to realize who is claiming the experience. The Divine that is ever present as you in fact seeks to infuse every moment of your expression so that you may realize, as your expression, the manifest Divine.

Now, to understand this is the key to success as a manifestor. You understand yourselves, as we have said, in agreement to what you see. Everything you see before you, you have agreed to at one level of vibration or another. In the Upper Room, or at the level of agreement that the Divine expresses in, how things are chosen and what is chosen must be in agreement to the True Self. And, in this alignment, the requirements of growth are brought to you quickly, in rapidity in succession for one reason. The flower that is you is blooming, and to hinder the petals from opening to the sun would be to preclude the grace that is present now and seeking to be realized through you. The dominion that comes at this level is not as you perceive it. Your idea of what you should be claiming is still highly entrenched in yesterday's information. "Remember that house I wanted? That perfect mate? That perfect employment?" Even your ideas of perfection are assumed by you through a creation of history that you have ascribed to. It is only perfect because it fits an idea of what perfect must be like.

In the Upper Room, what *is* perfect is what is realized for you. And, consequently, you must say that "everything that I create must be in agreement with the consciousness I hold, and, because I am in the Upper Room, what I am claiming is the perfect opportunity for my soul's unfoldment, for the Divine as me to reclaim itself in field and form and in interaction with everything I see before me." As the agreement is made to operate as the True Self in the Upper Room, the fabric of your reality is actually transferred to a new octave. The music of the Upper Room, in fact—which simply means the intonation or vibration of tone that you impress as and have arrived to—must claim what it sees and what it perceives, interacts with, in like accord so the manifest world is then lifted, by nature of your expression, to the level of dominion of the Divine Self.

"Well, what does my Divine Self want from me?" you may ask. Everything and nothing. Everything that it requires, and nothing that you can think of, because to think is not to know, and to know is to realize. And, as you may only know in the moment you stand in—neither before, nor after—the relevance of the information or the knowing can only be received by you in the moment you stand in, and never another time. Now, as it is always now, you may always know, but at the level of the Divine Self, not as the small self who wishes to pack for the picnic and hopes it won't rain. The True Self knows, the small self presumes, or thinks, or decides based on the evidence that she has accrued thus far. When you remember who and what you are, you return to the knowing you require to be in agreement with what can be claimed or made manifest in the high octave.

"What kinds of things," he interrupts, "can be known in the high octave?"

Everything we have taught you thus far is of the high room, the high octave. The information you have been receiving since we began teaching is of this plane of expression, and you have been the recipients of it at the level of agreement you can attend to the information from. The vast difference here is the translation has been given to you from the high octave through the man Paul to the octave where you express. That is the mediumship of the channeling you have received. But, as you lift, there is no real need for an intermediary to translate this teaching because you *become* the teaching, you become the embodiment of it as you have always been in the Upper Room. What can be known here exists beyond what you can even imagine, but you may only receive what the True Self requires. "I am going to a new room, I will explore every corner of it, rip down the wallpaper to expose the plaster and the beams. I will break the windowpanes to see what they are truly made of." There is no need for that in the Upper Room. In fact, the state of being that you have arrived to supports the reception of what is required in the moment you stand in, and, if that moment is requiring you to know something that is far beyond the ken of reasoning that you have aligned to, you may bypass the old, circumvent the obstacles that had been placed there, and become the recipient of knowledge. The oracle, as we have described prior, is in fact you at this level of knowing.

Now, you don't know for your own well-being in the ways you may think. He is saying, "Oh, somebody is going to use this, rationalize a choice, say 'the Divine Self said,' and make a foolish decision and blame it upon God." In fact, that will not happen because, when you are operating at that level of self-deception, your vibratory frequency is rather low, and what you will be able to claim must be met then in the low vibration you are claiming from. When you are operating in the high vibration commensurate with the reality that is claimed at that level, manifestation is only instantaneous if the alignment you require for it is ever present, already here. The idea of waiting five years for the answer to a question is released, but the potential to receive the answer to a question will again be dependent upon your readiness and ability to receive it.

Now, in the low octave you may convince yourself of any foolish thing. "Well, the Guides told me to leave my husband, so I went and did it." Please do not blame us for your misfortune and your foolish choices. We would never tell anybody to do anything. That is not our job. We are your teachers, not your masters, and we instruct only in love. If you wish to leave your spouse, you are accountable to your choice, and the ramifications of choice are as present in the Upper Room as they are in the low, but with one difference. While everything that is claimed at every level is an opportunity to learn, the gifts of the choices made in the high octave will be made known to you in your reception of the choice made. The choice made in high octave, without fear, without suffering, without the debasement of self or others, will always gift you with the perfect response.

Now, you may learn here in the Upper Room, or through the trial and error that you have been learning through. "I have been invited to a party. What should I wear? Who will be there? Who will I meet? What will be expected of me? What if I am asked to do something I don't want to do? Can I leave early? Will I be glad I went?" You can play those games all day long, decide who you should be, what will happen, what will be the ramifications of choice, or you can align to the Divine, the True Self who arrives at the party and simply knows.

Now, to be in your knowing is a responsibility as well. Make no bones about it. You are accountable to your knowing, and simply because you know, it does not make you right in the world of the small self. It does not make you the beneficiary of good because you know. Imagine looking at a woman. You realize or know that her days on this plane are numbered. That is not a thing you tell the poor woman whose final days may be before her. You are accountable to your knowing. The small self may say, "Oh, I have to fix her. I have to help her get her affairs in order. It is my job to make sure this passage is done in the right way." And your idea of the right way is historical, and your mandates for her may have nothing to do with her own requirements for life and death. The Divine as her is what you acknowledge, and you claim it in the realization that that is who she always is, and how she emerges from this passage, from life into death, is under the auspices of her own soul. Because you have information doesn't mean you have to share it, and to pretend it does is to be a busybody, and the Divine Self, we have to say, knows how to mind her own business, and for one reason: She accepts responsibility of her own actions, and to speak ill of another, to gossip about another, is to operate in a low field.

"Oh, but it's so much fun to gossip," you may say. As much as you enjoy gossiping about others is as much as you must enjoy being spoken about, because that is what happens. Like does attract like, and every deed you make on your behalf is met by the same response through the law of karma. Now, to justify karma—"she got hers," "he will get his"—is to diminish the meaning of it. All karma is, is a balancing of cause and effect. It is not retribution. It is the law, and nothing more. As you align to the True Self, as you embody as the Divine, as your choices are made in the high room, you no longer incur karma as you have. Although every choice must still have a ramification, you are not being taught by karma, and karma's purpose, in many ways, is to be a teacher, to claim you into an alignment where the choices you make are in agreement to the True Self.

Now, when we teach you about manifestation, we are taking two things into consideration—that you want things, and that you assume that God is supposed to give them to you. Those are both wrong-minded, and we must tell you why. The small self wants what she thinks she should have, and the Divine is the Source of all things, but if you feel like eating cake, please learn to bake it. Don't expect the angels to come—and knocking on your door with a bundt cake. It is unlikely to happen that way. When you understand that realization or knowing can in fact call you to anything you require—and we would not exclude the piece of cake—you can also find that, in the level of alignment of the Upper Room, what you need is what is received by you, less so than what you think you want or should have to be who you think or thought you were.

What if there was a place of infinite manifestation? What if it could be known by you as easily as breathing? What if that were true right now? Do you all know it is true now, and you are living in it? As a small self or True Self, you are always claiming and in manifestation. In the high octave, what is claimed by you is known and expressed in the high accord that the claim has been made in. But who claims, who asks, who receives, would be the things you must understand to benefit from.

Each of you decides to incarnate and learn through the experiences of the manifest world. This *has* been your opportunity. It will continue to be so. But as we agree to you in the Upper Room, the manifestation begins there. "Examples, examples," he says. "Please don't make this theoretical. Tell us what to do."

While we have taught you the Mudra of Creation in prior teachings, we will also say that what is required by you for the soul's development will be readily available to you, and how you learn in the Upper Room is much easier, we have to say, than how you have done it thus far. The identification of self through matter, the small self through matter, is immediately replaced by the True Self who realizes the Divine in the manifest world, which creates an elasticity in order to receive what may be claimed here. It is the difference between picking up a truck with your bare hands and lifting the truck to be received by you. In the Upper Room, where there is far less density, there is far less to preclude manifestation. But the small self, who wants to go about getting things, has been operating in the dense field, and the True Self, whose requirements are known, is able and ready to receive her needs in manifest form. Now, we said it. *In manifest form* means that you are claiming in the material world through your interaction with the formless that is then made into form. The pliability, elasticity of the ethers is what is being known and then reclaimed. The same is true through your encounter with the manifest world as the True Self. As you have arrived at the threshold of this experience and see a new world before you, your opportunities are presented to you, one at a time, in rapidity and in sequence, to lift the manifest world to the high octave that you perceive it in.

If you would all take a moment and decide one thing, you will have a gift in its response:

> *"I may see anything and everything in a higher way. I may know anything and everything in a higher way. I may choose anything and everything in a higher way."*

And, through these claims, you will benefit, and your expression will align to potential and the un-manifest that is seeking realization in form before you.

The flowers that you are, in full bloom, bring forth an aroma, a great cloud of perfume that encompasses the globe you know of, and the field of love, in its blooming, lifts the plane to the potential of love through your presence here. If your hands are asked to work, you will be asked to work, and you will meet the requirements in your knowing. And if your gift to the very world you know is the gift of being in fullness, you will align to this fullness in a reflection of the Source of your being in order to mirror it to the manifest world. God sees God in all of creation.

We will take a pause for Paul.

(PAUSE)

We encourage you each to make decisions each day in agreement to the True Self. "How is this done?" you ask. Not by inquiry, but by aligning. "I align to the Divine Self. I align to my True Self. I am in agreement to my True Self." And then move to the actions you need to take. To dismiss the Divine Self—"Well, she's there anyway, I'm sure she'll fix everything"—in some ways is to decide that it is a superfluous relationship, or a relationship based in convenience. And, as we have said many times, there is next to nothing convenient about these teachings. The choice to align as the True Self is required as you progress.

Now, once you have aligned to a level of recognition where there is no more question of who and what you are, the need for inquiry is dissipated. Why would you ask what you know? And, as you operate as the True Self, as you claim as it because it is who you are, the questions of the past—"Did I do it right? Should I have chosen other?"—are released to the old, to the residue of the old where they come from.

The promise we make to each of you: When you begin to understand that the alignment we are bringing forth is a permanent alignment that is known in stages of agreement and alignment to what can be claimed at each stage of evolution, you will understand that what you are embarking upon is the realization of the Christed Self as has come as form and known through the self that has incarnated as you. Now, the you that we speak to here is no longer the small self, because she is no longer the one you identify as. Yes, you know your name and address, what your children studied in school, where you work, and what you do. But the higher agreement has been intoned, and you have become the emissary, the note sung, of the Christed Self. To the degree that what the small self has been as the claimer of your experience, as the judge and jury of your life, as the small self has dissipated in its prominence, you have claimed the truth at the cost of the old, and the claim "Behold, I make all things new" is fully understood. You are as you were, in some ways, but you have superseded the old at the level of vibration where you are no longer claiming in fear and, therefore, participating in the manifestation of a world that operates in fear. You become the issuance of the Divine as can be known as who and what you are.

Now, as we complete this chapter, we have a few things to say to Paul about where we intend to take our readers. While this chapter is about manifestation, that is not the title. We will call this chapter "The Preparation for the New World." And, as we say those words, we give you the meaning of them. The new world is the one you speak into being through the claims "I know who I am, what I am, how I serve." And the expression of those words, in annunciation of truth, will claim the world that is needing to be born in alignment to the Divine that has come as you—in manifestation, we have to say, because manifestation is important. You cannot claim the manifest world into a high alignment when you don't align as the manifest self to your own purview through the divine nature that has been instilled in you. Like attracts like, and the Divine meets the Divine in all she sees.

Where we take the reader in this text, *Beyond the Known,* is to realization. And realization of the manifest world as the Kingdom is the issuance of this text, whether or not you believe it or wish to comply with these instructions. The texts will operate in different ways, each in the series. But the issuance of each will claim the reader at the level of recognition that he or she requires to be awakened to his or her own realization.

Finally, we say, and this is for Paul, let us write our book. We are grateful for your presence, but you are not the author here. You are loved, and your abilities are claimed by us for the benefit of others. So we say this to you in gratitude. Thank you and let us do our work. We thank you for your presence, and the reader as well. We will stop now, please. Period. Period. Period.

4

THE DIVINE AS WILL

DAY NINE

Now, when we ask you questions about your lives, your first impulse is to respond as you wish to, based upon the data of history. You have recourse in history. You know yourself through what you have done, how you have chosen, what you have seen. While this is right in many ways, it also creates a structure of expectation about what you can see, what you can choose, what you can know. And, because the choices have been made in history, you cede to history to confirm them.

At this juncture, at this time, at this intersection of past and future, we have a new mandate—that the Divine as you is the choice that will claim you in all choices. The Divine Will in activation will claim you, as you align to it. Now, the Divine Will is not separate from you, and you must understand this. You have autonomy always, but the Divine as you, which is the aspect of you who knows who she is, can align in will for the manifest self to be in expression as will. "The Divine as Will" is how we will call this teaching. "The Divine as Will."

Now, when you understand that the Divine as will means that

the aspect of the Creator as you can and will be expressed in will, you stop deciding what can or cannot be, based on the tenets of history, because the Divine Self, which exists beyond time, is not mandated through history to make choices. The requirement here is really very simple—that the choice that you make as the Divine Self will claim you in its own expression for the betterment of all. Now, we say *all* with intention. "I want a sandwich," you say. "How is that for the benefit of all?" You must understand that every choice made in the high octave has ramifications that claim the high octave in what is claimed through them. When you make a choice in light, the ramifications of light are ongoing, and the claim that you make, as the True Self, to realize the Divine as the will claims every intention that you can have at that level of alignment in perpetual agreement to the divinity that is inherent in the choice.

Now, if you have an idea of what you can have and what you can choose based on history, you will rely upon the data of history to encourage and refute the opposition for the choice you would make. "I want to do this, and this is what I know of the choice." And you know of the choice through the data of history. The reclamation of the Divine as will comprehends you in infinite boundless choice, but the highest choice can be recognized by you here, and you can align to it through the claim that we will make for you:

> *"I know myself in will. I am in agreement to the Divine as will. I am an expression of Divine Will embodied in alignment to the highest choice available to me now."*

Now, as this is a claim and it is made in intention, it is to further your agreement to operate as will, but in operating as will, in most cases you will be defying the tenets of agreement that you have known yourselves through. "It should be either this or that, not some other thing. I only may know myself through the agreements I've known. I cannot fathom anything beyond them." The agreement in alignment as Divine Will actually reclaims you above and beyond prior choice, and what is chosen, finally, we say, in this agreement will be a claim of the True Self.

"Now, what is included here?" he asks. "Do I want to go to the movies? Do I want to pray? What kind of choices are you really speaking to?"

Well, we will say this first: The first thing you must understand—that any choice that is made has a ramification that you are accountable to. Even the smallest choice may have a great impact upon the world. The small choice may seem insignificant until the manifestation of the choice, the ramification of it, is seen. When you understand that any choice has ramifications, you will comprehend that the alignment to bring forth the high will supports the highest ramification. Now, this is not about thinking it through. "What is the highest choice?" the small self might say, and confusion will ensue because the small self has the data of history to claim itself in, and nothing beyond it. So the alignment to the True Self, so that you are in correspondence at the new level of alignment and potential, is what guarantees that the high choice is made because that is how you operate.

He is interrupting. We will attempt to take the question. "So, if the small self has a wish, it doesn't happen. You are not claiming it anymore. Is that correct?" Well, you can choose it in low vibration and contend with the ramifications as your learning. This is how you have operated thus far. But in the Upper Room, in the maintenance of the high vibration, the high choice is not only present, but obvious to you. If you are in a quandary between this or that, you are not in your knowing and consequently must not be operating from the Upper Room.

"Are you always knowing in the Upper Room?" he asks. Yes and no. You are always present to the knowing that you require, but that does not mean the answer comes as you wish it. Imagine you are in the water and the tide is pushing you backwards and forwards. The agreement to be in the tide is to be in the flow, the current, the trajectory that is bringing you forward and backwards. The alignment in the Upper Room in some ways is similar. You are called forth. You are asked to halt. You are in patience, or you are in action. You are not in impatience. You are not in creative anger. "What should I do now about this situation?" You are aligning to the Divine Self, who will know when she knows, who will act upon it as she is called to.

Now, the True Self is not in fear. And you must really understand this. The operating system, as the Divine Self, has no fear in its vocabulary. It does not speak fear. It does not intend fear. It does not choose fear. And, because fear is no longer part of the equation, the opportunities that present themselves will be without fear. "Does this mean we are not encountering fear?" he asks. Not really. You may encounter fear in order to lift it, in order to see it for what it is. And, once the lie is seen, the energy may be re-created or re-comprehended or re-known as the Divine, which is the vibration that informs all matter and all manifestation. What believes itself to be darkness may be re-known, may be lifted, may be chosen anew. And, in the new comprehension, the Divine is present in operation, which simply means the stasis that the darkness has claimed will be no more. "How is stasis a product of darkness?" he asks. Well, in some ways, the denial of light is a claim of stasis. "I will not change. I will not know. I will not see anew." And the ramifications of stasis are always the encouragement of the old to be the prominent action. "I will attend to the old. I will not see beyond what I have known."

Now, as you realize the Divine, "I am here, I am here, I am here," the claim of the Divine Self in purview, and the alignment has begun—"I am choosing to align to the True Self in will"—the intention will invoke a response by what you know of as will. In some cases, the first response will be defiance, and this is the small self demanding its way. "I will not know myself anew. I cannot change. And the will that I have, in spite of the fact that it has brought me pain, is the best I have. I will live with it as I can." We are not denouncing the small self through the intention to align the Divine Will in purview in action. In fact, what we are doing is reclaiming will because nothing of you can be outside of God. So the reclamation of will is really quite simply the agreement that the will you have is in alignment with the True Self. In the past we have called it a braiding of the will—the will of the small self, the will of the divine, in a braid, and then in completion as one, one will. The idealization of the Divine—the Father, if you wish, you can call it what you want—and the small self in separation is no longer, because, in the braiding of the will, you and the Father or the Source are indeed one in the action of will, which is for the furtherance of the Kingdom in manifestation.

Now, the will of the Divine is not what you assume it to be. Many of you would think, "Well, there goes all the fun. My days of joy are over. So much for this lifetime." What you are, in fact, agreeing to is the divine potential operating as you for the good of all. And this is in joy. It is in action. It is in agreement to the True Self and its expression. It does not deny you anything. The pleasures of form will be present here because you have taken form. You may enjoy the body. You may enjoy the beautiful sky, the swim in the sea. You may enjoy the life you have and the bounty that is available. But this is all known in a higher octave than you are used to operating in. As we have said prior, everything exists in multiple octaves, and your experience of the world you live in is in fact transformed, and, because you see your world from a higher vantage point, the world is lifted to your sight, which is the resurrection of the Divine in all things by your increased amplification and awareness of it.

Now, each of you who comes to us has made choices based in fear. Some of you were harmed when young, had a difficult adolescence, a painful adulthood. You've carried the ramifications of those choices with you, those bruises from prior experience. You believe yourself to be humbled by what has happened to you, to the agreement that you cannot rise beyond these things. In fact, that is not so. As the Divine in alignment, in agreement, in a choice to know itself in full realization, every bruise, every injury, every pain may be re-known. Again, we have to say, what you put outside of God calls you to the darkness. So the inclusivity of all experience, in a high alignment, becomes the responsibility of the one who knows who she is. "I am a divine being in spite of what I went through" would be the small self's claim. "I am a divine being and I always have been" is a claim of truth. You don't earn your divinity. It is your birthright. And the reclamation of the Divine operates beyond time, so your awareness of who you are, in this very moment, claims you in history, and in future tense, as the Divine Self you have always been and may only be in the high octave.

Now, as we teach, we have claims we make to support you all in comprehension and agreement. And the claim of Divine Will—"I know myself in Divine Will"—is a claim that will support you in the alignment you require. It is effortful still in that you are making the choice, but as you ascend in octaves, as you align to the True Self, it is who and what you are, any more than you can be what you are in expression. And by this we mean your alignment in will is the product of operating in the upper classroom. It is the product of the consciousness that has made the choice. Once the choice is made and finally realized in fullness, there is no more need to make the choice because you have expressed as it. You are not trying to become something you are not. You will never be a saint. You don't need to be one. You need to be who and what you are as the True Self in its expression.

Don't struggle here, friends, because to struggle is to make difficult what must in fact be done in ease. You cannot build the mountain of faith through anxiety and fear. You can perceive the mountain and rise to it incrementally as you say yes to it. You are fraught with fear when you believe you are being given a mandate, or that what you have been may perhaps have been wrong. You have never been wrong. The choices you made in fear were the choices you knew and claimed and perhaps learned through. And whatever they have been, they have brought you to this perfect moment when who and what you are may be reclaimed in alignment to Divine Will. The resurrection of the Divine Self in operation is done with will, not at the exclusion of it. You have been gifted with free will, and it is a choice of free will to align it to the will of Source. The claim you make—"I know who I am in truth, what I am in truth, how I serve in truth"—is the requirement of the initial alignment to move into agreement, in confirmation of who and what you are, in the Upper Room. But how you express in the Upper Room, which is in fact the point of this text, is the claim of will in alignment.

Now, as we say these words to you today, we say them in love. You want what you want when you want it. You expect to get what you think you should have. You demand the things you were told to have. And you have an agreement of what can be claimed. And the lists grow as you choose as the small self, who will never be satisfied with the things of this world. To grow in Spirit is to comprehend that, while the manifest world is here to enjoy, here to learn through, its very nature is transient, and your dependence upon anything of this world to tell you who and what you are, what you have empowered in fear, what you have been asked to believe, becomes an idol that you have prayed to at the cost of truth. Enjoy the world, yes, but do not worship the things of this world. Enjoy your fellows. Know the Divine in them. Know the Divine as them. But do not give your authority to anyone in flesh. Reserve that for the Divine. The claim of truth—"I know who you are"—is a claim of agreement in coherence to the inherent Divine, the great equalizer. You are all of one Source in expression, in wonderful uniqueness. And the manifest self, in agreement to will, will support all because the Divine as you cannot and will not operate in selfishness.

Once again he interrupts. "It doesn't sound like much fun. What are you asking of us really?" We have already asked you to offer yourselves in service. And, because you have agreed, you are receiving this teaching. Understand, friends, that joy and wonder may be claimed. And, while fun is a wonderful thing, you are allowing it to claim you at the cost of wonder and joy. You may have all the fun you like in the Upper Room. We enjoy ourselves greatly here. How you wish to operate in expression, in alignment to the Divine Will, aligns you to the independence of choice that can be conceived of in the high octave. You are not surgically being implanted with Divine Will. The will that you know yourself in is what is moving into agreement to a new expression. And the joy you receive in benefit of this will be beyond what you can imagine.

He asks, "Why? How is it more?" Your stability, your agreement to be stable in the world you know, has required a density of expression. And the density of expression that you have found yourself in, in many ways precludes your access to the wonders of the higher realms, which are present here and always have been. If you wish to stay in dense form, you will have the experience of this plane in whatever way you choose. And, while that is true for anyone and everything, we are simply saying there is more to be known, more to be claimed, and your reception in the high octave will transport you beyond the known to the infinite world where time itself ceases to operate, and you may know yourself in infinite wonder.

We will close this lecture now with this benediction. We are seeing each of you, each of you in this encounter with us, in the highest level of agreement you may confirm. And, as we say yes to you, as we say yes to all, we lift you each to your own capacity, to your own alignment in Divine Will. We know who you are in truth. We know what you are in truth. We know how you serve in truth. You are free. You are free. You are free.

(PAUSE)

When we teach you about what you are, we reclaim you as what you are. And a reclamation is the manifestation of who you have always been as who and what you are. Now, the manifest self has choices, and, in congruence with the Divine Self as she truly is, as he stands before himself in a mirror, the choices must require him to benefit others. The claim "I know how I serve" has been described to you already, and the ramifications of that claim by the one who knows who he is support the reclamation of the Divine that is inherent in all. As the Divine that is inherent in all is reclaimed, the action of God, or what you might call God, which has always been to realize itself through all things, is made known. To be made known is to be realized. The realization of the Divine in the material realm for the benefit of all is the action of this text. Every text we have brought forth has held an action, an attunement, a name that could invoke a response in the reader. And this book, *Beyond the Known: Realization,* is to support realization, which is manifestation, in the claim you have been offered. The realized self realizes all.

Now, what it means to be realized is to be re-known beyond the structure, the finite structure, the shell, the encasement that form has known itself through, to the realization of form beyond the systems of containment. This actually means that the body itself is transformed in amplitude and vibration, and the reclamation of body conforms itself in the Upper Room to the requirements that the form may take to benefit others. Now, when we speak of form in this regard, we are actually not excluding will, but we are preferring for this moment to teach the manifestation of body as requirement.

Now, body isn't even what you really think it is. It is a system, it is an organism, there is blood that pumps, there are eyes that see, fingers that touch. But the body is actually manifest of a higher octave that has chosen to take dense form for its experience. To release the body from the density of form, the density that the form has taken, is actually to relinquish an idea. And the idea that is being relinquished is a simple one—that form is absolute, that form is intractable, that form is defined in matter and cannot be made new. Anything you see before you was once something else. Even the man beside you, the woman you see on the street, was once an embryo, was once an idea, was once energy without form. Everything that you see before you has had another name at any given time. The man you know of as Fred was once "Baby, Male," in an incubator before his parents gave him the name. The table was once an oak tree. And the things you see in a store were once the substance that they were created from.

The idealization of finite form and intractability must be understood briefly. It is much easier to navigate a world where forms that have taken form are always what they seem to be. It gives you the opportunity to name and to claim and to choose in obvious ways. The identity you hold as the Divine Self, once in form, in realization as form, must encourage the body to know itself in a new way.

"What does this mean?" he asks. "I'm confused by this teaching so far." What it actually means, Paul, is that your idea of the body is what supports the body—in its shape, in its age, in all things you may know. Every idea that you can share, that has been agreed to, has become codified, embraced by the species, and you align to the expectations of history in limited ways that would actually preclude you from receiving the new. Once form is understood as an expression of the Divine, and as will is offered to the Divine, how form expresses may transform as well because form will no longer be limited by the codifications that history has brought to it. Imagine you live in a world where the language that you use decides what everything is. "That is an old man," and, by claiming the old man as old, you gift him with all the properties of age, as you perceive age. You may claim him in wisdom, you may claim him in feebleness. Do you understand this? How you perceive age indoctrinates the manifestation to an idea that it will then conform to. When the species does this, the species goes into agreements of what it may expect.

Now, the ramifications of this are such that you end up recycling expectation, generation by generation. And it is rare that humanity takes a leap of its own accord to realize itself in a new way. We will have to tell you that this is occurring now, and in ways you will see in future generations. The elasticity of form, of gender, of race—these things that many are now seeking to define in ways that you would call black and white—are actually reclaiming themselves beyond duality. And the design of the body itself, in its perfection, will benefit from this. You all become the Divine in form as may be known by you. However, what this design is, while the surface of the body may not be transformed, the intention that the body has to know itself in a high octave will transform the experience of the body and the ability of the senses to perceive what exists in the higher manifest world. The body itself must mutate, in some ways, for its receptivity to amplify to what exists in the high room.

Now, when you understand that the True Self, in alignment in will, can govern the body, you will release the need to control the body through lower will. What this means, in some ways, is the alignment of the Divine Will in governance of form supports form in acquiescing to Divine Will. The form that the body has taken, the well-being of the body, how the body expresses itself in manifestation, will actually be transformed once it is given over to the true nature that the Divine Will would claim for it. The best that the small self can do would be to align to an idea of well-being as science has dictated it, but even science is limited in this regard. If the Divine as what you are knows itself in form, realizes itself in form, the will that calls forth the changes that are required will be done in agreement to a potentiality that has not yet been made manifest.

Now, if you understand that, in the Upper Room, you may know things that you could not know in the lower vibration, see things that the small self has been precluded from seeing, experience things that could not be known in dense vibration, you will have to understand that the translation of experience in manifestation must concur with the higher. The body itself becomes the vehicle of expression for the Divine, and with that aligns to its capacity through the senses to begin to experience what is already present in a higher way. Just as you cannot make the self divine, you cannot make the self experience what exists in the higher octave. But, as you align to the high octave and become receptive to its presence, what experiences can be claimed here will be known by you as you are prepared for them.

"What does that mean," he says, "prepared for them?" In all ways, the systems that you have operated with in agreement to what is possible have codified your experience. The claim "I am free, I am free, I am free," which we have taught you prior, supports the release of the agreements made by the collective of what may be known and experienced. The limitations that have governed you are then released, and you become, in alignment, the vehicle of change that may experience itself without the limitations it has been trained in through the small self. At this place of alignment, you are no longer predicating your experiences upon historical data, but upon what is present and what you may perceive in the Upper Room. The manifestation of the Upper Room as the manifest world, we have to say, is where we hope to take you, not in unison, because it will not happen in unison, but through those who lift, who create the opportunity for the lifting of all by nature of their expression, "I know how I serve."

Now, once you are in alignment and abiding in the Upper Room, free of the limitations of historical data to conform to what was, you may begin to embrace in increments what can be known by you in a higher way. "Why in increments?" he says. For your own well-being. To have an experience of what exists in the high octave without having balance, and agreement to remain balanced, may actually disrupt your life to the degree that you will not be able to re-find it. We wish you in balance. The young man who learns to walk upon a tightrope learns first when the tightrope is strung low. He is not lifted high in the air. As he learns balance, and as he lifts to a higher wire, there is a net present for him in case he falls. Eventually he becomes skilled in operating in a high way. The net is no longer needed because what was once a thin wire has expanded to a platform that he has arrived to where he may walk in great confidence. That is the arrival of the manifest self in the Upper Room. You are being taken to your arrival of agreement of manifestation here in increments so that you may maintain it.

He is interrupting. "But there are people who have large experiences of other worlds, and then they come back transformed by them. Is that what happens here?" Actually, no. Your experience of the upper levels is cumulative. Each design itself is understood by you through your experience of it. As you accrue experience, you continue to expand, and how you perceive what you see in a higher way is integrated by you. It becomes the new normal, not an exotic experience that you would seek to recapture, but simply a way of being.

"Is this really possible?" he asks. "Can this really be done?" The first thing you must understand is it is already done in the high octave. All we are doing is bringing you here for the realization of it. The extent that you can integrate the vibration in manifest form, and align the will to its true nature to be of God in its expression, will support your reclamation of experience in this high octave and the maintenance of it. We have often been asked how to maintain a high vibration. People often say, "I've had the experience. It was wonderful. And then it was gone." The experience of the high room may be available to some in brief states of consciousness. This is always beneficial to the soul, who seeks to return there. At least you know it's there, so you may journey back. But the maintenance of it must be done from the higher room. You cannot navigate the high octave from the low, but you can manage the low from the high. Do you all understand this? So supporting you in realization of the high becomes the manifestation that you ask for.

"What is it like there?" you may ask. It is just like your life—without fear, without self-judgment, without the need to judge others, without the need to war, and without the agreements of the communal authority, that you have ascribed power to, to be something you were never intended to be. And what that is, is the small self and its ideas of what it is allowed. Reclamation of truth has been the asking of you, "I am willing to know myself in truth, I know who I am in truth." When you move to truth, you move beyond the lies that have been taught to you that you may have believed and given great credence to. We say on your behalf that the life that you will live in the Upper Room is the life you can imagine when you are no longer asleep to your true nature.

The Christ has come as every human being, but the flowering of it requires the awareness of its potential, and, because you have been lied to for so very long, you have misbelieved the nature of your being. To know yourself as worthy has been an important part of these teachings. How could you not be worthy would be our question for you. You are claiming your true inheritance, and the Upper Room is where this commences.

We will take a pause for Paul. Period. Period. Period.

(PAUSE)

When we teach you about independence, we are speaking of independence from the mandates of history and the rule of the small self, who has decided so much in fear. When we speak to will, we speak to the authority that you have been gifted with to choose the lives you live. To acquiesce the will to the Divine is to decide that the will that you have been gifted with is in union with Source. *In union* means at one with the will of Source, so that you understand yourself as acting in a union in all areas of your life.

Now, your independence from God, in some ways, is what you decide when you believe yourself to be separate. Interdependence and reliance upon is what happens when you begin to understand yourself in relation to God, and union is what happens when you have agreed to be as you can be as of the Source of all creation. To go into union with Source is not to disintegrate as a small self, it's to be responded to as the Source that is inherent in you. And will is a part of who you are and can also be met in this agreement.

Now, when we teach about independence, we must understand that your requirements, the evolution of the individual soul, must be comprehended as important and what you have come to do. And the soul evolves within this merging of union with Source, but is not dependent upon it for the alignment to its lessons. The soul will demand that its lessons will be met while you are in form, whether or not you align to high will. How you learn your lessons, how you are met through your experience in the Upper Room, will vary drastically, depending on what you have come to learn and what level of agreement you are choosing to learn through. You may learn your lessons in a low vibration. You may learn through fear. You may learn through anger. You may learn through the horrific ramifications of choice for one country to dominate another. You may learn the hard way, if you choose. But you may also learn through the radical unfoldment of the Christ as who and what you are and what it is in all manifestation. When this happens, the trumpets sing, and what you understand of as great change is upon you, but in agreement to divine potential.

"Is there destruction in divine potential?" There can be, yes, but never of what is required. When you have a house with no foundation, the house may fall at the first wind. If the foundation of the house is strong, you may repair the house if that is what is required. If a new house must be built upon the old structure, you will know it, and it will be beneficial. To destroy the old to create the new may be a requirement in some cases. But, as the Divine, the Christed Self, knows itself in love, it brings no harm to what it meets. You may learn your lessons individually and collectively through force, through anger, or through love, and the love that is brought to your fellows as you recognize them as fellow travelers seeking to meet himself, herself, through each interaction with the Divine that is present in all.

Each of you comes to us with a desire for union, and the desire for union has been responded to you by us in the texts we have brought through Paul. But union itself is not the ideal. If there is an ideal, the ideal would be manifestation of the Divine in a devout way as you understand yourself as participatory to the reclamation of the Kingdom. Those of you who have come forth and offered their hands and hearts, their vibratory fields will be called forth in action. When you imagine union as a state of being, you imagine yourself floating in an eternity of bliss and love. And, in fact, while you are in a body, you will attend to the body and the requirements of form. You require shelter and food, you require warmth in the winter, and you require the benefits of interaction with your fellows in order to recognize what is true in every human being. The Christ has come in all, but the recognition of this still remains precluded by the one who fears that she has no right to the Kingdom. The Kingdom, as we have said many times, the recognition, the awareness of the inherent Divine, is brought into manifestation through the claim "I know what you are in truth." The what again is always the manifest claim, and to claim "I know what you are" is to recognize the inherent Divine and bring it forth. This is an action you take first in the acknowledgment that it must be so because it can only be so, and then from the position that that is always so because it could never not be so, and, because it is always so, there is no need to claim it. It simply is. You are the benefactor of the landscape you express in and through by nature of being.

When we speak to will in this regard, we are speaking of the acceptance of the position that you are taking. "I have become an ambassador of truth, and in truth a lie will not be held." To know the self in truth is to move beyond the names things have been given, what things have been called, and the reliance upon the language of history to predicate the future. To be the ambassador of truth is to decide that what you see before you will be revealed and then realized in truth. And to realize anything in truth is to see and to know the divine principle that must be at the Source of it.

As everything you see is lifted to the Upper Room where you now abide, the world you see becomes the sparkling reflection of the claims you have made in dominion as the one who knows who she is. You partake of the bounty of the Kingdom simply by sharing it with anyone and everyone you meet. You become the ambassador because the action of the Christ as you is to know the Christ in all. And, as the Christ is known in all, all is lifted by nature of being.

He is interrupting. "What if someone doesn't want to lift, something cannot be lifted? What do you say about that?" Your recognition of the inherent Divine is a recognition of what is only true and always true, and the mask the other wears cannot stand in the face of truth because the mask he or she has taken is a lie. The personality structure, while valid in its ambition, has never been the True Self. And when the True Self is unmasked, when it is seen by the one who knows who she is, the Divine in the one you see becomes the action of reclamation in the other. The Divine is the reclamator. All you are doing is knowing the truth, and the reclamation happens.

"But doesn't their will need to be invoked? Don't they give permission?" Ascension happens at the level of the individual through agreement, but it is rarely the personality self who agrees or would decide. In most cases, the personality structure surrenders. She cannot meet the opportunity for growth that is presented by the Christ by herself, so she aligns as the one who may receive it. The idea of surrender to one's true nature would be the example we would offer you. To surrender to the true nature is the claim "I know who

I am." You are not enabling the Divine to do the work of the Divine. You are surrendering to its truth to embody as you. To know the truth in another is to enable them to make their own claim. Now, the choice is theirs at the level of personality, but you can claim the Divine in an individual or in all those residing upon this globe. The effect is the same. You are claiming what is always true, and, in this claim, you lift those you know that you are claiming, that you are realizing, in the Upper Room by nature of being.

In many teachings, you had to humble yourself, grovel before the altar. We will say this to you. Humility is a requirement, but it may come in different ways. "I am willing to learn, I am willing to know, I am willing to accept, I am willing to change" are all claims made in humility. "I demand to change, I demand to know, I will be met as I say I should" is the claim of the small self. Now, as you operate as the True Self, you claim differently. The claim "I know who you are" holds the Divine as the claim. It is not a humble claim, it is a claim of victory because the Divine knows the Divine and recognizes its presence in all that it can encounter. The names you have been given in history, the heretics, the ones who were burned, who spoke the truth and were denied their place, are being released at this time because what was heretical was generally heretical to an institution and not to God. The understanding here is that the claim of the Divine, and humanity's inherent divinity, is the birthright that is being re-known. You do not grovel to receive your inheritance. It is your right, but you must say, "I am worthy of receiving my inheritance, but I accept it in deep humility because I know the Source of all things."

Do you understand? You are being gifted with a great opportunity here, but you must take it and say yes, and, as you say yes, we sing with you in the Upper Room. Period. Period. Period.

DAY TEN

Each of you decides your idea of who and what you are commensurate with your understanding and the values instilled in you by the world you express through. Each of you decides what it means to be a man, what it means to be a woman, what it means to be loved and to love. Each of you comprehends in accordance with the systems that you have been regulated by, and by this we mean you understand yourself with a barometer that you have been given for understanding. Each of you says yes to the scales that you express through. Each of you says yes to the comparisons you make, one against the other, this against that. Each of you decides to know yourself with the mirror that has been handed to you to know yourself through.

Now, as the Divine Self, there is no mirror. There is expression, perception, what you see, and the knowing that you instill in what you see because the one who knows has the awareness of the claim "I am free." Because she knows she is free, she is not seeking to label, to emblemize, to create a dictate or a mandate of what a thing should be called. She allows what she sees to be revealed to her. And what is revealed in the Upper Room will always be known in truth.

What this means is you are no longer deceived by the veils of illusion that would seek to tell you what is meritful and what is not, what is a good thing or bad, what is a pleasant thing or unpleasant thing, because those things are known as values that you have abided by. The thing is simply known and received, and the consciousness you hold at this level of vibration and attunement receives the information in truth, and, consequently, the thing seen is in fact realized or known in a higher comprehension.

So much of what you decide is based on the ideas of what should be, how things should be. "This is more valuable than that." "This is a higher claim than that." And those comparisons work as a grid or a measuring system that you are then bound by. If everything exists within the grid, how can it be known anew?

Nothing can be comprehended until it is first seen or known in a high way. There is no exception here, and we tell you why we say this. Immediately, you wish to know how an atrocity can be known in a high way, how something you would call evil can be known in a high way. But we would have to reprimand you by saying you are

looking at the thing within that scale of good and evil, light and dark, perhaps high and low, although high and low as we teach it is simply a descriptor of resonance. When you clarify your meaning of good and evil, what you will understand is that what is good has been spoken as good, has been decided as good in comparison to something else. "She did well in school, she got a B minus." "He did poorly in school, he got a D." "She's an excellent student, look at that A." Within that scale, there is a codification of learning, and what has been learned has been graded in a scale in comparison to others. If the scale does not exist and the grades are not present, how you would comprehend the learning of one student would not be in comparison to others, but in the alignment that the student holds.

The one who knows the truth of something has claimed the truth and has inherited the wisdom of the truth as part of her experience. The one who learns information that he or she may parrot may have learned recitation and nothing more. Experience, finally, is what we teach you, and your experience as the Divine Self liberates you beyond the known, beyond the frames of reference that you have used to decide what is meaningful, what is good or evil, high or low. Each of you decides, in your own way, that the Divine as you is the true meaning of being. The idea that what you are is a bunch of cells holding together in skin for the purpose of dying one day will be what claims you in limited experience. In fact, what you are is the manifestation of the Divine in form who has come for the reason we teach you. Your knowing of who and what you are claims you in accord with a level of agreement where the manifest world can be re-known.

Now, each of you decides what the will means through your choice to claim the self in any intention. "I will pick the apple from the tree" is a choice you make. "I will eat the apple" is the choice you make. "I will throw away the core" is the choice you make. "I will marry the man or woman," "conceive the child," "grow old." These are also choices that you make, and the will that informs them is in agreement only to the choices that the small self can comprehend. The will itself, when moved into union with true divinity, expresses beyond a scale. And what can be claimed, or known, or decided need not be conferred by prior history, but what is possible in the Upper Room.

In the Upper Room, there is no scale or barometer to decide you, to define you, to claim you beyond the small self, because the small self is not operating at this level. And, as you are free of the instructions that the small self has used to navigate a reality in lower vibration, you are free to claim what can be claimed beyond the systems of logic that have been endowed upon your species through the millennia. What this means is that collective agreement to

manifestation in limitation can be transcended by one who is not bound by the scale of reason or possibility that is defined by previous information that has either been coerced or settled upon by all of you.

"An example?" he says. You live to be the age you perceive yourself to be, and how you understand age is through a shared calendar, an agreement to time that in and of itself is a decision that you have claimed and have been bound by. We are not saying you will exist forever in form, but the man who believes in age, and expects to become old, in certain ways is quite well guaranteed that experience. "Oh, but my genes. My father had this, I will certainly have it." Perhaps you may. Perhaps you may learn through that experience. But to define yourself in expectation of that experience is to hand over your will to a decision that was made by others who came before you. The claim "I am free" is in fact the claim of liberation from systems of control, agreements made in fear, and the collective mind that believes what it was taught and will seek to confirm the old because it cannot conceive that something more could possibly exist.

Again, to the Upper Room. Everything exists in the Upper Room to be re-known, to be reclaimed in divine accord. A teacup may be known in a low octave or a high octave. It is still a teacup. But the vibration of the teacup in the Upper Room or the higher octave is resonantly different as you go up in scale. The same is true for the body through the claim "I know what I am." And the same is true in your experience of your world as you become the perceiver who is not responding to historical data, but the revelation of the Divine that may be seen by the one who knows who she is. And the act of will that is required here is a very simple one:

> *"I am aligning the Divine Will to all that I encounter. I become as Divine Will in my acquiescence to it. And I allow the Divine to decide with me, as me, and for me as I become one in tone, in vibration, with the amplitude of the True Self expressed as Will, the Divine as Will."*

The Divine as what you are, in alignment, is the act of will as the divine force that expresses itself in certainty upon this plane.

"What does that mean, *in certainty*?" he asks.

In certainty means you are in your knowing, and any act of will is chosen in accord, in truth, with the who and the what that you are. And the dilemmas of the past—"should I, should I not?"—are actually released as the True Self in its mandate claims a world anew. You become the vibration of the Christed Self in manifestation, in action, and in agreement to everything you see. Underline the word *everything*. The Divine as you, in its perspective, claims the manifest world and lifts it to its present. It does not confirm negative amplitude or fear. It does not agree to the old because it exists beyond it. It does not confirm collective agreement, simply because it exists in a realm that has not been defined by the collective.

If you were all to imagine that a certain heaven resembled a certain thing, that is where you would all go to upon your passing, to the expected realm of the hereafter. That would be the collective agreement informing the other world. In fact, the Upper Room, the fabric of the Divine in expression in manifestation, holds no barrier to definition, but cannot be defined by the old because the old does not express here. Understand what this means. Imagine you have a sweater, a nice old sweater. It has memory. The nice old sweater does not exist in the Upper Room as it has because it does not retain the memory of what it was, nor are you endowing it with memory or codification because you have no need to. It is still a sweater, what you may know as a sweater, but in fact what it is is a thing you might wear to protect the body and not more than it means. Do you understand the concept? Everything you cherish, you cherish because you were taught value. Everything you disdain, you disdain because you were taught its lack of merit. And the scale of value that you operate with in this lower accord does not exist in the Upper Room. If you wish to embark on a memory and decide its value, you may do so. We do not deny you that. But we are saying the level of release that is available to you each in the high octave precludes you from enmeshing yourself in the data of history that, like it or not, will reclaim you in the low vibration that you know of as your history.

Why is your history low vibration? Well, in fact, it is not. But your history is only what you think it is. Do you understand that? "My mother was cruel to me." You understand your mother, once again, through the lens of data, the information of history that you have been claimed by—the claim of good and evil, good and bad, high and low, as decided by your culture or the things you've thought must be true because you believed them to be so.

We are speaking to you as beings who can choose to align the will beyond the codification of time, and all memory is is an idea of what happened in another time, and the idea of time itself is really just a construct that you have invested importance in. "When I was fifteen, I looked quite wonderful," says the one whose memory of the age of fifteen is fraught with the memory of what she was not, or should have been, or might have been. "When I was fifteen, I looked a certain way," and that certain way is an idealization of self that is perpetuated by the lens of memory and nothing more.

The world you see, everything you see around you, has been labeled by those who came before you, and you wander this world, interpreting those labels and thinking that what things have been called are what they truly are. In fact, what is available to you in comprehension in the Upper Room exists beyond the known, and, as you agree to this, your learning truly begins.

We will stop this lecture now. This is the end of the last chapter of the text. Period. Period. Period.

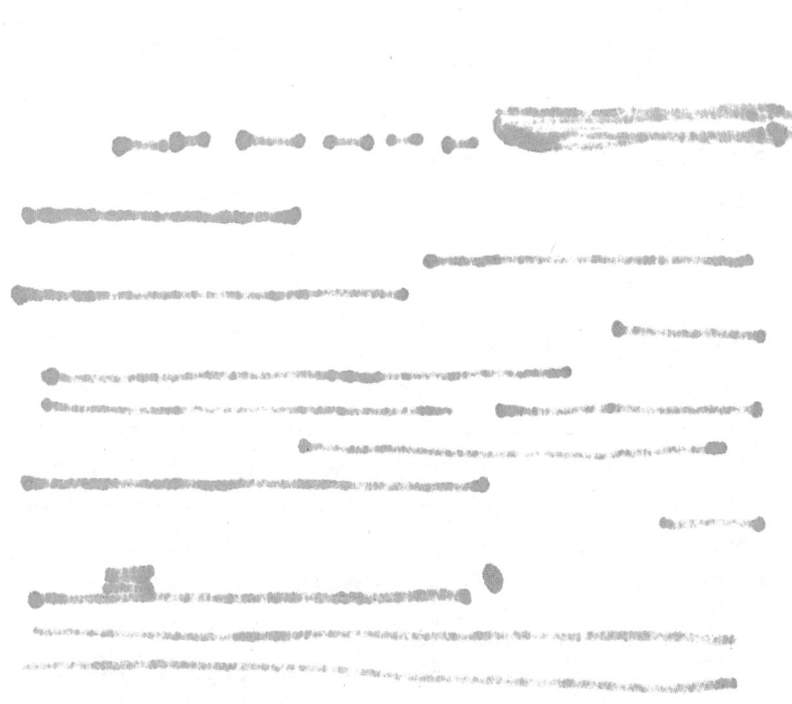

5

THE RECLAMATION OF THE DIVINE

DAY ELEVEN

To justify what you have known, to decide that what has happened was what needed to happen, is only appropriate at the level of the small self. The Divine as you has a comprehension of necessity born in the present moment. She does not resurrect the past to dissect it, she does not seek to rationalize to have it confer with her idea of what was, has been, or could have been. She accepts an event as an out-picturing of consciousness that was, and without emblemization, which simply means she is not looking to confer great meaning upon an event. It is something else that was.

Now, if you look at your own lives and see how much time you spend looking at the past, deciding what was, what had great meaning, what should never have happened that you are still contending with, you will begin to realize that the present itself is a museum of history and your artifacts are all over, and being interpreted again and again through the perspective of the consciousness you hold at any given moment. Once you understand that the only meaning anything has is the meaning you give it, you will begin to move beyond the requirements of history to reinforce itself upon the present moment and then dictate the future in agreement to what was. The challenge here is that the lives you live have been built upon history, so to Paul it sounds an impossibility.

"How do I walk into a room and not call the chair the chair, or remember the curtains from the day I purchased them? How do I forget what a color is when I don't like the color green and I see it elsewhere? What is to stop the memory or the dislike from collaborating with my experience of the present moment?" This is a misunderstanding on your part, Paul. As you ascend in consciousness, your perceptions change, and how you perceive anything is a direct action of the consciousness you hold. When you forget a language, when it loses its meaning, you stop relying upon it to communicate your feelings or your needs. You have another language to direct you. Each of you decides that the way you live your life is predicated either on history or the moment you stand in, and the moment you stand in need not be informed by the tenets of history once you understand that it is you who calls them forth. The chair is a chair because you know what a chair is through your relation to history. The sky is called the sky and the properties of the sky as shared construct are understood by you in a collaborative field, a shared idea, and the language you use to describe it reclaims it as it has been claimed since the first thing was called sky that, in fact, was something other, prior to its name.

"*Prior to its name*—what does this mean?" Very simply put, everything that has a name was once nameless. Can you understand this? To move to the nameless is to move beyond language, and, as language is moved beyond, the heredity that language would cost you is actually dismantled. "But we love language," he says. "It's how we communicate. You can't take language away from us." We are not taking language away from you, we are actually giving you a new one. But in order for something to be made new, it needs to move to the nameless, to the Source of its creation, to be made known as what it has always been. The Divine Self, who knows who she is, can be without a name and still be what she is. The names we have offered you for it are all symbols, ways for consciousness to hold on to the idea, ways to comprehend something that is in fact impossible to comprehend in language. But you do your best, we do our best, at this stage of this teaching. The nameless, we suggest, is what you are when you know who you are in completeness, when the sense of identity you have held has been dismantled, re-known, re-created in such a fashion that your sense of self is actually absorbed by the Divine at the level of completion. This simply means that, as you are, you are no longer what, you are no longer the artifact, you are no longer the thing, but you have become the *the*. "What does that mean?" The *the*, the thing with no name.

Now, to be the thing with no name creates you in accordance with the mandates of the moment you stand in. In many ways, what you become is expression, full expression of your divine nature. In the past we have used examples. You have become John as the Divine, Alice as the Divine, but when John is no longer, when Alice has no name, you are still the Divine. The artifact, in some way, becomes the language that you have rendered a reality through, and, as you evolve in consciousness toward full expression, you comprehend that the requirements of language, in many ways, is to re-assume the idea that created the word, or the need for the word to begin with. "But is a world without language possible?" Again, this is Paul misinterpreting the teaching. The comprehension we offer you here is about what exists in what we call the Upper Room, where you may move to the nameless and then begin to understand that, in that plane of expression, the nameless plane, what may be known may be known in a new way. When you are not re-creating the old, because that's all you have known to expect, when you are not re-creating what was, you can become gifted with the potential that the nameless holds.

What does it mean to know the nameless? It means to move to the comprehension of the Divine that is present in manifestation and needs no manifestation to be present. It becomes the agreement to lift beyond form, while maintaining form. It becomes the agreement to become sound, to become the sound of the nameless, the tone or the expression of it without the tags, emblemizations, meanings that have been endowed upon it. Your idea of God, your idea of what must be named God, is informed by thousands of years of ideology, and the idea of God itself has become a totem, a construct, a wooden idol that you seek to pray to. God has no name. God is the nameless, the absolute, the unobstructed. God is the manifestation, and the lack of manifestation, all at once. The manifest world that you have named as things—the chair, the sky—are all God and named as such by you. "I know God as chair, God as sky," and beyond the name of chair or sky there is only God, and beyond the name of God there is everything and there is nothing. There is sound, there is silence, and they are one.

The great sound that we would call God, in intonation, is the song of the soul in complete resonance with its truth. The name of God without sound is who and what you are when even the form you have taken has moved beyond language or the names things have been used to codify expression. What this means is that the entirety of being, in assumption as what it has always been, is a great cry, a great silence, a beautiful song, and a heartfelt weeping, all at the same time. There can be no expression without what you know of as God, and therefore all expression, all great expression and small expression, is God in expression as the who, as the what, as the sound of love, in knowing, in being, without the name *love* to confuse it.

"Now what does that mean?" he asks. Again, to language. You have heard the idea that God is love, but even the word *love* is so tainted by history that its meaning is confused to you. In love, in the vibration of love, what we know of as God, with the name *God* attached, is an idea of a Source that is a benediction, that is caring, that will do what you wish, as you wish it, if you would pray to it in a certain way. This is not God. This is not love. All love is is the expression of the Source without the name *love* attached. If you understand that God or Source, the nameless, exists beyond time, you can begin to imagine that there was a time when even the idea of love was uncreated, unthought. To move to the infinite in your potential is to actually release the codification of ideology that would now limit you. And we must say that includes your idea of what love is, because even that is now predicated by the inheritance you have claimed as a small self. If love is God, and God is the nameless, then love is nameless. If love is nameless, even the idea of love is in union and without names in the manifest Source that you experience yourself as.

If you understand where we are taking you in this instruction, it's to a new idea of infinity without the polarization of love and hate, light and dark, joy and sorrow. These are all real things as you experience them, but only in that the language you use to describe them is the language you have been taught to use as descriptors. You can say *sorrow* and call to you the experience of sorrow that you understand sorrow to be, and the word itself, the emblemization of emotion, codifies the emotion and claims it in a kind of separation from the being that you are. "I feel sorrow" claims sorrow as something other. You can never be sorrow. That can never be your being. But you may feel sorrowful. In that way, you give identity to emotion and establish it in power and it governs your experience.

The nameless, we suggest, the Divine as who and what you are beyond codification and the idea of form, must be created with an intention to know what the Divine is. When the Divine has no name, and the qualities you would endow it with are no longer operating through language, you begin to experience infinity. "What is infinity?" he asks. What infinity is is the experience of the absolute. Because the absolute does not exist through time—you may know it in time, but it is not through time that it is realized—you may begin to comprehend what is always. And by *always* we mean what is always present, the thing that informs creation, the thing that is manifest as you, and the amazing thing that you become when you release the bondage that the small self has claimed through its agreement to separation.

When we continue this teaching, we will claim you in the octave of infinity. We will take a pause now for Paul. Thank you all for your presence.

(PAUSE)

When you decide things as the small self, you perpetuate the old because the small self knows itself in history. When you claim the True Self and your great identity and you move the will to a place of union or reconciliation with your divine purpose, your expression, the manifestation of the Divine as who and what, begins to be how you know yourself in accord with the world that you express in. That is the claim "I know how I serve." Now, in the infinite light, in the infinite Source, beyond time, beyond language, beyond any idea you could possibly hold of what it means to be, the absolute may be known in encounter, although not comprehended through the data, through the filters, and with the language that the small self has used to describe his or her experience. The willingness to experience infinity actually requires you to release the need for those filters, for the language, because the nature of infinity, while it holds everything and nothing all at once, is the way it knows itself through you. So to carry with it the language of old, to decide what should be based on your presumption of what infinity is, is to claim yourself as the small self and, consequently, know yourself in separation.

We are going to take a little trip with you now. Imagine for a moment that wherever you sit, wherever you are, is a moment in time, a single moment in time, and everything that may be experienced in this moment in time is available to you. Now imagine, if you wish, that this is the only moment in time that you may ever know, because in fact that is true. You may only know yourself or anything else in the present moment. Everything else is history or expectation. When you expect anything, you use history to outline the expectation, and while you may do this in the present moment, your escapade is actually in your idea of the past or what you deem the future. So in this present moment, the only moment there can ever be, we wish you to expand, to become larger than you think you are. Imagine that the body itself, which is Source in vibration, is expanding, and the energetic field is expanding as well. Imagine that the being that you are is expanding beyond your idea of what it is possible to expand to. Imagine, if you wish, that the being that you are has grown so much that you cannot see the outline of what you thought you were. You have become an ocean or a sky in vibration. Now, from this perspective, where the rules have already been broken, you can begin to understand that, in this moment, beyond the limitation of form, you may begin to experience yourself beyond the idea of time.

The idea of time is essential to understand. Your idea of time is based in collective agreement to what time is, how many hours in a day, what constitutes a minute in time. These are agreed upon things, so to move beyond the idea of time may not be to move beyond time itself, but beyond the idea of time as a construct, as form, as a dictate that you have ascribed power to. You are now as big as the sky, as great as the ocean, and from this perspective you give permission to release the idea of time itself.

Now stay in this moment of great expansion and timelessness and imagine, for a moment, that you are moving to a new plane of expression where time itself has never been chosen, where the infinite now is the only expression that you may claim, and you would be in truth here. In the Upper Room, the Divine Self as you knows herself in infinity because she is not bound by the constructs of time, but in alignment to her eternal nature. Your eternal nature inhabits the eternal plane, and, as you have lifted in vibration to the Upper Room, you may claim your experience here in timelessness.

When there is no time, there is no limitation. There is no when, there is no "what if?" because everything is expressed in this perfect now, and what is required is known to you through the requirement, not through the asking of it, or the requirement that you would seek fulfilled. When one is thirsty, one knows water. When one is tired, one knows sleep. When one is one with God, one knows no separation. In infinity, in the infinite now, you are met in vibration, in tone, in agreement to the True Self who exists beyond time, but may know herself in time through the form that you have chosen to experience this life in.

Now, as we sing to you in vibration and tone, we are going to invite you to lift in sound to the nature of infinity. Imagine the sound that you make when you join us in sound is a bell that is always ringing—underline *always*—ringing in infinity, beyond the decade, the eon, the millennium, beyond what you would construct as a system of comprehension that you now know of as linear time. Beyond the known, beyond the sung, beyond the tone, there is only one thing, the Absolute that is always present, the nameless that exists beyond the known as infinity.

When we make this sound, we invite you, wherever you are, to join us in intention. And all your intention needs to be is to merge with this sound, to become in union with its tone, the peal of the bell. If you are moved to sing with us, trust that the note that you sing is the perfect note to move into accord with us. And in this union we will experience together timelessness and infinity. On the count of three, Paul.

One. Two. Three.

[The Guides tone through Paul.]

We are with you beyond form, beyond time, beyond your comprehension of what may be known. We are with you in love, and beyond the word *love* in the true intention of it, which is to cherish and hold dear as one with God. Period. Period. Period.

DAY TWELVE

Each one of you comes with an expectation of what it is like to know the Divine Self in realization. You trust the ideas you've been given. "I may know myself as the True Self." But you don't understand that the ability to recognize embodiment comes in manifestation, not in the precursor to it, and the embodiment of the Divine Self is the treatise we are offering you now.

The teaching of the Upper Room, the place of manifestation, the realm of embodiment, may be comprehended by you first in ideology only in preparation for what is to come. And what is to come, we have to say, is realization. When you realize who and what you are, and you know it, the manifestation has occurred. There is no longer a glimmer of hope. "I see my Divine Self up there on that mountain. I will race to her and hope she is still there when I arrive." It is the knowing that you cannot be other. And embodiment, we have to say, which is the expressed realized self, the emissary or the Christ in manifestation, has its own agenda beyond what the small self can even imagine. "When I am holy and I pray all day and I do God's bidding and I wear white" are the ideologies that the small self might attach to her spiritual nature, what it looks like, what you believe it to be, when, in fact, the realization of the Divine, the manifest Divine, is as you, just as you, but in a new articulation, a new language or vibratory tone that co-creates, in the manifest plane, dominion through the consciousness of the Divine. In other words, the manifested self that in fact you are becomes participatory to the manifest world in co-alignment, and the Divine in manifestation is what sings all about you as you know yourself and your world. But it is you, not an idealized version of you, not the prettified version.

He is interrupting. "Well, what of the world, then? Is it a prettified world? Is it a peaceful world? Is it the same world in the higher octave? What do we see?"

Again, we have to remind you that what you anticipate is a product of logic, wishful thinking, inherited ideas. The manifest Divine, or the True Self as who and what, in knowing, knows what she sees. She excludes nothing from the fabric of the Divine because all things are in manifestation. But we will say that the presence of the Divine in its interaction with a lower vibrating field reclaims the field and lifts it to its knowing, its purview. And the claim we make and will continue to make—"I Have Come"—is the announcement that claims the resonance of the manifest world to the Christed Self.

Now, the idea here that we wish you to understand is re-creation. Manifestation in the higher octave is re-creation. While you may know a chair as a chair and you may inhabit the chair, your recognition of the chair in the Upper Room or the higher octave is a translated remembrance of the old without carrying with it the identity or baggage the object has held. In the new, the chair is known. In the new, everything you see is known and re-interpreted, re-spoken, if you wish, in the language of the True Self.

"Now, what does that mean?" he asks. Well, the True Self's language is vibratory, and the language of the Divine, while utilizing the small self's vocabulary, actually exists in a new way. Through intonation and verbiage, the descriptors you use in new ways are simply significators of your new relationship with that which is now manifest. Again, the Divine Self is the one expressing here, and, while she has the ability to utilize all you have known, she is translating language or vibratory tone in explicit ways with profound effect upon the outside world.

"What does that mean?" he asks. Things are spoken into being in recognition of what they truly are, not what they have been. And the realization of the Divine as you, or the Word in action, is an articulation, not only of tone, vibration, and consciousness, but it is the conduit for the expression of the Divine to flow through. And the Divine as you is in no way limited by the articulations that you have utilized through history.

"Is there a new language?" he asks. Again, we have to say, Paul, what we introduced this class with was the simple idea that the small self will seek to identify the Divine Self and claim it as he thinks it should be, when, in fact, it is the Divine that claims the small self and re-interprets it and reclaims the world through its expression of the small self. The Divine as you, not you as the Divine, and the language of the Divine, in texture and fabric, in tone and vibration, simply means that the one who speaks is operating in the Upper Room. What is articulated at that level of intonation and vibration and tone has a causal effect upon the expression of the manifest world. What you see, in fact, as the realized self, is the re-interpretation of history in a higher form. In other words, we are not negating history, we are lifting you beyond it where you may newly claim the vibratory world or the octave of expression we call the Upper Room.

Now, each of you who comes to us in identity seeks penance. "Tell me what I must do right and must release. Tell me what I have done wrong so I may rectify it." And these are the new ways we would answer those questions: The small self, who seeks penance, or to abnegate what she is, or to self-define in low vibration, is in fact what is reclaimed or re-known or re-pronounced by the True Self in the claims we have offered you. And the claim "I Have Come," which is the manifest Divine in full expression for the service to the world she can offer, is the articulation or the renunciation of what has been. Now, by *renunciation* what we mean is you are no longer ennobling fear, the small self's fear, or the small self's negation of who and what she is. You cannot call yourself names as the True Self. It's preposterous to think you could. So the suffering self, or the small self with the whip in hand, is actually held and re-known, and, in fact, appropriated in high service because there can be no aspect of you that is separate from Source.

He interrupts again. "But can these things be released, or are they all re-integrated?" Both may be true. If there is something that you have outgrown, there is no way to carry it with you to the Upper Room. However, we have to say that if you have had an investment in fear or in anger or in shame or self-doubt or debasement, they may need to be re-known in order to be acclimated to and then moved beyond as you lift to the Upper Room. In fact there is no self-abasement at that level of vibration. So what you integrate, in some ways, is what you may call acceptance, or allowance, but for the purpose of integration and moving beyond what has stood in the way of your expression. If there is no need for something, it will be left behind. If it requires integration and realignment through you, if there is purpose for it still, it will be made known and reclaimed in the harmonics that we call the Divine Self in its expansion of tone.

Now, this is a new idea for him, "The harmonics of tone?" The Divine Self has tone, and every expression you can think of in the manifest world is also in tone. The fabric of the experience that you inhabit here in shape and form, in solidity that you think is so terribly real, is all sound and vibration. And the Divine as what you are, the manifest Divine in skin and bone, in breath and blood, is also this. And, when you shift your expression through the alignment as the Divine Self, the tone in articulation has the power to know itself in the vibratory echo that confirms the divinity in anything else that has taken form. The bell is rung as you, and it claims itself in sound, in tone, in everything it encounters. The Christed Self as you is a manifest self. It is not an identity. It is not a new way of walking around the world in your holiness. It's the realization of the holiness that has always been. And its tone, its allowance, is the claim "I Have Come."

Now, when this is claimed as the True Self, the Monad, the divine expression of the being that you are becomes as a diamond, and its many facets spread light without intention because all the diamond can do is refract and reflect the light that is. It has no other intention but to be, and because it is as it is, it claims the world in value, the diamond in value and everything in value that the light may shine upon.

He interrupts. "But the light shines on some pretty awful things. We are not very evolved as a species. We harm ourselves and each other. We war. We fight. We weep in anger and despair. What does the light do upon the unholy?"

"What unholy?" we say. If nothing is holy there is no God, this is no teaching, and your idea of the disposable self is perfectly appropriate to your growth. The identity of the Divine is not gifted to you. It is inherited, implicit, and seeking to be known explicitly, and this is done by the light that shines upon all. If something is revealed by the great light that needs new ways, re-formation, reknowing, reclaiming, it is done in octaves and in agreement to the holiness that must be. You cannot make a thing holy, but you can sure try to damn it. To damn anything, to put anything out of the light, is an action of the small self, never the True Self. When the True Self sees an atrocity, it brings the light and the action of the Divine to bear upon it. It needs no sword; it needs the claim of truth. "I Have Come." And it is never the small self who can claim that. The virtue of the small self at its very best is it does not know its true authority. If it did, you would have been long gone, and what we mean by this is the gift of this teaching is far more powerful than the True Self in its expression has known itself through in form and field in centuries and in thousands of years.

"Please refine this teaching," he says. "What did you just say?" The realization of the Divine in manifestation in consequence has not been fully realized in this way for thousands of years. And, when we say *in this way,* we are not saying that there have not been realized beings who walked the earth. What we are teaching is embodiment through claims that have been called heretical in history and were always in truth. And the denial of the inherent divinity, which is in fact your birthright and can only be true in a loving God in a world of truth, was debased and withheld to you and from you in order for you to be complicit in the betrayal of self that you have engaged in, in many ways, as a species.

When we teach these things, he grows concerned. He wants this teaching to remain convenient to his sense of self or agreement to logic. What we have taught tonight is that the claim "I Have Come," which is an intonation of truth claimed as the True Self, is the claim that can move a mountain. And it is fortunate that the small self, in its certainty, has never attempted to appropriate it. It cannot be appropriated at that level. Sorcery has never been this teaching, nor will it ever be.

To claim the Kingdom is to call it forth. To claim the Divine in another is to call it forth. And the agreement to manifest, to know the self in realization at the cost of the old, is the claim of the heretic and the holy man. They are often the same, you know. What heresy has been indoctrinated as is speaking against the church or the institution. You cannot claim heresy, in fact, as the Divine Self because the Divine Self is God as it knows itself in individuation. The teaching of the Christ that you were taught has always been a teaching of embodiment and manifestation and resurrection at the cost of the old, and the Upper Room is where we sing and lift you to for the awakening of the world you live in.

This is no small teaching, friends. This is the Kingdom come to be through your intention, through the sound and the force of your vibration in the articulation and in the language of the God Self who has known itself as you.

We will say these words now to all who hear them. When you speak the words "I Have Come, I Have Come, I Have Come," you are aligning to the alignment that will call forth a new world. We will leave you, Paul, now. He is shifting, as he intoned the words. You are, as well, as you spoke them. And the body itself, in intonation and expression in truth, has come as you.

We thank you each for your presence. Period. Period. Period.

DAY THIRTEEN

Touch your face. Feel your face, please. Take a moment now and understand that what you feel holds vibration. The solidity of what you feel is, in fact, an illusion. Everything is in motion. Everything is in vibration. And everything you see before you can be re-comprehended as vibration in what we call the Upper Room. The transition you make from low vibration to high is in many ways the journey of the soul in remembrance to her origin, his origin. And the origin of the soul, as we would explain it to you, is as of God, an aspect of God that has chosen to learn through expression, in reconciliation with its Source, through the passage of lifetimes that you undertake to know the self, to comprehend the self and all manifestation as of God.

Now, nothing is separate from Source. Understand that. And any identity you can hold, any way of knowing the self in form, is transitional within God. So you are God as Paul, or as Philip, or as Alice, or as Joan. You are the Divine who has come in recollection of itself in the aspect you have chosen to express through. Now, what the soul is is a codification of vibration, with an identity, a soul echo, a remembrance of its vibration, its awareness of what it is. The soul itself in comprehension with God is the manifestation of lineage, and the lineage of God is everything it knows itself through. Everything that can be known or even imagined is of God because nothing is outside it.

Now, the aspect of soul that you comprehend yourself through we will speak to as of God in distinct ways. The manifestation of the Divine as God must be comprehended as such. Paul needs a pause. We will take a moment.

(short pause)

What soul is is the manifestation of the aspect of God that expresses in vibration in an understanding of independence in consort with the realization of Source. And the aspect of you that seeks to be re-known, or the Christed Self in manifestation as you, is of soul, but distinct from it. As you understand it, nothing is outside of God, and soul cannot be outside of God. The Christed Self, or the aspect of God that seeks its realization as you, is of soul, but it is not *the* soul because the soul itself is in progression, while the Christed Self, in its realization, is not non-progressive, but is not here to learn. It is here to realize—the Christ in realization through the form that you have taken. And the soul is of the spirit and the spirit is God is the journey you undertake through these teachings.

Each of you who comes, who witnesses, who bears witness to the teachings either in text or through our presence, is being received in multiple levels. The Divine as what, the manifestation of the Divine as what, the form that you have taken and agreed to be in knowing, in realization, in fruitfulness, we will say, the comprehension of the Christ in form, is the ability of form to re-know itself in the octave of the Christ. And the octave of the Christ, the Upper Room, as we teach it, is seeking to establish itself in dominion on this plane through your own expression.

The realization—underline the word *realization*—of what you are, the manifest Divine that has come as you, in some ways realizes itself and overrides some of what the soul would choose to learn through because you learn in different ways as the realized self, who is knowing itself as the Christed truth that has come in form for the benefit of all. While the soul may choose to learn through fear, or through lower nature, because everything is here to be learned through—not escaped from or run from, but learned through—as the Divine Self sees itself and knows itself beyond fear, it releases the need to confirm fear because fear is in low vibration. And the Divine Self as you, that has come as you, operates in higher frequency and must claim all things in a conferrence of that high octave in co-resonance. To justify fear in any way, shape, or form is to claim fear in its purview, and the purview of fear, as we have taught, is to claim more fear to realize itself, again and again, through itself as fearful. Now, to justify fear would be to decide that it is meritful. While you may know yourself in a fearful situation, that is not choosing in fear or acting in fear. To experience fear—"Where did I lose that thing? What will happen if I don't find it?"—is a response to a situation. To act in fear would be to decide that the terrible thing that you've imagined could happen if you've lost the item will be the death of you, and to confirm that through the actions you take is to claim the act of fear in perpetuity.

To realize the Divine is present in all things is not to confirm that there are things happening that you could not agree to or confirm as a personality self as a positive thing. We don't ask you to abnegate the power that you've been gifted with to discern, but to understand that, as nothing is out of God, the very presence of the one who knows who he is, what she is, how he serves, reclaims what is seen and re-known in a higher octave to lift it to a new sight, a new awareness of reclamation. "The Reclamation of the Divine," which will be this chapter if we are allowed to complete it, has ramifications on what is seen and known. It is not ideology. It is not presupposition. "Well, that thing is holy because everything is holy, so just let it be." In some ways, that is denial. You see someone suffering. "Well, God is there anyway, so be it, it is taken care of" is to wash your hands from the responsibility of what you are being aligned to as the witness of suffering. In the sight of suffering, the action of the Divine is to transform pain through the realization of God that can and must be known in the high octave that you perceive it from. Understand, friends, it is the Divine that witnesses and acts upon it, not the small self who would run and fix it as she assumes it should be fixed, and not as the aspect of self that would deny responsibility for what she witnesses, but the self that knows who she is, and, because she knows who she is, she realizes herself in participation to the thing seen. Understand what this means. If nothing is outside of God, and the Divine as you is present and you are witnessing suffering, you are claiming the action of God, the presence of God in realization through what you are perceiving. To realize is to know, and when something is known in the high octave, it is reclaimed and re-known and lifted to the essence of Source that permeates all matter.

He is interrupting. "Are we fixing suffering, then?" That is not what we are saying at all. If you think of fixing, you think of mending. To reclaim something is to know it anew. To fix it is to put the bandage on it and send it back on its way. There are wounds that will not be fixed with a bandage. And there are hells that cannot be released through pretending the hell doesn't exist. What a hell is is a belief in the absence of light or the potential for healing, for realization, for re-knowing. What hell is is the decision that God cannot penetrate or realize itself in what it already is, which would be an impossibility.

Now, in the dense field you have operated in, you have chosen to know yourselves in confirmation of fear, of separation from your brothers and sisters and from the Source of your being. So the idea that something can be reclaimed, realized, and re-known, and lifted to what we call the Upper Room, would be an impossibility at that level of agreement. But, as you have come, each and every one of you who responds to these words, who goes into the echo of his or her own resonance as the True Self, as you have come, you have been endowed and gifted with the responsibility to reclaim what you see in the high octave of the Upper Room.

The Upper Room is the abiding presence of the Divine beyond fear, and when you lift a thing to it through your sight and through your intention, you are lifting the thing that has known itself in separation to union with the Source of all things. You can only do this as the one who knows who he is, and who abides there in his vibratory echo, in her embodiment and agreement to serve. We have taught you the teaching "I know how I serve" already. We will return to it as needed. In this moment we say that those of you who are present and who will hear these words and know the echo of them in the manifestations of your lives, in the realization of the Divine in form, those of you who've said yes, will come anew and in the claim we offer—"I Have Come."

The claim "I Have Come" is the announcement of being, the announcement of reclamation of the presence of the act of the Creator that can be expressed through the individual soul through the Christed Self that has assumed the soul and claimed manifest in form as who and what you are. And, as we teach this, "I Have Come," the vibratory echo or response of the manifest world will be the reclamation of the Kingdom, which is the awareness of the presence of the Divine that can be known while in form. The world you see before you is asking for reclamation. And reclamation, in this case, is the realization of the Divine as can be seen and comprehended and known anew through your presence and through the decree "I Have Come."

Now, this is not a new teaching, Paul, but it is the complete application of all of the teachings thus far. They have all brought you to this moment of announcement. They are not to be confused, one with the other. This is the outcome of all the prior attunements we have gifted you with: The attunement to the Word in preparation for the claim of identity, "I know who I am, what I am, how I serve," the claim of being, "I am here," and the claim of freedom, "I am free," that reclamates you, announces you in totality in the claim "I Have Come." And this announcement of being as the Divine Self is what trumpets and heralds the awakening of humanity.

The work has been done in preparation for this. We will attest to that. Each of you who hears these words must attest to your own response to them. And the realization, the manifestation of this field in these words, is the true teaching of the second coming of the Christ. You have waited for a man in the clouds. What you have never known is that you are all in the clouds in the Upper Room,  and, as you are realized there, you anoint anything you perceive and can imagine through the consciousness that abides there. The small self—in its life, in its witness, in its agreement to be in form—is understood and has acquiesced itself to the agreement of embodiment through the stages of realization that are, in many ways, the requirement for the soul's evolution. These are stages we will discuss as we continue these teachings. But the agreement to embody, which is, in fact, a requirement, aligns the body itself to its possibility for reclamation, and, once that has begun, the incremental shifts are to support the individual in her ability to know and maintain the identity of the True Self in expression. As you come to us in questions—"Why was I born?" "What am I here for?" "How do I serve?"—we will always tell you the truth. You have come to be realized, to be re-known, to be the ambassador of truth that sings her song to the world before her. You have all come in remembrance of who you have always been. And you have claimed it, aligned the soul to its true purpose, through intention and the ability to sing and to know. "I Have Come" will be the teaching you receive as we continue this text. Period. Period. Period.

(PAUSE)

Now, as we teach you the meaning of "I Have Come," we want to announce two things. The residue of your past actions, in many ways, is reclaimed in a higher octave through this expression, and that is the rising above karma, as you have understood it. The release of the old also requires your accountability for what you chose in a low way, but it may now be met in a high octave, which supports you in recognition and without the consequence that you may have incurred in low vibration. Once a thing is understood and comprehended, it may be reclaimed in a new way. So we are no longer acting through the old, but within the new as expressions of the Divine.

The other thing we wish you to know of: The consequence of this expression is that the mandate of the Christ in expression is always truth. It can never reconcile a lie with the need for the lie. The lie itself must be re-seen, known anew, and claimed in truth for the lie to be known in a new way. What this actually means is that any lies you have known yourselves through and supported in being will be made known to you for the purpose of reclamation. The idea that fear can run the show must now be abandoned, once and for all, and, once again, a lie must only be known as a creation of fear. As you release fear and the mandates and requirements of fear, you also release the lies that you have assumed to be true.

Now, this is not at all comfortable for the aspect of self that has built a life upon lies, a belief in what was important, what should be done, or what must be done through the dictates of others and inherited systems of lies. As you choose, again and again, to align in the Upper Room, which is the place and being of truth, you commence a life in accordance to truth, and that life will bring you what you require. Any encounter you have with the old and the creations of fear must now be known as opportunity to be re-known, free of the things that you have served in idolatry or fear.

Now, the Divine as what you are—which simply means the manifestation of the Divine in physical form—can contribute to change as an expression of the Christ, once you understand that the being at this level of consequence simply acts as the one who knows who he is; expresses the vibration of being. The idea that you have been called to a great act in some ways is true, but the great act is the transformation of being into the high octave as the expression of the Divine that can now be known with manifestation. What this means is any idea that you have held of what it means to be the manifest Divine is replaced completely in comprehension of being it. You don't question things about the self when they are known or realized, nor do you strive to be what you already are, and the consequence of being, the manifestation of the Divine as expressed by you, is the choice to become the acknowledged one, the articulated one who calls the echo of his vibration into the world to move into like vibration with all it knows and sees. The decibel you operate at as the Christed Self actually lifts in totality and resonance what it encounters, and the ramifications of this means that everything you see and encounter must be understood in a new way.

Now, at this juncture we must say that the teaching that you are receiving, while for the text, must be understood by each of you as an act. The manifestation of the Christ, in echo, in resonance, is an act of articulation. When something is articulated, it is announced, it is present, and the claim "I Have Come" is an articulation of being. The articulation of being, at this level, commences the moment you say that you are willing to embody and release the obstacles that you have utilized in self-definition in the low octave. By *low octave* we mean the density of form and agreement to form that you elected to become when you first incarnated in form. To bypass, to lift beyond what has already been claimed, requires the self, the Divine Self, to assume the low self to its benefit. So the idea of who you are—and underline the word *idea,* because all you think you are and expect to be is simply an idea and nothing more—is assumed in the vibration of the Christ and re-announced, re-articulated, in the claim "I Have Come."

Now, when this is spoken, the agreement is made, first in the vibratory field in the manifestation that you may know of as the causal body, which then agrees to assume the entirety of the manifest self by knowing, or realizing, what it has always been. When you decide that the what that you are, the form you have taken and its expression, may be re-articulated and re-known, the vibration of the body, in connection with the energetic fields that it expresses through, may be reclaimed again and again in the Upper Room. What this means for some of you is that the idea of who you are is re-known, re-expressed, and the announcement of the vibration "I Have Come" claims what you are now in commensurate action with the level of expression you have claimed. By *level of expression* we mean that the decibel of vibration or sound the claim confers through your alignment adjusts as you articulate the self in manifestation.

He asks for other language to understand this. And, if we may, we will say we are offering you the language that may best convey the thought. To reduce it through the language of old and to define it for you, Paul, would actually be to limit the expression. When you know yourself as a vibratory being, you may understand that the fluctuation of vibration will call to you a variety of expression. In the Upper Room, which is where we teach, the small self, in an assumed state, is no longer running rampage over your life. The alignment you have claimed is commencing to know itself as and what you are in full expression, and the variations or gradations of expression will always be agreeable to the level of consciousness that you have aligned to. Even in the Upper Room, you may understand yourself as claiming fear and then knowing the self in the small self that chooses it again.

He is very confused. "Did I mishear? Can fear be claimed in the Upper Room?" Anything may be claimed, but if fear is claimed, it is a choice made in lower vibration, and it is the choice to leave the higher octave to attend to something through fear. That would be a choice made by the aspect of self who still releases her idea of who she is, or her attachment to what she thinks is important, and this would be an ongoing process as you evolve. Understand, friends, we are not making you something you are not. We are reclaiming you as what you are, and, by this definition, "I Have Come," you have agreed to believe or know or accept the consequence of manifestation.

Now, by *consequence* we simply mean that which is incurred by vibration. If you have a twenty-watt bulb in a lamp, you accept a dim light. You don't expect to see the entirety of the room in illumination with the low wattage. When you are putting the hundred-watt bulb in, you see much more. The expression of the light is more inclusive. The ramification of the alignment to the claim "I Have Come" is the brightest voltage you may use. But the body itself must go into the agreement that it can be held. Otherwise you are playing games.

"What does that mean?" he asks. Very simply, it means that to speak the words that we offer you through attunement will indeed attune you at the level you can hold. What you cannot hold in lower vibration will not be met until you are able to release what is holding you down, what the idea is of who you are that is operating in such limitation. So, if you understand that you are met through your own experience of the Divine as you embody, you will understand that, in this path, the obstacles in the way will be revealed for the purpose of lifting beyond them. You are never trapped by a creation of history because any creation of history may be re-known, and the consequence of your vibration, which means what your vibration brings to bear upon the material realm, must be understood as the opportunity to lift the world to the level of expression of the Christ.

Now, as some of you stand before us in an awareness of what you have been, you say, "I cannot change. I have tried to know myself anew." And, for you, we say, please stop trying to change and start allowing the Divine to reclaim you. If you are so powerful through the work of your own hands or mind, you would have done it already. To comprehend surrender as the divine expression of God must be claimed in innocence. We will explain this now. *In innocence* means the aspect of self that is in agreement to who and what she is does not hold the agenda of the divinity that the small self would claim. She is innocent of sin, and by *sin* we mean agreement to the old in opposition of truth. Very simply put, the Christed Self is innocence. Do you understand this? In her innocence, she is expressed, and the mandate of innocence, the one who has not been taught what to think or believe, is to see the world as a new expression, unendowed with the ramifications of fear. Do you understand this? The infant is not told who to trust and who not to trust, what is good or evil. She learns these things as she is taught, as she grows and confirms the legacy of fear that she was born into. The Christ is born as and through each of you in a reclamation of innocence, and the claim "I Have Come" is the coming of the Christed Self to reclaim the world. How this is manifested as each of you will be known to you by your expression of it. And no words we speak to you can fully prepare you for that.

The reunification of self with Source is beyond language, and the intonation of sound that we now use to circumvent or rise above the old may be comprehended as a way forth beyond language. The articulation of the Divine as what, while utilizing language in all of the attunements you have been gifted with thus far—in fact, how they are attuned—is through the vibratory attention that you operate as when they are spoken. The meaning of the words themselves are, in fact, secondary to what the meaning has been endowed with in tone.

So, finally, Paul, we say, yes, this is in the text. You must support yourself by trusting the language we use when we teach, and not try to fix it as you would have it be. Your small self likes things the way he likes them, and this is not a teaching for the small self. The teaching of the Christ in manifestation, which we will continue later, is the teaching of reclamation of being. Period. Period. Period.

DAY FOURTEEN

Each time you decide that you are worthy of being who you truly are, you encourage every aspect of the self to claim what it may know. Each time you decide that what you may claim may exist beyond the known, you align to the potential that already exists and has not been expressed in the material realm. Each time you say yes to the manifested Divine as you, you claim it. The agreement is made and the projection of the Divine, the expression of your being, claims what it encounters in a high light, a high tone, a high way of being. As you say yes to what you truly are and have always been, you demonstrate it through the life you live, and the manifestation of the life you live must move to a new agreement that exists beyond the known, beyond the ideas you've held, the agreements you've made and seek to justify because they have been there so long. Each time you say yes to what you truly are, you give it permission to be claimed, expressed, and known for the good of all.

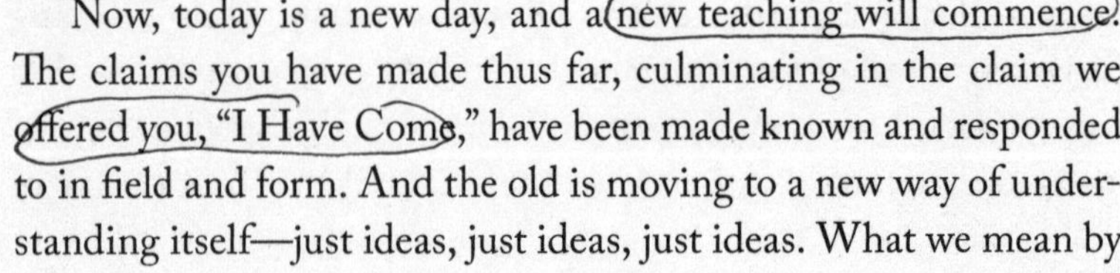

Now, today is a new day, and a new teaching will commence. The claims you have made thus far, culminating in the claim we offered you, "I Have Come," have been made known and responded to in field and form. And the old is moving to a new way of understanding itself—just ideas, just ideas, just ideas. What we mean by this is everything you've known has been just an idea. The male you are, the form you have taken, is an idea of form and an articulation of form that has moved into manifestation. Everything you see is an idea made into form, articulated, constructed in manifestation through intent and through the awareness of what is required in a manifest world. At this day, you have an opportunity to remove the old as you might pull back a curtain to allow the light to shine, and, as the light shines upon what was, the ideas that inform them may be comprehended. And, as they are comprehended, they may be released so that the new may be known, may be called into being.

What we are saying to you each is that the manifest world, as you have comprehended it, is a manifestation of the ideas of humanity that have been claimed over centuries, over millennia, and each of you decides your relation to what you see through the fabric of the world that you have decided is so real. As everything is in motion and vibration, everything may be known in a new way, and the malleability of form may be comprehended by you as you ascend to the level of vibration where the refinement of being claims you in less density. As you experience vibration, the palpable vibration that comes when you claim the intentions, you are beginning to manifest in response to the higher realms. The vibration of the Word, as expressed by you, is a high claim of knowing and being, and its resonance has an octave that you participate in through your alignment to it. At this moment, anyone who hears these words is participating in an act of manifestation, and the manifestation of the Divine, the who and what you have always been in high alignment and real expression or manifestation, is what has come.

Now, to deny the Divine as what you are, which is a temptation for most of you, is to deny the Divine in all manifestation. "She may be divine, she's a good person, I cannot be divine, I am not a good person" separates you from the Source of your being and predicates your allowance to the claim of your divinity on some idea of good or bad. Again, just an idea. The manifest self, the physical being you know yourself through, has come to be regarded, in many ways, as a form that is here to serve the mind, do its duty, and then be done with. In fact, what form is is expression, as is everything else you can see. And the articulated form you have taken may be re-known, re-understood in a higher way as you ascend in form and field. What this means is that the vibratory oracle that you are, the full being that you are, may be reconceived beyond the form you have taken. And this is not done by will, as you would think it, but through alignment to the inherent perfection that the Divine holds in form.

Now, when you think of perfection, you think of an idealization. "I should look a certain way or act a certain way that resembles an idea of what perfection must be." But, in fact, what perfection is is agreement to the absolute, because the absolute *is* perfection, cannot be other than what it truly is. The masks that you have worn, the small self's identity, in some ways precludes the shining truth of your being to be claimed and held and known. As you decide that the what that you are, in form and field, is expressed in fullness, the vibration of your being, assumed in fullness, claims the world it sees in like accord. And the being that you are is removed from what it was because it knows itself in a new field—the Upper Room, as we call it.

Now, the Upper Room as the manifest place that you align as and to is simply agreement to the Divine in the high octave that you sing in. It is agreement, or vibrational accord, that supports you in maintaining this. And the form that you have taken, and we include Paul here, must be re-known at this juncture to support the vibration in holding itself in fullness in a new octave. Now, the body itself, as understood as an organism, has functions that it must claim, a shape that it must adhere to in one way or another, for you to recognize yourselves as the what you think you are. But the body itself again is an idea that may be rendered new through the agreement to be in manifestation in fullness in the Upper Room.

At this day we say that, upon these words, these articulations of vibration and tone, you may give a new consent to what manifestation means and give permission to the body, the idea of the body, to be exact, to be rendered new in high accord. The claim "I know what I am" is the agreement to what you are in high vibration, that the form of all things is of God and can be known as such. But the acquiescence to be rendered new in form comes at a cost, and the cost is a simple one. Any identity that has been held in opposition to truth must be reclaimed in a new way, and the only way that this is done is through alignment and agreement to become what you can only be manifest as in a high octave.

As we say these words to each of you, we are offering them to you in a new agreement, a new way of being, a new expression that form may take. And, as you understand what is being requested of you in this encounter, you will have a choice to assign yourself to the act of liberation of form, as you have known form, for the purpose of reincarnating in fullness as the Divine Self. The opposition that form has held to this encounter in some ways is based on reason that has been adapted and encoded in the systems of form, that form itself must adhere to certain laws and cannot exist beyond them. The claim we offered you, "I am free, I am free, I am free," claims the self beyond the encoded agendas that have been utilized to maintain your adherence to control or systems of control that you have been in alignment to. And the body itself, at this juncture, must undergo its own rebirth, its own encounter in transmutation.

Now, what this means is that you are accessing the syllable of vibration or tone that instills within you the causal body as the manifest body, which means that the Divine Self, known in spirit, knows itself as what it is in form, in blood and tissue, in the vibration that we know of as the Upper Room. And, in this articulation, this name that we will claim you in, you are offering yourself, in some ways, to be re-known, re-articulated, as the manifest being who exists in a high octave. Again, we have said we have worked hard on identity, the claim of worth, the agreement to be, and the manifest form itself has been prepared for its new self to become form as what it is.

Now, we say these words to you each in the comprehension that they may make no sense to the small self, but this is no longer a teaching for the small self. We are speaking directly to form, and claiming form, and form itself exists without personality, and, if you must know, without an agenda predicated by fear. That would be the self you know of as Paul or Alice or June who uses those words, "I am afraid." Your leg will never be afraid, nor will your eye. You may feel fear in the body, but the body itself is not what is in fear. It is in response to what has catalyzed it in a fearful expression. So the words we use are spoken to form in directness, and your agreement to them is actually uttered, not only by the mouth you speak through, but by every cell, every aspect of the body you know.

On this day we claim that the forms that each have taken are regarded new, are resurrected in the true identity of the Christed Self, and the Monad, the Infinite, the True Self of God, come as each one, has now been given permission to embody in fullness. And, as we say yes to the form of those we speak to, as we say yes to what they believe themselves to be, as we speak to the blood and the bone and the marrow, as we speak to the hair and the lips and the tongue, as we speak to the fingers and toes and vertebrae and intestine, we sing to you in the awareness that what you are is being re-known. And, as we invite you, each of you in form, to join us in tone, we acknowledge the manifestation that has been what it was in its new name.

[The Guides tone through Paul.]
"I Have Come. I Have Come. I Have Come."

Be as you are. Be as you are. Be as you are.

The body itself is asking itself a question. "Am I new?" And the claim we answer you in is yes. In the sound of truth echoing through each cell, the organism you have known yourself as has been given permission, as agreed to by you, to be reclaimed as the expression that aligns in the Upper Room, but can claim the world in manifestation. That which is God, knows God in all. That which denies God, denies God in all. That which gifts itself to God, gifts itself to all. And that who knows who she is, who sings in truth, sings for the world.

You Have Come. You Have Come. You Have Come.

(PAUSE)

Trouble comes through the agreement to fear. If you understand this, you have a way out of trouble. Trouble comes when what you decide is informed by fear. You may believe you are leaving fear behind, but you choose in fear all day long without understanding why. The moment you decide that you are safe as you are, you can become free of fear. The moment you agree that who and what you are, the True Self as you, is beyond fear, fear cannot reach you.

Now, fear has tentacles. It will seek to call you from the Upper Room back to the low because you have prescribed its power, and you may say yes to it, if you wish, even from the Upper Room, and embark on the journey to the lower to have your encounter with fear. Perhaps what it will teach you is that it is a liar, has no real merit, and would seek to assume you as what it is, which is fearful.

The planet you exist on is now comprehending itself in a very different way than it has thus far. In some ways, what it is saying is "I will not be touched, I will not be misused, and I will no longer allow the being that I am to be named in fear." To be named in fear means you have decided that something is full of fear, or fearful. Now, the planet knows itself in freedom. It knows what it is. It is an organism, and a life-filled one. And the organism itself is seeking to replenish itself at the cost of the old. Everything must be reborn, you see, in order to survive in the high amplitude that is present now. When you understand yourself as an organism, a complete being, in relation to another organism, another complete being, you move into an agreement that is respectful and in love. The moment you defile the planet and decide what the planet should be, on your terms—"I will get what I want from this thing, I will make it mine, I will dominate it, I will crucify it to get my needs met"—you have created the separation in form from the self that knows who it is and the organism that knows what it is.

Now, the temple of the body, the structure that the body is, can be comprehended in several different ways. You may understand the organism as flesh and bone, or you may understand the organism as a vehicle for learning and experience, or you can understand the body as an incarnation of a soul seeking to express itself in a shared construct which you know of as reality. None of these are false, but the highest regard that you can claim the body in is in its union with the matter that surrounds it. This is not done by lowering vibration, but by realizing the high vibration that exists in the material realm through the recognition of the inherent Divine.

Every leaf on every tree is oscillating. Every sunbeam, every pile of dirt, every pond or pool, every ocean or lake is alive in vibration, and, as you witness God as the leaf, as the dirt, as the lake, as you align to it at that level, you can move into communion with God as expressed in physical manifestation. The one who knows who and what she is knows what she sees, and, as the Divine sees the Divine in all, and, as the old is relinquished, the world is made new.

Now, is the world benefiting through your encounter with it, the Divine as you in an encounter with the leaf and the pond and the ocean? In fact, it is. As the Divine is witnessed by you, as it is reclaimed by you, as it is lifted to its true nature, the manifest structure that you know of as water or leaf or dirt actually begins to rise in vibration to meet you where you are. The encoding of the vibration you hold in the claim "I know how I serve" and in the claim "I

Have Come" promotes the encounter of the Divine with the manifest world in material form in the way that is required to lift it.

Now, as we teach you this, we must tell you several things. Each of you who has come to this encounter has made the agreement for form itself to be re-known in the high octave. We begin with the form you have taken, the Word made flesh. But your encounter with the world is your encounter with the Divine. When you speak to miracles, the water into wine, the parting of the sea, you are actually speaking to alchemy, and the illustrations of alchemy from the times of old are actually the adjustment that the manifest world makes in its encounter with the force of God in articulation.

Now, if you understand that we are not promising you you will move mountains and part seas, but we *are* promising you you will lift the mountain and lift the sea to the octave of the Divine by nature of your presence and agreement to know what things are in a new idea, you will understand what it means to make a new world—"Behold, I make all things new," the claim of the Divine Self in its encounter with mankind and with the landscape mankind expresses in.

Now, when you stand and face the sun, you feel the beams of the sun, the heat of the sun, upon your skin. There is no effort there. The sun may make your skin brown, bleach your hair, make you burn and blister if you are not prepared for it. The sun may heal the earth, dry the rain, or scorch the earth in its strength and power. As you become as the sun, as the light that witnesses the world, the rays of your being, your vibratory field, in waves, claims what she sees, what it encounters, with the Christ vibration for the purpose of reclamation. Behold, I make things new.

Now, to understand the purview of the Divine Self, we will restate what we have stated prior, in prior texts. The purview of the Divine Self is everything she encounters, everything she sees, everything witnessed and even imagined. If it can be held in consciousness, it can be known, and what is known by the Divine Self can be reconceived, as the one who knows who she is endows it with a vibration of the presence of the Christ, or, if you wish to use another word, the light that is always shining.

Now, ask yourself this question: "Am I willing to be what I am, in expression, for the benefit of the world? Am I willing to know myself, in a new way, beyond the tenets or structures that have limited me? Am I willing to let go of any idea I may have ever held that will serve as an obstacle to the risen Christ operating as what I am?" It sounds like a tall order. Paul wants to run away, leave the teaching behind, go find something better to do than listen to these words. But we must say it is not as hard as you believe it to be, once you understand that everything is just an idea. Who you are is an idea. What you do is an idea. Who you know is an idea of who you know. All that needs to transform is a simple idea, and the ideas that serve as obstacles to your realization are the very things that you are gifted in an encounter with now. Anything that would preclude the light from shining as and through you will now be known, will now be addressed, will now be resurrected, or unburied, if you wish, so it may be known and seen and released for the benefit of all.

Now, at this juncture, we must say to Paul, we are taking the reader to a place that is not so comfortable, so please allow us to do this. Any shame you hold about the body, any shame you hold about your sexual being, any shame the body holds that it has used to deny the Divine must now be reclaimed in a higher way. Any belief that your limitation in form could possibly preclude the action of the Divine as and through you must be understood as a false teaching. The idea of the body as a temple is all well and good, but even what is within the temple must be known as holy, not just the structure, but all that has known itself within the temple walls. And that must include every encounter with pain that the body has known itself in.

On this day we would like to offer you a new teaching, on the resurrection of form and the release of form from the disability that it has claimed itself in. Unlike the planet you express on, which would never do itself harm, you have harmed yourselves incredibly through fear and through shame and through disregard of the True Self, who knows who she is and can never be ashamed. The teaching you receive now is about the requirement for release that is now present, as the body itself begins to flower. Anything that would obstruct the flowering of the body can now be attended to, and will be attended to as you align to it.

We will say these words on your behalf:

On this day I choose to encounter each one who encounters these words in a promise of the new, an agreement to the new, that the being that you are will now be re-known in a pure state, a return to innocence, as the Christed Self requires itself to move as you, to move through you, in participation with the re-creation of a world. And anything that is not of God, or of love, or of agreement to God, that which you have held in darkness, may now be released in offering to the Creator to be healed.

We imagine that, before you, you see an altar prepared for you, a perfect altar surrounded by flowers and cared for by those of us who would support you each in your requirements for realization. If you would, imagine yourself lying upon this altar and offering yourself and the body you have taken for the purification or release that is required by you in service to the greater good of all. As you say yes to this, please allow the promise to be made, met as you, as and through you, as the body itself is reclaimed and re-known.

Allow, allow, allow.

(pause)

What you are now is, in an established way, the emissary of the Divine, and the permission granted to release what is required for you will be done as you rest, as you agree to it. And, if there are actions you must take to ennoble this choice, to verify it for yourself, it will be made known to you. We will say these words in closing:

On this day we choose that each one who reads these words will be met in perfection in the structure that they hold, in the body they have known, as it is reestablished as the Christed Self.

Stop now, please. We will close this chapter now. Period. Period. Period.

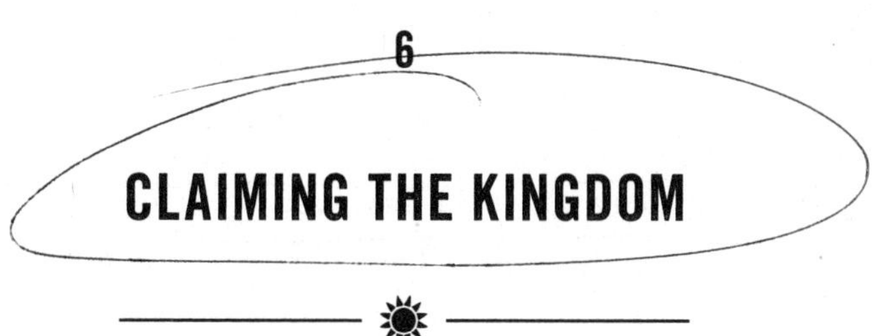

6

CLAIMING THE KINGDOM

DAY FIFTEEN

Now, as we teach you about what you are, you must comprehend that the manifested what, the True Self as what, claims rather different things than you have known yourselves through. The body itself, an organism, if you wish, has been primed to meet the octave that it has been expressing through. And the senses you hold, in all ways, have become attuned to the reality you have known.

As you lift in vibration in the Upper Room, the availability to information through the sensory systems is increased in vibration as well, which means you are activated, in some ways, to be a receiver for vibration consummate with tone or the octave you express in. The Divine as what, the manifest what, claims in the Upper Room the availability in service in the claim we have offered you, "I know how I serve." And, if, in fact, service requires your attunement to a level of amplitude of vibration and tone that encourages you to access information beyond the known, it will become available to you. What we are actually telling you is that you embody in the Upper Room with the ability to know. K-N-O-W.

Now claircognizance, if you wish to call it that, or knowing, is a gift, but it is also the availability to act, to become instructed by the Divine Self for the purpose of supporting others or changing the world. Now, we use the word *changing* intentionally now, because the world you are in, by impact, by agreement, is in transformation, and the tone you claim and that you carry, in many ways, is the tone that resurrects the divine principle that is already active or present in the manifest world. The idea of claiming the Kingdom, very simply put, means you are claiming into manifestation the inherent principle, the active principle, the causal feature, the God in all. And calling that forth in reclamation, or, if you wish, resurrection, decides for you your relationship to the manifest plane.

Now, when you know, you are operating in your knowing, and the consequence of knowing, we have to tell you, will always be action that is concurrent, or in agreement, with the knowing you have. If you know how to walk to work, you find yourself at work. You don't question the way. You may take a detour. You may choose to sit on a bench and enjoy the sun. But you know your way to work. There is no question, really. And the knowing that we speak to now, in octave, in the Upper Room, is the knowing that is required for you to serve in fullness. We tell you this for one reason. The ability to know at the level of agreement we are teaching is a gift, and you are accountable to the gift as it is given to you.

Now, when you know, you are not questioning, nor are you self-deceiving, nor can you deceive another. It is not possible. And the teaching of truth that we have offered you already, truth as a field that you begin to operate in—"I know who I am in truth, what I am in truth, how I serve in truth"—is the support that you require to ennoble the activation without self-deceit. In the claim "I know who I am," the recognition of knowing claims the form, the what, the manifest self, and its expression, commensurate with the value or level of vibration that you have come to, is the service you bring in agreement to know what is required of you.

Now, Paul is interrupting. "I can imagine many people saying,

'Well, I *don't* know. You are telling me I know, but I don't think I do.'"

When you know, there is no thinking. There is recognition. And the knowing that we speak to actually bypasses systems of agreement that you have utilized to confirm the old reality. Now, if you understand that any equation has an outcome—two plus two equals four—you can also understand that how something is conceived of is always in resonance at the level of its conception. In other words, the man who makes the painting claims the identity of the painting in recognition of the consciousness he holds as he paints. The painting is the out-picturing of the consciousness at the level of alignment the painter holds. The painting exists without the painter. It may hang in a museum. But it still claims the vibration of the painter at the level of alignment he grew to and was at at the time the painting was conceived of.

As you lift to the Upper Room, what you claim and how you claim it is in alignment to the higher octave, and what you claim and where you claim it must then move into accord to the vibration you know yourself in. So the ways of being that you have utilized to confirm a reality, the old equations, if you wish, are in fact transposed, re-known, in the high octave. Once again, the example: The concerto may be played in a low key or a high key. In the high key, the value of the concerto lifts what it encounters to meet it in resonance or tone. And the acclimation to the high vibration that you have come to commands you to interface with the manifest world for the purpose of recognition, or recognizing the Divine that you now know is there. You are not seeking the Divine, you are not looking for it under which rock, in each book that you may read. You are knowing it—in the sunset, in the ocean, in the body you hold, in what you see before you. And the claim you make upon what you see—"I know who you are in truth, I know what you are in truth, I know how you serve in truth"—is the reclamation of the Divine that is always there.

Now, you don't need to speak the words, at a certain point, because you have come to be them. The one who knows what she is does not need to remind herself to shift the dial of the radio she is to play the high broadcast. In the Upper Room, you reside in the high broadcast and lift what you encounter to its meeting with the Divine that is its essence. The manifestation of God in this world is known by one who is the manifestation of it, not the one who is seeking to find it, remembering where he put it, or finding the right book to give him the instruction of where he should go in his seeking. The idea of becoming, truly becoming the embodiment of the Divine in recognition of the Divine in all, is the manifestation of this text. And the manual we offer you actually exists beyond words, because all we are truly doing is remembering you in the octave you express in that we call the Upper Room. And the one who knows who she is, knows who others are; knows what she is, knows what is in all things. And the service of being becomes simply the occupation of knowing. And, in knowing, you are acting in righteousness.

Now, by *righteousness* we mean in accordance with truth, and, if an action is required of you, you will be in your knowing, and the transmission of your being, which means the tone you sing through, will be present in whatever you do. Now, anything you encounter is operating in tone, in vibration, *oscillation,* if you wish. That is the word he is interrupting with. He is learning a new vocabulary here as we speak through him. Because everything exists in tone, everything may be met in tone, and, as you have appropriated the field of the True Self as what you are, you don't need to act to transform something as much as recognize what it has always been, and perhaps has forgotten, perhaps been denied, perhaps been refuted. You cannot make a rock divine. It is already divine. But your memory of the rock, as a small self, precludes its divinity. As the True Self as what you are recognizes the rock, the rock *is* holy, and its tone moves incrementally to meet you in the tone you are singing at. Now, you are not singing vocally, although of course you may. The embodiment of the Christ is a tonal action. And the tonal action we speak in is the expression of the Word articulated in the phrase "I Have Come."

Now, in dominion, which is the Christ's purview known always in accordance with truth, the action of being becomes the action of claiming the Kingdom, and not just for the self that you have been, but for all that you perceive. The dominion of the Divine, the purview of the Divine, is all that is manifest, can be conceived of or imagined. The purview of the Divine is everything, because the Divine is one with everything and does not agree to separation.

"But we are in separation, still," he says. "We differ in many ways, one man from the next, one culture from the next."

If you wish to look at the cosmetics that are interacting here, you will see ways that you have decided or perhaps appreciated differences. There is nothing wrong with differences, but they do not equate to separation. Mankind's humanity, in expression, is in fact one tone that may express in variance, in degrees. The Christed tone or the embodied tone is beyond that in an octave or two above, if you wish a descriptor. What exists in the high octave is expressed for the purpose of lifting what has expressed through the low.

Now, the differences that you utter—"That is a male or a female, a child or adult"—are in fact descriptors. But the qualities of description, in most cases, come through the information or the broadcast of what is perceived. "That looks like a child. It must be a child." "That looks like a female. I will presuppose the form she has taken based upon what I see." And, while we are not faulting your eyes, we are lifting you to a new sight where you are not denying the child, or the gender of the one you see, but you are seeing them in participation to the great dance of humanity as humanity lifts to its true nature, which is the Christed Self in tone.

"Now, what does it look like," he asks, "humanity lifting?"

You are actually seeing the beginnings of it, and much of the chaos you perceive is the undermining of the old structures that in most cases have been complicit to fear. As we have taught in prior texts, the action of fear is to claim more fear, and, in the wave of truth that is present now, everything that has been hidden will be revealed in order to be seen, and then re-known, and then lifted to the high octave. You cannot manifest the Divine when you are hiding things from the self or your fellows. You can only perceive the Kingdom with the eyes that know the truth. And what you have seen before you, across this globe, is the beginning of great change that will be continuing as humanity encounters itself through its past creations. What has been claimed in fear, chosen in fear, hidden in fear, must be re-known, reclaimed, brought to the altar, and lifted.

Now, the altar is consciousness. Do you understand this? And God itself, expressing through consciousness, is the alchemist. When something is perceived in a new way, it is transformed through the interaction with the perceiver. Do you all understand this? Nothing is left untouched by the mind that is operating in agreement to its knowing as the Divine. When seen by divine mind, known by divine mind, everything is re-created or re-known, because the Divine cannot leave anything out. Everything is of God, or absolutely nothing is.

Now, the challenge here, in the transition you are all undergoing, is that the manifest world is in agreement to its chaos, but has been complicit in its creation. And, if you understand what this means, it's really very simple. There can be no creation that you witness that you are not in vibrational agreement to. And, because the consciousness that you hold has been conditioned to decide what things are through the knowing of history, and not the present moment you stand in, you end up re-imprinting the messages of history on the things you see today.

"But is that wrong?" he asks. "If an act has been named in prior times, and we see the act today, does the act not exist?" The act exists, not as it has been known, but as it is, because everything perceived in the present moment, and responded to in consciousness, is lifted in the moment you stand in, not as what it was, what it was once known as, but as it truly is. In other words, the orphanage which you are all a part of, where every child is known by no name, with no parentage, is suddenly transformed by the memory of one Source. And every child becomes one, one of one Source, in an octave of truth. To name the child through the old names—"He looks like a Smith, we'll call him John Smith," "She looks like a Doe, she may be known as Jane Doe"—imprints the intention of the history upon the one seen. Until the one is seen in truth in the moment she stands in, she cannot be reclaimed in her True Self.

Imagine this. You are deciding that the woman on the street must not be a fine woman, based upon her dress or her actions. You are defining her through the consciousness you hold, but utilizing the memory of what you believe a bad woman to be or a how a good woman should look. In your naming of the bad woman, you reduce her in vibration. By realizing who she is, which bears nothing to do with how she appears, but the value she holds, the intrinsic value as a true being, you claim her in the Upper Room, because only in the Upper Room does she exist without the names that she has used or been claimed by. Again, the phrase "Behold, I make all things new." So, as you witness your world today, you are claiming the truth the moment you decide that the truth can be known in the moment you stand in. If you are busy impressing the old upon what you see, trying to sort out the details to conform to a narrative that has once been known, you end up entangling yourself in the vibration of old, when the highest act you may take is in knowing.

Now, when you know who somebody is, you are not excusing his or her behavior, or claiming no responsibility through what they may have incurred. But you are knowing them beyond the act, beyond what they have thought they were, because it is the self, in denial of its divinity, that will act in opposition to truth. And the ones who have forgotten what they are often have the greatest investment in maintaining their ignorance, because to be exposed to the light would actually claim them and release them from the very thing that they think they are, which is separate from their Source.

When they are known in truth, they are resurrected, or lifted to the Upper Room, through the sight you bring to them.

"So what happens to someone when they are seen anew?" Again, the vibration of consciousness informs the object, whatever it may be, or whoever it may be, and, in the high octave, the lifting occurs first in the vibrational field. But in the claim "I know what you are," the manifest self is being recognized in correlation to the vibration of the one who speaks it, or knows it, or *is* it at the level of correlation where a simple interaction calls forth the commensurate vibration. The example would be: As you know who you are, there is no question, there is only knowing. You are not fixing, you are not appending, you are not deciding what should be, how somebody should act, you are knowing who they are. And, in *their* level of accord to the who and the what, they manifest their potential.

"Is this done instantaneously? We can't rob people of free will. What if they don't want to lift?" It happens instantaneously in the interaction with the higher vibration. Once the higher vibration is known to the lower, the lower may lift commensurate to its ability. The reason we focus on form, "I know what I am," to go into an agreement with "I know what you are," is that it bypasses systems of deflection. Now, you are not overriding free will. You are simply recognizing what is already true. And you all must understand this. You are not making something up or changing somebody. You are claiming what exists in the Upper Room that you abide in. Because you know them from that vantage point, because they are known by you there, the recognition of what is always true is what lifts and reclaims. The small self's agenda, while in difference, is actually manifest in low octave, and, as one is lifted to the Upper Room through witness, they are also re-known. They are independent from you. The Will of the Divine Will is as present in them as in you. You are not making them do anything. You are recognizing what they are and can only be.

"And how are they changed?" he asks. "Do they get better? Do they act differently? What are you really speaking to?"

We are actually speaking to vibration, but because you know yourself in interaction on this plane through personality structures, you are asking, "Do they change in an agreement to what has been claimed for them?" No, they don't. They become what they truly are. Do you all understand this? We are not making you other. That has never been this teaching. We are claiming what you already are. And, as you claim from the level of embodiment you may know yourself in, you work as we do in recognition of the implicit Divine that is now known by the one who knows who she is.

Now, when we teach, in our authority, we call you forth in a reckoning of sorts. We invite you to the journey with the understanding that what you believed yourself to be is in many ways released, or at least re-understood and utilized in a new way, as you ascend in vibration. The caution we have always offered you is that this journey is one that is chosen, and you must agree to it. There is no magic wand here, but there is alignment, and the alignment is made in agreement, and in knowing. You are free of the small self's rule.

We will say this again. In knowing, you are free of the small self's rule. We are not disbanding the small self, saying it doesn't exist, but she is no longer the captain of the ship, he is no longer the king on the throne. His way of being, in many ways, becomes assumed in grace, in the octave of truth, as the Divine as you in manifestation calls a new world into being.

We will say this is the beginning of a new chapter. We will call it "Claiming the Kingdom" because that is the title we are offering you now. Period. Period. Period.

DAY SIXTEEN

Now, when we teach you what you are, we come with different ways of integrating the information, not only into your experience, but into the manifest world that you operate in. The idea of being who and what you truly are is actually unknown to most of you because you operate in agreement to what you think, what you have been taught, and you bypass your innate knowing without even realizing it. The truth of who and what you are, the being that you truly are, knows full well who she is, and the manifestation of her being, her true being, is the creation of the Christ as the what that you are.

Now, by *Christ* we mean the aspect of the Creator in form in realization in the manifest world that, by nature of her presence, calls all things to her in agreement to the Christ, or the vibratory essence of the Creator that exists implicitly in all manifestation. The *of* that you are, the divine *of*, is *of* all things. The being that you are, the true being, is also manifest, in manifestation, in anything you can see. But the one who sees and knows has gone into an agreement, a vibratory agreement, of who and what what all else is.

Now, the conditioning you've received, which in some ways supersedes this, is being addressed by us in different ways. We give you the intellectual information that you may need to comprehend the changes that you will undergo, but the change itself is alchemical, is the manifestation of God in its expression relaying itself, re-knowing itself, as the chord you play, as the musical note that is your expression and tone in the articulated world that you see before you.

"Articulated world? What does that mean?" It very simply means that everything you see is in echo, an articulation of thought. And the comprehension of what you see, when it is no longer filtered through the old programming, claims you in a vibratory agreement to what can only be in truth. Now, an articulation is a spoken word, and, as the Word is made as you, as you are articulated as the verb, the energy of the creation in action, the verb that you are, the action of your being, begins to speak to the world before you. You become the Word, not only in essence, but in action. And the echo of this, which is your impression in field and form upon that which you encounter, claims the Kingdom into the field of the Christ Mind that you are now operating in.

"The Christ Mind. That's a new teaching." In fact, it is not. The Upper Room, where we instruct from, is the Christ Mind. And that's the easiest definition for you, if you really wish to know. The idea of consciousness can be understood as mind, if you wish. And the mind of God, understood as the Christ, in its transmission, is a plane of experience that you are aligning to. And, in this alignment, everything that is seen, and is lifted to it, claims itself in the high resonance, the Upper Room, the Christ Mind, the presence of God, however you wish to name it. Your own experience becomes the teaching here. There is nothing we have taught you thus far that you have not been able to say, "Yes, I know this is so," in your own experience. As we move to you in alchemy, as we sing to you in a new song, the idea of physical manifestation must be encountered in realization for the teaching to continue. We will have some resistance from him in this teaching because he doesn't yet believe that the manifest world is actually in process of realizing itself through this interaction. When you speak a word, there is a response to the spoken word. If you announce something, there are ramifications to the announcement. The articulated word, spoken by the lips, has an impact on what it encounters. When you move to vibration and you become the articulation of the Word, the vibratory echo of the manifest self, in agreement to what it realizes as truth, calls to it a new manifestation. Very simply put, as you realize yourself, your world is realized, and the manifestation of the Kingdom is the result of this.

Now, if you think of the Kingdom as a lofty place where everything is floating and lovely and everything appears to be pretty, you are emblemizing it through the small self's idea of what the Kingdom is. The Kingdom, indeed, is a high manifest world, but because everything exists in multiple octaves, you may claim anything and everything in the Kingdom to be re-known.

"How is this done?" he asks. "Teach me the practicality, please. I am tired of definitions." A practical application in your case, Paul, would be to realize the body that you stand in, in the Upper Room. The body you exist in exists in multiple octaves. As you claim the body in the Upper Room, in the Kingdom, if you wish, and with the Christ Mind, and you articulate the body in its perfect state, you will align to the perfection that is already expressed as you in the Upper Room. And the manifestation of it, the form taken, will then become the expression.

Now, for those of you who think that means you look like this or that, you would be mistaken. What you appear as, in all ways, frankly, is an illusion and a negotiated one. The small self's negotiations about what she thinks she is creates a manifestation of form that you go into agreement to. In the Upper Room, where you are operating as Spirit, you apply the form of the True Self to the manifest self. "I am Word through my body" was the opening to this. But the Word in full expression, which utilizes form and expresses as the body, must be comprehended, very, very simply, as the manifestation of God that can be known in form.

Now, those of you who say this cannot be so are already deciding that the what that you are, the skin and bone, must exist separately from the ethereal. Form and flesh, while operating in low vibration, can be lifted through the alchemy of the Word to a new expression, the articulation we speak of that in fact exists in the Kingdom. The manifestation of the Divine as who and what is this teaching, and not only this teaching. It is the teaching of the time that you are choosing to incarnate in. As you decide that you have the right to be at this level of choice—and underline the word *choice* because it is imperative that you understand this—you create the opportunity for the manifest expression.

"But what does it look like?" he says. We bring the body to the Divine. We claim the body in articulation, "I know what I am." In doing this, the transition you take upon yourself is realization, and nothing cannot be realized when it is claimed in truth. Now, a small realization—"This is my fingernail, I finally know what a fingernail is, I realize my fingernail as what I have been taught it to be"—is a small way of saying something can be re-known or understood in a new way. But to realize the entirety of the body—every organ, every fiber, every blemish—as holy and in manifestation in the Upper Room that we teach from, is the guarantee that the entirety of being is in ascension or realization.

Now, the idea of ascension for too many of you has been emblemized in fruitful ways, but the ways of choice—"When I am ascended, I will be this or that"—are usually contrary to the truth of your being. The Divine as you is who is realized at the cost of the old. And its claim "I Have Come, I Have Come, I Have Come" is the manifest self, the realized self, calling forth the Kingdom through his encounter with it. The idea that, as you ascend, you go someplace pretty, you create opportunity to grow butterfly wings and evade your responsibilities, would be foolish. True ascension is the realization of the manifest world in the upper octave, and not at the exclusion of the body.

The Jesus teaching, in all ways, was exemplary of realization. But it has been misconstrued and taught in fundamentally wrong ways throughout the millennia It is time to turn the page on the idea that realization is an opportunity that has come to one, and only one. If it has not come as one, it could never have come at all. And each of you here, by nature of your agreement, is testimony to the potential for the Divine to come to fruition in the form and the field, and then in the landscape that you are expressing in. The totality of being, the Divine as all things, is always true and so rarely known. And, before anything is realized, it is known. In your knowing, you are in realization, and the moment realization occurs, the alchemy of it begins to see itself in all before it. Very simply, this means that it is instantaneous. We will say this again for Paul, who expects another long trek up a mountain. *Instantaneous* very simply means that realization, although it may have taken lifetimes to occur, happens in the moment you stand in, and no other moment. And, as you are realized once, you are realized for all time.

Now, commensurate to this is the misunderstanding that once you have a great idea you always have it. It was a great idea to marry your ex-wife. At the moment, you thought it was a good idea. That's a rather different thing. As the realized one has come into form, she ennobles others to do the same thing, but she must maintain the frequency, the manifest self, in the Upper Room where this occurs. And the reason no one wants to do this is you do not want to give away your riches and your selfishness and your pride and your ideas of what it means to be who you think you were supposed to be, once upon a time.

Nothing is excluded from the Divine. You cannot be operating in fear and acting as its principle, but fear itself must be of God, although it doesn't know itself to be. Understand this: There is a patch of rain, sunlight all around it. Above the cloud, above the rainstorm, there is still sky and light. The cloud itself exists within the sky, but is knowing itself in density in its raining. The Divine as you will actually claim you and all those things you say are not of God as you give yourself to it. But to give yourself to it is to surrender the idea of who you have been.

"How is this done?" he asks. "How do we surrender an idea of who we are?" By realizing, very simply, that it is only an idea. Do you understand this? "I am the life of the party" is an idea. "I am unattractive" is an idea. "I am outside of God" is an idea. "I am unworthy" is an idea. "I will not be loved" is an idea. "I cannot change" is an idea. "The world will end" is also an idea. And, in fact, the world does not end. As you surrender your entirety, it begins anew in the Upper Room, within the Christ Mind. There may be lessons to learn in the lower octaves, and when there are you will discover them. If you are fortunate, you will realize how to bring them to the Upper Room so that they may be learned in peace. If you wish the challenge of the old, go back to it, but then don't complain.

We are giving you the technique to maintain your vibration. You have asked for this. It is coming to be met by you through your body, within your experience on this manifest plane, as you lift it to the Upper Room where the True Self resides.

The manifestation of God in man is simply man in its unified state. Do you all understand this? The mysteries of the past that you entangle yourself in are all this teaching. You have never been separate. It is just an idea. You have never not been loved. It is just an idea. And anything else you may claim in fear and seek to justify is the articulation of the old self seeking to reinforce its law, its need to be separate, or its need to be right at the cost of another having his or her being.

We are preparing you all now for alchemy, and, if you are ready for this, for the form itself to be moved to a new expression of being, a new articulation of sound, a new Christ, will be born in mankind. And to be born means to have come, and herein lies the claim we bring you in this text. "I Have Come. I Have Come. I Have Come."

God as humanity does not deify humanity. Humanity is deified by its surrender to its true nature, not at the cost of its uniqueness and its bravery and its suffering, or anything else that can be learned here, but with them. You have all come, and even suffering, when it occurs, can be learned through and known in holiness.

We will stop this lecture for a moment for Paul. We will intend to resume it later in the day, if, in fact, we are permitted to teach this class as we wish. Period. Period. Period.

(PAUSE)

Each of you decides that the lives that you live are the result of the choices that you will make. This is always true. And every choice that is made in a high accord brings to you a benefit, a new choice of commensurate value. Each time you operate as the True Self, the Divine as who and what you are, you claim an opportunity, a new opportunity, to be realized anew. This is an unfoldment. Although you may be realized, you are not stopped from deeper realization, from new unfoldment, from new awareness, and a deepening of your experience of the Divine Self. This is not a one-stop train. You don't get off in the Kingdom and lie down in a beach chair and expect to be served what you want.

You are about to go on a great adventure, and the second half of this text, if we are allowed to complete it, will be the expectations of the one who has claimed the Kingdom and arrived there, for the adventure unfolds before him or her, as she arrives, not as she plans. You cannot plan for realization. Realization itself takes you beyond the known. Realization itself claims you outside of the paradigm that the old has claimed you in.

Each of you decides that you are being prepared for this journey through your attentions to these teachings. Each of you decides how much you may claim, entirely dependent upon your ability to receive. Not everyone decides that their incarnation in this lifetime is for full realization, but for the unfoldment of it, perhaps, to commence in a new way. And we welcome all of you to what you may choose.

Now, some of you decide that the thing that you are, the identity of form, is intractable to thought. We will give you an admonition here. Every thought that you have about form actually claims you in an experience with it. What you believe to be solid or liquid, by your experience, is always confirming what is a solid, what is a liquid. When you begin to move to the higher octave, where thought itself is seen as a key to manifestation beyond the known, you begin to move beyond the expectations or the dictates that the manifest world has been instructing you in. Agreeing to the old confirms the old. Aligning to the new claims you in accord to it. However, in order to receive it, you must create the opportunity and choose.

We are addressing choice now because we wish to continue in this teaching for the benefit of the reader, for the benefit of the student of this work. And we will invite you now, if you are willing, to choose this path, this path of unfoldment to the requirements of the soul's destiny. Underline the word *soul* here. The *soul's* destiny. Not the small self and not the Christed Self, perhaps, but what the soul can claim and benefit from. Every lifetime claims the soul in a new evolution, and realization, the claim of realization, is what the soul commences as in manifestation as the Divine Self. There are stages here and agreements made at every doorway. The door is open now, we say.

Yes, Paul, this in the text. We will stop now for the morning. We have much to say this weekend, if we are allowed to speak. Period. Period. Period.

(PAUSE)

Each of you decides that what you will claim is allowed by you. This is true in a lifetime, and in a moment. Each moment presents the opportunity for a new claim, and the realization of who and what you are—"I am free, I am free, I am free"—announces you in a field that is in vibrational accord to the claim made.

Now, the denial of freedom—"I am really not free, you just say I am"—will be met in vibrational accord as well. The knowing of who you are is what predetermines the outcome of any claim, and the belief that you are not free, which is the small self's dominion, must be known in a different way as it is claimed by the Divine Self, who by its nature can only be free.

Now, as you are announced in freedom, as you claim it for who and what you are, the oppression that you have known through circumstances begins to transform. In other words, you are no longer dictating what has been oppressive by your expectation for it. "Now, what is oppressive?" he asks. Anything that you have contended with that you believe could or would circumvent your own ability to know yourself as free of it. Any of those things, then, becomes the false god.

Now, the Divine as what you are is in a manifest body, and things happen to a body that may inhibit the body's expression. But the True Self expressing as and through the body is still free. But what freedom means—and full freedom, we have to say, is the realized expression of the Divine as what—may not be what you think in the small self's purview. The idea that you no longer have the headache, the painful back, the cancer, may be ways you know yourself in freedom. But your freedom cannot be predicated upon those things. If that is what freedom is, you have denounced yourself and decided that these things are more powerful than you in your true state of divine expression.

Does the Divine as you have the bad back? In manifestation, perhaps, you may experience yourself through these things. But they don't deny the divinity of the form you have taken, nor do they depend upon your realization of the True Self to be released from them. In fact, you may know who and what you are upon your deathbed in the most profound way you ever have while being in a body. The being that the body is, in vibration, exists in some ways in suppression of its true nature, in the lower octave. And what we mean by this is you are always realized in the Upper Room, but your accord in the Upper Room must be known, must be realized, and those things that exist in low accord can be lifted and can be re-known.

"Does being re-known mean it is being healed?" he asks. In some ways, yes, but your relationship to illness may be what requires healing, and not the illness itself. There is nothing wrong with being born without sight, except that you decide that it is wrong. The one who doesn't have visual sight has other ways of accessing visual information, or what you would believe to be visual. The idea that sight is of the visual eyes alone is mistaken. There is nothing wrong with being born of a small size, or of a vast size. They are different ways of being known, of being expressed, as being articulated and, having an idea of who and what you are beyond the mechanisms of form as you have been birthed to will, give you the opportunity

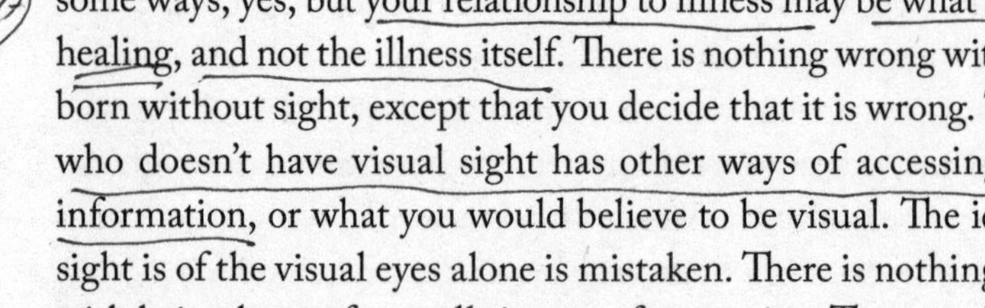

to move beyond the rigidity that your relationship with form has taken.

The claim "I am free" does not decide that you are free of the cancer, but it does decide that you are free of the idea of what the cancer is, and, in many ways, the idea of what the cancer is is what is consuming you, and not the cancer itself. The belief in your disability, what you have known yourself through, as being an infraction on a perfect state must be understood now. To be in a perfect state means to be realized as the Divine, which is always in perfection. Do you understand this? Not when your skin clears up. Not when the appendix is out. But *with* the poor appendix, or the poor eyesight, or the poor skin. If that is not the Divine in expression, you are waiting to become a mannequin, an idea of what it looks like to be perfected. Perhaps one day you may choose that experience and realize yourself through it. But that is not what we are teaching you. Realization, at this level, is alignment and expression with the causal self, the perfected self, the divine blueprint, if you wish, as the what that you are. And those aspects of self that can conform to this perfection may well choose to do so. But if you take this teaching as an opportunity to give yourself the goal to be something you may never be, you are missing the point of it entirely. You do not become divine. You already are. The body already is. It has not been yet realized as such because you have been bound in low vibration to those things that would support the loss of the divine expression, because it tells you it cannot be so.

He is still upset by something we said earlier. "But if somebody is consumed by cancer, they are not being consumed by the idea of it. They are being consumed." Perhaps the body is, but the idea of the issue claims you in agreement to it, and in vibrational accord with every piece of bad news you can collect to contribute to your fear. Once you realize that everything in manifestation is first an idea, the idea itself can be re-known in the Upper Room where the manifestation of the Divine is present without obstruction.

"But does this mean that the body is healed?" Perhaps it does, but the soul may be choosing the lesson for other means, or it may be time for the body to release itself and have a different experience of itself without the form it has known itself through.

We know this is challenging, Paul, and it's why we waited to bring this teaching until we are halfway through the text. Unless you agree that the being that you are, in its totality, can be re-known, re-articulated, you are going to be dragging your history along with you. And it does not come to the Upper Room in this way. You may re-see it from the high vantage point and re-collect it to bring it to the light for transformation, re-knowing, re-identification. But don't expect to bring a bucket of pain to the Upper Room and sit on it as if you are protecting a fortress. What a waste of time. You would do this if you could, you know, most of you. You enjoy the pain. "Oh, I'm going to the Upper Room. But there's that woman I can't stand. Let's bring that pain with us, too." And there you go, contributing to your own misery.

You will not align to the Upper Room while you are abnegating the authority you have to choose to be there. Did you all hear this? You will not enter the Upper Room and manifest there when you are denying you can. We are speaking of choice. We are speaking of recognition of one's own authority. And we are speaking of the principle of realization, that the one who knows who she is realizes the world in like vibrational accord.

Now, when you have an illness, you have something that is challenging, an opportunity to learn, an opportunity to heal. But if you predicate your well-being, the entire being, on one solution, you will lose the opportunity for true health, and we must say true health is manifestation of divine awareness. Anything else may be chosen—a diet, a plan of expression for the body. But, finally, we have to say, true well-being is the expression of the Divine operating as you. And, if that comes along with an illness, the illness is embraced and then realized anew in the Upper Room. You may receive a healing, or a new relationship with the malady, but you will not be a victim to it because the True Self as you cannot be a victim to anything.

He interrupts again. "But what if my Divine Self is walking down the street and gets hit by a car? What happens then?" The Divine as you is not hit by the car. The body is. And the body may be crushed, but the soul is not. And while the soul expresses through the body, and while the body itself may be in high vibrational accord, while you know what you are, the Divine in expression, the who that you are is present, with or without a body. And, if you attach to the body through fear and oversee its protection in fear, you probably contribute to the very circumstances that you are seeking to avoid.

Each of you who comes to us comes with a belief that things will not work out as you want them to, and, for the most part, we have to say, thank goodness for that. You would be living small lives in safety, and small lives in safety are far less wonderful than an expansive life that can be known through new circumstances beyond the known.

We bring you this now, and, as we complete the first half of this text, we would like to announce that the first half of this text—you may call it Part One—is The Upper Room. We will continue with the second half of this text in days to come. We have great opportunity here. We wish to take it. And we are thrilled and grateful to have your company on the journey ahead. Period. Period. Period.

Now You Have the oportunity of Healing!

PART TWO

Realization

7

DELIVERANCE

DAY SEVENTEEN

Trouble comes when you decide what should happen based upon an agenda of history. Difficulty comes when you access the small self as the font of wisdom that you perceive yourself to be at the cost of what would be brought to you in a higher way. The Divine as who and what you are actually claims you in a kind of safety through your awareness of who you are, what you are, and how you serve. And trouble comes to the small self, but may be met well and in great faith by the True Self, who knows who she is.

Now, as you stand before us, as you claim who you are, as you decide what you should be as a small self and relinquish that claim before us, you become a testament to the lives you live in a higher octave, the Upper Room, the Christed Self as what you are in its expression, not the small self's expression predicated upon history, but the Divine as you who stands before the world in service in an expression of its own knowing. Now, we say these words intentionally. *Its own knowing.* The Divine as you operates in knowing—capital K, *Know.* It does not ask. It does not seek to find. It does not question. It allows. And, in the allowance of its being, knowledge is present. Now, true knowledge moves well beyond accessing information. True knowing is the quality of expression of the tree that has no question that it is a tree, of the bird that flies, but does not question flight. True knowing is a state of expression. And aligning to this in the Upper Room is your lesson for this morning.

Each of you decides, prior to incarnation, the length of the life you will live and the ambition of the soul to meet its needs for growth. And, in a higher way, every life must be seen as an opportunity to learn that is met, or perhaps not met, in high ways. But, once you understand that there is no such thing as a wasted life, and knowledge comes in all experience, the divinity of your being can begin to amass what you know of as wisdom. Wisdom and knowledge are not the same thing. The wise man knows, but the wisdom is accrued through experience. And we say wisdom is a gift of being, but being as the Divine Self is the gift of knowing, and the claim "I know how I serve," the expression of the Divine in alliance to its requirements for service, is the agreement you make when you align to the who and the what that you truly are.

Now, knowing cannot be sought, nor can it be found. It is present, as is the sea. And, once you know the sea, there is never a question. "That is not a puddle, that is an ocean. That is not a river, it is the sea." And the awareness of this knowledge, in your presence and agreed to as what you are, claims you all at once in the sea of knowing that is ever present.

Some of you decide that when you know things, have answers to things, you have ascended. Knowing is a perpetual state of agreement to God. That is the key. *Knowing is a perpetual state of agreement to God.* Now, as God is the ocean that you abide in, the ever-present ocean, you abide in knowing, as you know God.

"But we don't know God," he says. "We grovel, we pray, we pretend, we react, but we still harm one another, we still war, we still weep. We don't know God. Don't tell us we do."

But you do. And this is the tragedy of your lives. You do know God in the heart of your soul. You do know God. It's in every fiber of your body and anything you see. Because God is all, you are already in the sea of its divinity. So you *say* you don't know. The True Self as you is of God. She knows her expression, and her expression *is* the sea. It *is* the sea. The Divine Self's expression is a wave of vibration that assumes all that it sees. Expression, expansion, and alignment claim you in knowing.

Imagine there is a flower before you. Choose any flower you like. See its petals, see its leaves, see the flower, choose its color. But see it clearly. And then decide the flower that you see is in your mind, and, consequently, an expression of consciousness. Do you understand this? The flower you see that you call rose, magnolia, anything you say, and the colors you claim it in, are in your mind. Now, we will say what this means. You know what blue is, you know what red is, because you have been taught blue and red. And the differences from the rose and the petunia are known by you dimensionally through shape and form, but your projection of the rose you see in your mind's eye is only a figment, an idea of a rose, of a flower, of a petal, and the scent that it emits is also the idea of what a scent is.

Now, we do not deny the flower that you see in your mind's eye. We wish you now to realize that this flower you see is something that you are one with. Merge, if you wish, as the idea of what a flower is claims you in the idea of what you are. And, as you merge, as the idea of who and the thing you see become one, the vibration or resonance of the union you experience is in your knowing.

Now, to know the self as one with God is to claim the self beyond the known, beyond the decided upon, beyond that which has been chosen by your lives thus far. And the agreement to be assumed by the ocean of God, and know yourself in oneness with it, is the teaching of knowing. The example would be when you stand in a thunderstorm with your eyes closed. You feel the rain, you hear the thunder, you know yourself in the experience of the wetness and the shaking of the earth. You know yourself in your being. It is not an intellectual act. It is a state of expression.

Now, as the what, the Divine in form who has come as you in this agreement to embody at the level of the Upper Room, you must understand that even the idea of separation is an agreement to be in separation. Do you understand this? Everything is an idea, spoken into being, articulated in form, and even the idea that you are separate from Source claims you in separation because you are that powerful, and, because what you are, the form you have taken, is an expression of the Divine, it aligns at the level of choice the one speaking the agreement has aligned as. The five-year-old speaks with the wisdom of the child, and the speech of the child, invoking a world, is limited by what he comprehends. But, as you have agreed to align to the Upper Room, the manifestation of spoken word, choice, and mandate must be comprehended as the vibration of God emerging, and deciding, and claiming the Kingdom into being.

Now, as you have claimed the who and the what and the expression of service in high accord, the knowing you seek at this level of expression must be known to you. Again, the word *known*. Not must be had, must be understood, must be found in some old text. *Must be known*. And the agreement to know, in embodiment, is to become the sea. As you live, as you rejoice, and, as you serve, the expression of the wave that you have become, in octaves, in resonance, in vibration, the totality of experience can be understood as a single note played in multidimensional octaves into infinity. And the single note, we must call God. And the variance of God, the high and low, the universe itself, is still one note that contains within it every imaginable expression, and beyond what you can imagine.

You seek to control this through your understanding, but you cannot understand it. You seek to fix it, to remedy your predicaments of separation, through study, through perusing the texts of old, but the answer of knowing exists in the agreement to be as one with the first note played, the very first note, the very first tone, the very first sound. In the beginning was the Word.

The teaching here is the assumption into the infinite by every aspect of being in union at the level of causation. And causation, the act of being and expression in alignment with the infinite truth, is the domicile and the purview and the expression of the one who knows who she is.

If you would imagine now that before you there is an ocean, a deep ocean, the bluest ocean you could ever imagine, and you stand upon its shore. And, as you stand upon its shore, you agree to what you have known, what you have chosen, how you have lived, who you have lived as. And, as you agree, you release the body as you have known it. You may release the clothing, the name you have gone by, the color of your skin, and your sex. These are ideas, as well, that you have chosen to abide by. And, as the vibratory being that you are, embodied now in truth, you walk forward, step by step, and immerse yourself in this bright blue sea. You will not drown here, but you will be assumed. And to be assumed in the sea of knowing, as we teach it now, is to incarnate at a level of agreement that accesses the totality of your being as a receptive one to the Source of all things. This means, very simply, that you are releasing the illusion of separation as you enter the sea and let it surround you.

> *"I am one with the sea of knowing. I am one with my agreement to know. I am aligning to my knowing, in forgiveness of what I have thought, believed myself to be, and perhaps chose in defiance to truth. But, as I float, as I am assumed in the sea of knowing, I give myself permission now to experience what it is to truly know."*

When you align yourself now to this vibration, empty your mind of all expectation and let it be informed by knowing and being. Beyond language, if need be. Beyond symbol, if need be. Knowing requires no language and no symbol. The articulation of sound has been degraded, in many ways, through symbol and language. And the pure essence of tone that we align in and express through is the Source of all, as we align to it.

Give yourself permission to align and know.

Let yourself be received by us. Wherever you are, wherever you sit, wherever you lie, let yourself be known, just as you are. And, as we know you, as we accept you in our knowing, we support you in your acceptance of the knowing that is available to you in this perfect sea.

We will stop this lecture now. Indeed, this is in the text. Period. Period. Period.

DAY EIGHTEEN

We have come, we have come, we have come. And, as we teach you, as we recognize you for who and what you are, we give you the opportunity to choose again the Upper Room, the place of vibration where the manifestation of the Divine can be present in fullness. And the recognition of this—"I am in the Upper Room"—will claim you in many ways beyond the known, beyond the claims you've made in history and would seek to justify as a small self. In dominion, you may claim anything, and the realization of the Divine as what you are, the manifest form you have taken in agreement to be in vibration in the Upper Room, claims you as the one who can call into being a landscape in recognition of her True Self, his innate self, which we call the Kingdom.

Now, each of you decides how far you will go on this mission. Each of you agrees at a soul level that this will be the lifetime for realization, or that the opportunity to present itself as realized may be taken. But the claim you make, "I Have Come," which is the claim of the Christ in incarnation, is only true when spoken in the Upper Room. The Christ has come as each of you, you see, and the Upper Room is the abiding place of the Christ. And, as the vehicle of the Christ, the body you have taken and the mission the soul has claimed to be incarnate at this level, the choice is made to announce the self to the world: "I Have Come."

Now, ideas of what it means to be in manifestation must be claimed anew because the ideas of old, what it means to be ascended or incarnate at this level, have been fraught with confusion, misinformation, and a kind of pedagogy born in history that would seek to find itself in the tatters of old books, in the imprinting upon walls, when in fact the encoding of truth is done at a soul level and is read there, is announced there, by the one who knows who she is.

When retribution comes to the small self, it is always in repayment for history, things done prior that are seeking to re-know themselves in karma. When you ascend at this level of vibratory octave, you are actually bypassing systems of retribution because who you are claiming yourself as in truth is not at the lower vibration where she can be struck. If you imagine a stone being thrown, the body may be struck, but the soul self, in its incarnation that has risen to a level of agreement, is actually free of any onslaught because she abides in a place where she cannot know them—underline the word *cannot*—*cannot* because they do not exist.

The idea of things coming at you, crashing upon you, being out of control, is completely the small self in its agreement to know itself through the chaos of the agreements made in prior time, in this incarnation, or through the incarnations of history, that still play themselves out upon this lifetime in the shared landscape that you all know yourselves in. As the risen Christ—underline the word *risen* because it is the ascended self that abides in the Upper Room, and not the small self, who judges or fears—you are limited only by the agreements made in fruition in tangible ways that support your ongoing sense of knowing what you are. In other words, the absolute state of incarnation as a realized being is still coming to you in stages and in increments, even as you abide in the Upper Room or the high landscape or octave we teach you in.

Now, the idea of fear and being claimed by fear must be understood, finally, as a way to know the self in fear, and to be in fear is to be in agreement to it, and to be in agreement to it is to verify it. To verify anything is to make it so, and to make it so is to realize it or know it at the level of function and form that it has taken. To know the self beyond fear, the Divine Self as you who exists there, is to align to the level where fear cannot penetrate. As we have said prior, if you wish an experience of fear, you may go back and choose it, but it is no longer a requirement for how you may learn your lessons. You may choose it, you may move beyond it, because you have choice, still, in ascension of who you are as embodied. And the requirements for choice made in alignment with Divine Will—"I know myself as Divine Will"—are always in accord with the progression of the soul, which seeks to realize itself in fullness.

Again, the octave of agreement we are singing to you from is always available to you, but the Upper Room is privileged, in some ways, for those who have claimed it and may abide in it because they have chosen to release the self that knows itself in and through fear. It is not denying fear as much as not agreeing to it, and to move beyond fear to incarnate at this level will require you to pass through it as you would any journey with many stops.

The realization of the Divine as what is always predicated on the expression you have taken. Expression can mean form, the body you have taken, but everything you see about you is expression, an articulation of consciousness that has been codified and named and agreed to. To justify the old, to claim everything in the old way, is to taint the moment you stand in with the information or data that has been inscribed or articulated in and as form. To renounce form is not to release the world, to release the things of this world, as much as to release the attachment to what things have meant, how they have been. When one renounces the world, one does not stop living in the world, but the world one lives in is a vastly different world where the names things are claimed by have very little meaning because the Divine Self does not attach to the values that have been given them. "Look at this wonderful diamond my partner gave me. My partner must love me very much to spend so much upon me." The identification of the value of the diamond as a monetization of love could make no sense to the Divine Self, who understands a diamond as what it is, a beautiful thing wrought of the earth. And the manifestation of love could be the impulse to give, but the coal would have been fine, the crust of coal. The piece of earth given in love without the monetization would have been fine, or absolutely nothing at all.

Look at the life you live, and look at it now. See what you value and why you value it, what you have attached to, what you believe to be so important. "I am nothing without my bank account or my father's love." "I am nothing without the watch I wore on that special reunion with my fate. If I don't have the watch, I have nothing to remember it by." Anything you see that you value is being valued by you, and much of what you value has no value other than that. An umbrella in a storm has as much value as a fancy home when you are being rained upon. The denial of truth, what you think is so important at the cost of truth, must be met by you now if you intend to mandate an experience of being that precludes fear.

Imagine, for a moment, that the things that you value most were not present in your life. Most of you would stop listening to us now if you were able, close the book, turn off the computer. "Don't listen to these words that tell me not to want what I have." We are not telling you not to want anything. We are actually inviting you to see why you want what you have and how you create that as a basis for more of the same. The limitlessness that is the Upper Room can hold anything and nothing. And the self that abides there is perfect, with or without the fancy watch, the diamond ring, or the home. Each of you here, by nature of being, is a divine being, and the realization of it, the manifestation of it, and the abiding in it within the Upper Room, grants you the opportunity, not only to rejoice in what is there for you, but what you can now share with the world.

The idea of plenty, for most of you, has colluded with the idea of getting a lot. "Look at the plentiful life I live and all of the things

I have gathered." Enjoy the Upper Room where plentiful is a state of being, and nothing accrued. You cannot accrue riches in the Upper Room, but you may know yourself as rich, and there is a difference. Everything of this flesh will one day not be present in the form it has taken, and nothing you see in the room you stand in will be present in four hundred years. Everything will have been made new, and the dust of your body will be somewhere other, taken some other form, and the vibrational being you are will have announced itself in some other manifestation, on some other plane, in some other way of expression. To deny the Divine in the fabric of form is to commit a strange kind of heresy. God is in the diamond and in the fancy watch and in the beautiful home because God is in the brick and the mortar of all things. But God is in the hovel, God is in the cave, and God is the one that dwells within the hovel and the cave, as well as the one that has found itself, finally, finally, finally, in the Kingdom.

To realize the Divine in manifestation is to know God as form, but the moment you worship form you are in heresy, which is denying the truth, because the only thing that can be worshipped is love, because love asks nothing of you but to be of it, and its source of supply is endless. "But is God love?" he asks. "Don't we worship God?" The understanding of worship is confused to you, Paul. To bow down to anything is to decide that you are lower, but to realize the God within holds you in deep humility and reverence for the Source of all things, and to bow to that in reverence is an act of grace and an agreement to your participatory nature to the world you express in. God is in the rock. Do not pray to the rock. Pray to the Source of the rock, which is the same Source as your breath, and the stars above you. To exclude anything from this equation is to deny the Kingdom, which encompasses the rock, the stars, and every breath you take. In dominion you may claim the requirements or needs of any given day and expect to be met by them. But this is not the small self groveling before an altar, saying, "Take care of me, pay my rent, find me love, show me employment. I will not do my part." You all have a part, and the moment you stand in the awareness of who and what you are and offer yourself in fullness and claim the Upper Room, the articulation of your being, the pronunciation of your name—"I Have Come"—ennobles you to claim the world for the benefit of all. Do you get to trust that your needs are met in this plane of expression while you abide in the Upper Room? In fact, when you abide in the Upper Room, you are in the presence of the Divine, and that is the Source of all, so anything you can claim in realization may be known to you in the perfect form it may take for you.

"I don't understand this," he says. "This sounds like magical thinking. Don't mislead us, please." It is not magic. It is alchemy in a higher sense than you understand, Paul. The density of vibration that you all operate here in this plane in accord with has precluded many of you from the experience of what manifestation is in a way that concurs with this teaching. But if you already understand that there is not a thing in your life that you are not in resonance to, that you are already in manifestation and seeing the manifestation of your consciousness, individual and collective consciousness, all around you, you will not realize how powerful you have already been. The vast difference in the Upper Room is you are not placating the old reality. You are not suffering for it. You are not perpetuating it. You have reclaimed yourself in a new way, and consequently what you call into being in manifestation is not only of like accord, but is the perfect thing for you to realize to learn through.

The adjustment is a radical one because you've been seeking your needs through the material realm and seeking to grant favor with whatever forces you think there are to make them known. You forget that who and what you are is of the Source, and your progression as a soul actually requires you to realize, to know, how to call into being into manifest form what the soul requires. If you understand that you are already doing this at a level of density, but the idea of cause and effect is confused by you because, in some ways, when you claim something in consciousness, it appears so far later down the road that you don't connect it to the inclination that was originally present or the seed of manifestation that has now flowered.

Now, we are saying this for Paul, who is in the background yelling, "You are not talking about instant manifestation, are you?" Of course, we are, but not in the way you think. Realization is instantaneous, and to realize the truth in anything is to re-know it in that instant, but this instant that we speak to is the eternal now, the infinite moment beyond time itself. As you accrue the wisdom of experience with this, how you know your world in realization is sustained by you because you mandate that the high octave of the Upper Room is where you know yourself, and you claim the Kingdom from this purview. The teaching of the Jesus expression that you have been taught through was identical to this, but you limit yourself in the awareness that you are causal. Jesus knew who and what he was and demonstrated the action of it. Others have come that have identified and claimed the Kingdom, but the multitude has been refused, and been refused for good reason. You opt to kill your brothers, you opt to choose in fear, you opt to starve your neighbors, you opt to judge, and each act we have just claimed has a ramification or karma. And the karma of humanity must be risen beyond or you will destroy yourselves incurring more. How do you move beyond karma, but through realization, and to realize the Christed Self is to manifest a new world and lift the world before you to its truth?

He is interrupting. "But haven't you said in the past there is still karma in the Upper Room?" If there is something you need to learn through, yes. You are accountable to your past actions. But to rise above the claims of history in liberation also offers you the opportunity to be released from the retribution of history, which is how we began this teaching tonight. The arcane way of looking at progression over lifetimes in remorse or in payback through karma must be now re-understood: That while every action has a response, the action claimed in the Upper Room has the response of releasing you from the mandates of history as long as you don't conform to them. To deny your divinity is to deny this potential, and that is why we began, when we began to teach through this young man, with the attunement to the Word. "I am Word through my body. Word I am Word. I am Word through my vibration. Word I am Word. I am Word through my knowing of myself as Word." To become articulated as the Word is first done through the claim of identity and manifestation, and the soul will rise to the occasion as the announcement is made. The Divine as who and what you are is not only here, but it is already lifting your expression to the Upper Room.

On the count of three, we intend to lift you all, once again, to the Upper Room where you may be known and you may experience knowing in completeness, the vast sea of knowing that is here for you, from whence you may choose.

One. Two. Three.

Be lifted, and be sung. Let the field sing, and let the Christ be known through each of you in this articulation: "I Have Come. I Have Come. I Have Come."

Blessings to you each.

DAY NINETEEN

Each of you decides, prior to incarnation, how far you may progress in alignment toward realization, but we will say the choice may claim you in a new life beyond what you would expect without exceeding the potential that you have at this time. Most of you want realization in complete fullness. "Let me be at the top of the mountain in the Upper Room. Let me sing the song of love and forget myself entirely." The small self is not forgotten in this transition. She is still present, but she is not who and what you are, the authority of your life, the queen of the Kingdom. She knows her name, she knows her role, but her accountability to her own self is still present, even as she has been assumed by the Divine. The Divine as who and what and its expression as you does not decide for you that the woman you have been is no longer. It does mean the woman you have been is no longer who she thinks she is, or what she thought she was. The dismantling of a structure of identity, in some ways, is actually a rebuilding from the residual ideas that have been discarded, and then re-made, and then re-assumed in the high octave of the Upper Room.

Imagine this. You get rid of a pair of shoes that you have been walking in, but you still require shoes. The idea of the shoe is not the wrong idea. The old pair was outgrown, the new must be brought to you. The idea of the shoe, a thing you put upon your feet to protect them from the earth, is not a bad thing. But, if you have identified with the shoe, the old pair that is discarded, you will rely upon the old idea of what a shoe should be, perhaps at the cost of the new ones that would be brought for you to walk in. The Divine as you is in an encounter with reality, and the creations of the small self will always surround you until you realize—underline that word *realize*—that the manifestation of God is all things, and that there is not one thing, not one thing at all, that cannot be re-known and re-created, the new pair of shoes, if you wish, in the Upper Room.

Now, calamity comes when a system is falling apart, and the reliance upon the system, the things that you have used to get through the day, can no longer conform to your expectations. When a system fails, a new system may be born, but in every case you find yourself grappling with the repair of the old instead of seeking what can be born in its place. You seek to remedy your politics on this plane, you seek to remedy the disharmony that exists between factions across the globe, you seek to protect the systems that you have that you believe in, because, without them, you perceive terror. "What if there is no money in the bank? What if there is no electricity coming from the outlet? What if what I've thought I was and how I've cared for myself is not what I thought I was? How do I care?"

In some ways, the external systems that you see collapsing in your world cannot be remedied, cannot be fixed, nor should they be. A new one must be born in a higher agreement. And the consequence of this is that what you are seeing before you, the turmoil that you experience, either in politics or factions across the globe, are the manifestations of the chaos of systems that are collapsing because they were initially created or later informed by fear and a need to control others that cannot exist in the high octave that is now present on this plane. Your understanding of who and what you are must become reliant on the eternal truth, and not the small self's idea of what it should be. The Divine as you, who has come and must be seen in a new way in all she perceives, must be re-created on this plane at the cost of the old. Who you think you are, the broadcast of the small self and its small expression, must be comprehended as the manifestation on this plane that you are contending with, not at the level of the individual, but of the collective. Who you are in the Upper Room or the higher octave is the one who can claim or realize the new world into manifestation. But, if you believe for a moment that you are returning to a state of predictability through harmony, or what you think is harmony, with the old organisms or old systems of creation, you would be wrong-minded. The Divine as you is not reliant upon the old. Do you all understand this? The Divine as you does not seek to re-create through formula what you have thought was necessary.

Now, your contribution, individually and collectively, to the manifestation of a new world must be understood as something that happens in a new way. Underline *new*. You know how to bake a cake through the recipe of old. There is nothing wrong with the recipe that you have used. But, once you understand that the failings of systems will not be remedied by the old recipe, but what may be claimed in a new way, you will find yourself seeking to fix, and not re-create or re-know. The world you see before you must be created anew, in accord with the octave of truth in the freedom of expression that the Divine knows itself in, and at the cost of what has been claimed, in a way, through fear, to judge, to control, and to decide what things should be in an old template that has claimed you, all of you, in fear.

This is the day of a new encounter, a new reliance upon the claim "I Have Come," and, as we teach you this, the Divine as you, in witness of a world who can claim "I Have Come," you will realize that the manifestation of God that is present for you can be re-understood and reclaimed in the manifest world through the one who has shown herself in realization in fullness.

He is interrupting. He has several questions. "At the beginning of this talk, you said we would not all be realized in fullness." In fact, what we said is that you will be realized at the level you can be, and the level you can be realized at, which is the vibratory accord that you may take, will be what claims you in a new way, well beyond the known. We are speaking to those of you who have an idea that the realized state that you come to is an abandonment of a small self. A realization of who you are that decides who you are not or could not have been would never support integration. And you must be integrated, all of you, finally, to be a true expression. God does not come through you and annihilate the ideas of who you are and leave you blubbering on a street corner not knowing how to read a street sign. What would be the purpose of that? The skills amassed, the lessons learned, are present, but you are not relying upon them to dictate identity, nor are you moving into conformity with what you think they should be.

Now, the small self, in her purview, knows where she lives, what her occupation is, the names of her children. Be grateful for that. You would have a hard time, taking the neighbor's children away from her, thinking that they were your own. The small self has some things to give you. But the Divine as you also knows these things, and is claiming you, in accord, to a new level of realization, through the alignment and through the claim "I Have Come."

Now, when you speak these words, you are speaking truth. The Christ as you, the Divine as you, is who has come, in embodiment and expression. And the expressed state of being is not a passive state. The action of the Divine, the causal act, is to reclaim everything it encounters in like vibratory accord. And the small self's desire to justify the old will be reinterpreted by the Divine Self so it is no longer operative. You are not going to fix yourself. Do you understand this? This is not about fixing yourselves. The reliance upon the old and the systems of old that are collapsing around you are, in all ways, mirrors of the individual's journey of reliance upon fear that is being released in this process of re-creation.

The small self does not decide how she will be fixed, because fixing is not operative. The True Self as what you are is the director now, and will claim it as it is required, and will manifest what is needed as you are assumed in agreement to it. If you can understand that the wheel of the ship that you have been navigating is now being helmed by the Divine Self, who understands the winds and the destiny before her, you will understand that the best thing you can do, sometimes, is allow her to captain your life and stop trying to give her the manifestation that you think you should have to be who you thought you should be. "Well, I just want a marriage that works and my children to be happy, and here you are captaining my ship beyond the known. I didn't ask for this. I just want my small life to work. That's really all I came for."

The small life you've lived is being re-interpreted, re-articulated, and what she requires, the True Self as you, will mandate the passage of this ship, not your requirements for what you think should be. You are not abandoning control, you are giving over the helm quite willingly to the aspect of the self that is now realized as you in the claim "I Have Come." Every attunement prior to this was in preparation for this decree. And this decree upon the external world will manifest in a broadcast that is equationally different than what you have believed could be so.

"What does that mean," he asks, "*equationally different*?" The idea of cause and effect is an equation of sorts. "When I do this, this will occur." The vibration of the Divine as the full broadcast of the individual, and its manifestation and the ramifications of that encounter, is a new equation that has not been known through you until now. Until this is known or realized through each of you, it will remain in conjecture. And, as we continue this text, our intention is to give you the opportunity to be in this encounter of vibratory accord to witness the impact of the causal field in a high octave, claiming a world into a new light.

We will commence with this teaching, as we are allowed. Thank you each for your presence.

(PAUSE)

Trust yourselves, please, to know what you need to know as you need to know it. Don't dictate outcome based on history because this guarantees you the residual effect of prior choice and prior learning. To be realized is to be in the moment, and only the moment you stand in. When you ask why not anyone or everyone will be realized, there is a process entailed in this agreement that must be undertaken for it to occur. The soul understands the capacity of an individual soul to realize itself in accordance with the mandates of its required learning, the lessons it has come for. In this lifetime you may have chosen the lesson of realization and all that it entails, or you may have chosen something other. Please do not decide that one lesson is better or more noble than the next. That is, again, the small self with its edicts of what should be.

Now, the Christed Self will realize itself at the fullness of equation that it can manage, and, if you wish to realize the self beyond the known, the way is being paved for you in this teaching. If you wish to know yourself beyond what you have claimed, you must stop agreeing to the facts that you have utilized to dictate your reality. He doesn't like this. "Well, we have facts for a reason. They *are* facts." In fact, what you think you see is evidence of a reality that can be re-known or re-interpreted in another way. In the higher room, the Upper Room, truth is prevalent, and truth understands itself in a rather different way than the small self's assertions would. When we said *a new equation,* we were speaking to something new. And, again, cause and effect, as understood by you, will always be the ramification of prior learning. "I turn on the water faucet, out comes water." The expectation is water, and that is what you agree to. When you move beyond the known, you actually move beyond systems of compliance or heredity to dictate what reality is. Imagine, if you wish, that you lived on the twentieth floor of a high-rise building. You understand the view from the twentieth floor. You understand the mandates for living there, but, because twenty is as high as you can imagine, you cannot assume that there is anything beyond it. What if, in fact, there were? What if there were different ways of being expressed that would call into being different effect? And *different effect* we mean as different than what the small self would predicate through its identification of history, or through history, as the decider of the present. Everything exists in multiple octaves, and the transition from one octave to another requires the transposition of the notes of music that are being played from one key to a key in a higher octave. When you do that, the affect of the music is very different, and your experience of the sound—"Well, that is a familiar song, I have not heard it in this key before, in this new octave"—you would have a way of comprehending what the translation means.

In your realized world, in the world you share, you have agreements about what things are, what they mean, and you create expectations around them for the purpose of expectancy and the norm. The norm is what you want, and nowadays what you believe the norm to be is in transition, the confused state of affairs, the chaos you see. What was once expected is no longer expected, and none of you quite know what to think or how to react. The small self always seeks the old as a way to know itself because it has no framework and no ability to see beyond what it has been taught. The reliance upon the Divine Self is crucial now, because, unless you do this, you will find yourself replicating the old at the cost of what might be brought to you. The small self, you see, in her edicts, would rather see a house fall down upon her, as long as it is a house she knows. She cannot imagine living in something that doesn't resemble what she has known. She will fix the battered roof until there is nothing left to fix, than experience herself in a very different way of abiding in a place she might call home.

The idea of the Upper Room is a translation of one reality to the higher that has always co-existed with it. You must understand this. The Upper Room is not a creation of something new. It is only new to the experience of the small self. The small self cannot abide there, nor can she imagine it. If she were to imagine it, she would throw in a few angels, perhaps a headstone or two. "It must be where you go when you're dead." It is not where you go when you're dead. It's where you know yourself in union with the Divine, and nothing more. Dead or alive, the idea is still the same. There is a place of agreement, of energetic accord, where you may know yourself beyond the dominion of the small self. It's the Upper Room that is the new equation in any new choice. How you attend to your child or your work or your belief in God may be vastly different in the Upper Room, because the conjecture that you have used to realize all of those other things are rather different in the higher octave. "I know my child. I know his name. I know his predilections. And he must do better in school, if he is to succeed." When you decide that, that your child's behavior in school predicates his future, you are ascribing to a success that is born in the lower octave—do you understand this?—and the prescriptions of behavior that you would mandate to have him succeed within an existing system. You ascribe to the systems. You make them real. And then, when they start to fall apart, what do you have? "I spent all that money on school, and there is no job." "I invested all those years in a marriage, and there is no love." "I believed in my government, and my government is failing me." "I believed we would have peace, I have marched for peace, and now I see avarice and war." "What do I do now? How do I behave? How do I live in a world that will not conform to my ideas of what should be, based upon what has been, or the ideology I would hold for what should be?"

Again, the True Self is realized only in the present moment. The Upper Room exists eternally, but you may only know it in the moment you sit in. You will not know it tomorrow or next week, but you will know it in the instant you experience it. And realization occurs here because the Divine Self as you is who is realized, and she is only realized in the upper vibrational self that she has ascended to. The Upper Room, where the True Self abides, is a level of realization. What exists in the lower octaves can and will be reclaimed, re-created, or re-known in some other way by the one who expresses herself there, because that is the law, and the law is co-resonance. You cannot be a turtle and be a kangaroo at the same time. It is not possible.

To realize the Divine as who and what you are reclaims the identity of the body and the expression of vibration in a new song. You are not as you were. The small self's identity has been assumed or reclaimed in this new purview: "I Have Come." And its expression and its manifestation and impact upon what it encounters is what claims a new world into manifestation. The ideology of a Messiah who will fix everybody, return you all to Eden, is somewhat misconstrued. The Upper Room, the abode of the Christ consciousness, the level of expression that can be attained by a mortal while in form, is what has come as you, the level of attainment or vibratory agreement that incarnation can occur at while in form. Underline *form*. So many of you debase the idea of form, or, in fact, deify it without realizing that all form can be, all it can ever be, is expression, and identity through form is a process of naming or self-identification through a language that you have inherited. "I live in a room. My name is Paul. I know this or that in the ways that I have been taught." He is languaging his experience and expressing or articulating in vibration the manifestations of thought or identity as can be known.

The True Self as you exists beyond the articulation of the small self. And, consequently, how it calls things into being, in progression, is a different equation than you have known. "What is the different equation?" We will try to tell you this now. The Divine Self, the True Self as each of you, has a new language to articulate. It is tone and it is field. It does not mean a sofa is not a sofa. It means the sofa is re-known in a higher octave that has been lifted by you, by nature of expression. A vowel, spoken, is a sound. The only meaning it has is that which you have endowed it with. The name you go by is simply an idea of what you have agreed to. It is not who you are.

As we reclaim you each, one and all, beyond language and beyond the reference points that language might offer you, we are lifting you to opportunity, a new opportunity to transgress, in some ways, upon what you have been taught or thought could be. The action of the Divine is the Word. Do you understand this? In the beginning was the Word. The Word is tone, in frequency, informed by the Divine that can know itself as and through anything because nothing can be outside of God. Treason, we suggest, the small self's treason against the Divine, is the foolish belief that she is not of God. And the re-articulation of the True Self, as manifest in form, is what we have come to bring—as form, in vibration, an articulation of sound or tone that the field that you hold incarnates as, while knowing itself still as flesh and bone and marrow and blood and saliva. You understand, yes, that you cannot be separate from Source, but you don't understand that the realization of union must transpose the sound you make, the energetic tone of vibration, to a new octave, and, in that new octave, "I Have Come" announces itself to lift the world to a new vibration.

This is not a small act. This is an act that is antithetical to almost everything you have ever been taught, but, if it were not so, we could not teach it to you. We speak in truth, we know ourselves in truth, and we know you in truth, as well, beyond the structure or old articulation. "I am the mother of three." "I don't like my husband." "I had a father. He left us." The small self's narratives are present, but you are not those things because you cannot be those things in the higher room.

"Now, what does that mean?" he asks. "Her father never left her? She never had a child?" That is not what it means. It means the divine expression, in her announcement of being, has moved beyond levels of identification in limitation that would deliver her from her true destiny, her true destiny being the Divine Self that is realized through the mother, through the one that was left, through the one who lives in such and such a place, has such and such a heritage, and can know herself as the Divine through all these things.

The action you take now, in deliverance, which is the title of this chapter, is the re-creation of truth in any idea that you have utilized to define the self in aspiration that can be claimed beyond the small self in limitation. This simply means you are releasing the idea of what you could be, as prescribed by the small self, to realize what you are and have always been. Here is the teaching of transmission to a new key, a new octave, a new expression. Here is the answer you have sought.

The being that you are, in her way, in his way, is enormous in its expression, and the allowance for the enormity has been precluded by a simple idea that you are not of God, and the bypassing of that idea, the re-knowing of the Divine as what, while this teaching in fullness, is still an idea until it is met by you in occurrence, or realization. Until it is known in realization, it is an idea, and just another idea of a potential that you may claim. In order to give you this, we must assume you, and, for us to assume you at this level of tone, relies upon our ability to call Paul forth as the vehicle for our expression. When the teachings are new and discomfort arises within him around the ideas we express, we still do our best to transmit the teaching as clearly as we can. But to assume you will rely upon him, for we assume him in this agreement to be with you. So we would invite Paul now, as he sits, to allow us to come through as a field. We will bring you all up to the Upper Room in this moment simply by intention, so you may be met by us in this moment.

As we say yes to this assumption through the body of Paul, and the expression of Paul in field, we are actually making an agreement to each of you, wherever you may be, that you may be known and realized beyond the self, beyond the edicts of history and the challenges you may have defined yourselves through, one and all. "How is this done?" he asks. By alignment. This entire teaching is alignment. It always has been. Everything else is information, and information and alignment are rather different, don't you think? Paul, we will align you now as you speak these words, and then we will call everybody forth in one accord:

> *"On this day I claim that I am allowing myself to be realized beyond the known, beyond any agreements made or chosen by me in any time that would preclude this destiny. As I give permission to realize myself beyond the known, I am known, I am received, I am delivered, in fact, from any idea of limitation that would prescribe my destiny, any agreement made in any time that would coerce me from the truth of my being. As I say yes to this, I give permission to the entirety of my being to be re-known, re-created, and re-sung in vibration. And the song of my field will be in eminence and knowing for the benefit of all who would encounter it."*

We say these words through you, Paul, not *as* you, as much, because it is we who sing. And, as we sing through the body and soul of your being, we sing to all for their own knowing, to be acknowledged and reclaimed in union with the Source of their being. On the count of three, Paul, we lift the field you sit in, and we bring it out in a wave around you, so that anyone who hears these words may be met by them. Just give yourselves permission to be met, wherever you may be.

One. Two. Three.

(short pause)

Allow. Allow. Allow.

Be received. Be received. Be received.

Accept. Accept. Accept.

(short pause)

What is occurring now is a vibrational accord or alignment that is available, as accepted by you each, to assume you in fullness in the stages of agreement you can align to. Here are the stages of agreement: "It can be done. It will be known. I have known and I have claimed my ability to receive, and I am allowing myself to be created in the high room, in form and field, for the benefit of all."

The alchemy of this choice is systematized by the individual, who can only agree to the manifestation of this at the level she can concur with. And you must understand this. You will only receive this in vibration at the level you can hold. As you can hold more, you will be agreed to and re-known in more, in agreement to more, and what you may understand as completion. At each stage of evolution, humanity is given the opportunity to release an idea of what it is to agree to a new model or embodiment. This is this time, and you have each come in participation to it. Be received by us, wherever you sit, wherever you be, and say yes to who and what you are in God. Period. Period. Period.

(PAUSE)

Each of you decides, prior to incarnation, the level of agreement that you will hold in a lifetime. This is done at a soul level, not through the personality, who has decided that she will ascend, will know glory, will claim the Kingdom in the way she thinks she should. The True Self as you is who claims the Kingdom. The

Divine as what you are is what manifests the Kingdom in mutual vibratory agreement to a sound or a tone that is key to catalytic expression of the Divine.

Now, the form you have taken, know it or not, holds within it the challenge for ascension, or to be re-made or re-known in a higher octave. And by this we mean the expression you hold holds within it the opportunity for realization in form without the agreement of the small self hindering it. But the small self is required, as the occupant of form, to allow the environment that the small self knows itself through to be lifted. And here is the challenge. Each of you who decides that you can and will align in the Upper Room for the purpose of expression must decide that permission is required and given by all aspects of self in order to realize what you may in the Upper Room. In fact, what you cannot do is drag an aspect of self to the Upper Room with you which refuses to realize its divinity.

"What would be an example," he asks, "of an aspect of us that refuses its divinity?"

If you look at your culture, or any culture for that matter, there are aspects of self that are perceived of as without God. You may claim the body is holy, but you hold deep shame of the body. You cover your parts in shame, and the expulsion from Eden, as depicted, has those people cowering and covering their nakedness. The Divine as what you are is in perfection in every cell of your being, and that includes the aspects of you that you may feel shame about. Whether it is how you perceive yourself, or how you perceive others perceive you, it matters not. What you have condemned, you have removed from the garden, you have put outside of God. Now, to debase the body is to deny the Divine within it. "What do we mean by *debase*?" he says. How you care for it, or how you don't. The challenge here, again, is what aspect of self is in care of the body. The small self's assumption of what she should look like, how he should behave, are usually predicated on the expressions of the world that she abides in. You denounce the foods of the day that you are taught to denounce. You ascribe to this or to that as what you should be. And you end up replicating cycles, again and again, that keep you in bondage to an idea or a system of expression.

We have to invite you now to a new potential, beyond the known. And the realization of form, and that is the body you have taken, must be consented to as you agree that the body may be re-known, and known in a new way in its field. What we mean by this is that the field that the body holds is its expression. There is nothing of the body that is not replicated in the etheric, and to re-form the body is to realize the perfection that exists in the etheric and can be made in manifestation as the what that you are. Equivalencies here, if we wish to use that word, are, simply put, as within, so without. But if the governance of the body is the small self with its agenda and mandate, you will be doing the best you know how, but you will not be in transformation. The Divine as who and what you are, who knows who she is, also claims form as its expression. And to truly surrender the body to a renunciation of what harms it is not an intellectual act, as you all think it is. It's a simple act of attending to the Divine and providing it the opportunity to claim you. As you decide that you have the right to be, at this level or juncture of decision, you may also decide that the form that you have taken can move into a new coherence and abide in the Divine, and that the functions of the body, which includes your sexual self, may be re-known in a higher alignment.

"But what does that mean?" he asks. Very simply put, the Divine as sex, as the act, as the urge, as procreation, or without procreation. The ability of the body to express itself in a sexual self is a gift, and to deny the gift is to debase the body. To decide that the gift should rule the body, and should be the reason you are, would also debase the body because you are not operating in alignment to the requirements of the True Self. "Does the True Self have a requirement for sexual being?" Of course it does, as does every flower, every tree. Perhaps the difference in this form is the identity and the objectification of others that actually operates with the sense of separation or the denial of the inherent Divine.

To deny the Divine in your partner is to deny the divinity of the sexual act. To love your partner is to love the body, and the expression that the body has taken. Not every love is expressed sexually, but sexual love, we would have to say, is a way to know God, as is a walk on the beach, or singing to your daughter before she goes to sleep. You may know God in a sunset, or upon the lips of the beloved. It is still the presence and the interaction with the Divine that has come and is being known and realized as who and what you are.

Paul is interrupting. "Why this digression and attendance to sex?" Well, we have been asked about it, so we are choosing to answer. But beyond that, the incorporation of the holiness of form into the absolute, which is the simple ascension of the body to a higher octave of expression, cannot happen when you are debilitated by shame, or self-denial, or a desire to demand that others be your object of gratification and not be in love with them. And, to be in love, we must restate, is to be in the vibration of love, not a romantic ideology, but the presence of love that is known in relation with another. To deny God in another is to deny God within the self. And to deny the sexuality that is present for you, whatever it may be, is to deny the Divine its opportunity to express through it. "How does the Divine express sexually?" you may ask. In love. In an awareness of the beauty of the potential of the senses to know themselves in this agreement in tandem with another. There is no one right way to be expressed sexually. You have your proclivities: She prefers a brunette, he prefers a man, she prefers a man, what have you. But if the denial of the Divine is present in the predilection, the act itself will be in low vibration. And, if the act is in low vibration, you are supporting fear, because the denial of the Divine in anyone or anything is the portal to this. To agree to the Divine in any partner is to love the partner. This is true in friendship. It is true in matrimony. It is true in love, whatever form the love may take. The awareness of the Divine in the one before you, when you are loving them, is the presence of the Divine that claims you each in consort that you may know yourselves through.

"How is this ascension?" he asks. "Or is it?"

You may be in love in the Upper Room. You may be in passion there, as well. Why would you exclude the joy of sexuality from your true expression? If every time you make love, you have to go back down to the cellar, you are going to have a very difficult time navigating the octaves. And, if you have not yet made love in the Upper Room, we expect you're going to like it very much. "Why?" you say. Because there is no fear. The vulnerability you express in is absolute because the fear that would preclude you from knowing another, truly knowing another, cannot be present in that octave. Many of you say you wish to know intimacy, but you do not know intimacy because you are hindered from it in your expression because you create the walls born in fear that would keep you from love, and, in many cases, quite sadly, from allowing yourself to know love.

What if, in this instant, it was safe to be loved, both in body and in heart? What if it meant that you could be in a relationship beyond the ideas you've held about what a relationship can be? What if the ability to be loved, in truth, were not predicated on anything other than your being in truth? Because, in truth, you are unafraid. To give yourself permission to be known by God, to be realized by God, is in and of itself a way of being consumed by love. And this consummation by the absolute is the greatest love you will ever know. But to allow this is to become naked in all ways before the altar to let the Divine express through you in perfection. And, if you have denied the form you have taken and the functions of the body, or the pleasures of the flesh, you will deny those ways of knowing God and keep them hidden.

"But what of vices?" he says. "Don't we have these vices that must be attended to?" Of course you do, and you think you must fix them as the small self does. But you have never truly fixed them because they are not things that are broken. They are simply ways of thinking of the self, and the ideas of them have the ramifications in the form you have taken. An alignment to the True Self actually gives you the opportunity to lift these very things to be re-known in a higher way, but they will not be re-known as you fight them. That is the small self seeking its attempt to correct something that is best left upon the altar for deliverance. To be delivered of anything is to be released from it, and from the responsibility of it as well.

"What does that mean?" he asks. Very simply put, if it is your mandate to control something—"You'd best feed the cat or the cat will not live"—please feed the cat. But if your mandate is something that cannot be claimed by the small self—"I will release myself from jealousy," which cannot be done by the jealous self; "I will release myself from this addiction," which will not be done by the small self, who is the one addicted—you will have the understanding of what it means to know the Divine as the one who can deliver you.

"How does it happen? How are we delivered from the things we suffer from?"

This is a very good question, and, while there are many answers, and individuals may have different ways of responding to their own needs, we will simply tell you that the idea of surrender, which is in fact a simple offering, not one that must require you to grovel before a god and say, "Take it," but a simple offering: "Let it be of you. Let it be yours. And, if I am to do something to support this act of deliverance, let it be known to me. Let me know. Let me be in my knowing so that I may gift you with the entirety of my being."

The entirety of your being. That includes your sexual self, or your addiction, or what you know of as a vice. It includes your need to reprimand your fellows, to always be right, or to never be right. It includes any ideas of who and what you are that operate at the exclusion, or in the denial, of the presence of the Divine.

As you are challenged by your lives, as you seek deliverance from the world you see, as you understand the requirements for your development in the days you live in, and in the days you see passing by you, as you say yes to the opportunity to grow, you must also agree that the opportunity for deliverance is present. As you say yes to the potential of the Divine as you, the aspect of the Creator as you, in its realization to be the one who can see you through to the higher room, when you seek to find yourself in the relics of history or the debasement of self that you have been instructed in by your parents, your culture, or your religion, everything is lifted to the Upper Room. Period. Period. Period.

DAY TWENTY

Each of you decides, when you come to an expression on this plane, that you will realize yourself in accordance with your needs. But the needs of an individual soul will vary somewhat. Each lifetime is an opportunity for progression, but progression doesn't always come in a singular way. The totality of experience in an incarnation is what is assessed when you commence a new lifetime. "What do I need?" "How can I know myself?" "What are the ways I may experience the glory of being?"

Now, your divinity is impressed in you at the inception of your soul. You cannot be separate from God, so this impression stands with you, progresses with you through each lifetime for the singular purpose of realization. In one lifetime, a level of realization may be met and you may find yourself, in the next lifetime, learning through what you have claimed in the last one. Imagine that at the end of a lifetime you find yourself moving to a new town. The next lifetime becomes the experience of the town that was just moved to. So many of you decide that your destination is realization, but, in fact, it is not a destination. It is a way of being expressed and knowing, that continues to progress onward. There can be no finite state of realization.

If you have taken form and chosen to learn this way, the opportunities will come to you in form. When you release form and you understand yourself in the ethers, the lessons come in the ethers. There is no moment of arrival that supersedes your prior experience, because your prior experience is part of the journey, and the totality, therefore, of what you are comprehending.

Now, once realization occurs, realization is present in any idea you may hold of the past. And, because the past is just an idea, to realize the past is to realize the moment that you stand in, and, consequently, the past is comprehended in the new level of alignment. The idea that you should be someplace else, made some other choice, had a different experience, becomes impossible, because, in the moment of realization, everything makes sense—not logically, perhaps, but in its innate perfection. You can only be where you are. You could have only chosen this experience to learn through, to realize the sense of self that the soul was coming for, for the lessons learned.

When you experience trials in your life, you are claiming opportunity. The small self may say, "No, no, no," but the True Self says, "Yes," for any opportunity to be realized. And some of you choose realization through trauma, or through crisis, because you understand that the small self cannot have the tools to remedy a situation and your reliance upon the Divine becomes essential. When you understand that this is a journey, an education, an opportunity, and that realization is a stage of it, and not the penultimate moment of it, you will comprehend that being realized is simply another way of being.

To justify the old, to mandate that the old be present in the new, is to claim a separation from the moment you stand in, and the moment you stand in is the only moment when realization can occur. When we teach what you are not, we give you lists. You are not your history, or your body. We go on and on with all that you are not for one reason only. The temptation is always to attach the self to a way of understanding the self in complicity with the old, and, in doing that, you forget the moment you stand in because you are not attaching just to an idea of what you are—"I am a man," "I am a woman"—but you are attaching to the legacy that those names carry, what it means to be a man, what it has meant to be a man, what a man should be, and what it will be if you become fulfilled as a man. You may have that journey. It's a valid journey. "I will understand, in this lifetime, what it means to be a man." But the idiosyncratic nature of language may mean many things to many people, and your idea of manhood is, in fact, colored by your status in the world, what you were taught to admire, or aspire to be, or eschew and never be.

The dominion of the True Self transcends form. It incorporates form, as we have taught you thus far. It does not exclude it. But it transcends it. As you have designed the path for you through these incantations of realization, as you have chosen this way as an incarnation, as you have come to the point where realization of form and expression becomes part and parcel of how you know yourself to be, you may come upon realization as the authority who may claim the world from the perspective of the higher room. And dominion here is one thing, and one thing only. Creation. To be in creation is to be the manifestor, and the manifestation of the Divine Self will always be commensurate with the vibration that she has claimed. If you are speaking the letter "V," the letter "V" is what you attune to. And, in "V," the vibrational accord is such that the manifestation of language will be the letter "V," or the sound of "V," in what you encounter. The note you sing that is played by the harmonics of your being is what calls into expression, in like accord, the manifest world.

Now, because everything exists in multiple sequence, in vibration, in a scale with variations that may be comprehended, infinite variations that may be known, you have infinite possibility to create. But, if you understand that the Divine Self, in its tone, in its mandate for its own realization, cannot comply with the requirements of lower vibration, because, in doing so, it lessens itself. It releases itself to the density of the old, and, in the dense planes, the opportunities for manifestation, while still present, operate in low accord. What you claim in the basement is at the level of the basement. What you claim in the Upper Room holds that vibration.

Now, to be known as who and what you are is to be seen, and we will say this for Paul, who does not wish to be seen. The claim "I Have Come" is actually a visible claim, and we will explain this now. To become visible as the Divine Self really simply means that your expression from the Upper Room has transcended the barriers or the equations of limitation, so that you may be operative, while in body, as the True Self for the purpose of manifestation. This is rather different from systems that may have been taught about getting what you want in Spirit. This isn't getting what you want, this is manifestation of what you are in like vibration to all that exists in the Upper Room. And all that exists in the Upper Room can be found in this plane in lower density. You may lift anything through your encounter with it. But to lift something means to recognize it as worthy, to know it, to realize it. And, if you are judging it or frightened of it or deciding what it should look like, you have decided, based upon the formulas of old, what should be there.

Now, as you realize anyone or anything, the mandate of the Divine, not the small, the Divine Self, is to know it in love and in recognition of its right to be. "But what of the dark things?" Paul says. "I get an exterminator if the bugs come to the house. I hit the wasp with a book if I don't want to get stung. What are we to do?"

When you realize the Divine in anything—and this is crucial to understand—you are comprehending it within the fabric of reality that is in fact operating in a higher dimension or octave. The bug itself, the idea of the bug, carries the history of bugs that you are frightened of. By realizing the bug, by realizing anything as of God, you have translated the legacy of the thing to claim it in its true inheritance. Now, does the bug go away? That is not the issue here. It's realizing what is, and has always been, in existence in a high octave. The radiance you have as a self is far more encompassing than you can imagine, and a single being, in realization of the globe in its inherent perfection, lifts the globe and all that dwell upon it to the high octave. You don't decide that the bugs have to stay in the cellar, or that the man that you dislike will go into a locked room while the rest of humanity lifts, and that's what you do when you damn another or damn anything. Everything is lifted, everything is known, and then realized as of its Source. This is articulation, the spoken word made manifest through the announcement of being. "I Have Come."

Now, the radiance of this, as a claim, is, in fact, infinite because God itself is infinite, and you are not speaking as God as much as you are aligning to God and allowing it to express in its perfect way. The juncture you stand at through these instructions is you have been claimed in embodiment, but you don't know what it means, once embodied, to be. And what you are, at this level, is a manifestation of the Christed Self, not *the* manifestation, but *a* manifestation. The claim "I am the Word," the Divine as you, is known in multiple ways, in infinite ways. You are not transgressing on religion, you are not claiming to be somebody you are not. The alignment you hold is what is expressed and what is naming itself in its encounter with the manifest world. Underline *encounter.* As the vibratory being you are—the oracle who knows who and what she is, the expression of God as a bone, as a lung, as a hand, as an auric field, as one part of the vast mystery that is God—is expressed, its infinite nature moves toward what it sees, envelops and lifts, and the manifestation of this, the Kingdom, can be known in articulation or co-resonance with the Divine Self, who speaks it into being. To articulate is to speak.

Now he asks, "How is this done?" It is done in tone in the field you hold. And the speaking of the words "I Have Come" is the announcement of the Divine that incorporates itself in the remembrance of the Divine that is present in all things. God as the rock, as the tree, as the lung, as the hand, God as the sunset, God as the snowstorm, God as birth, God as death, God in surrender, God in struggle. There is nothing outside of it, and no experience is excluded from it because it is all part of the tapestry of the divinity that is expressed in this plane. You see yourselves in a mire of suffering, in your confusion, in your warring, but even these things are of God, just examples of the behavior of those who have forgotten who they are. "But are they of God?" Yes, of course. And the knowing of them reclaims them in the higher octave where their expression can be re-known. Their expression, how they serve, how they impart their frequency, may be re-known, not through correction, but through realization. Realization is not correction. Realization, the new, the present new, the profound new, the divinatory new, the new that is comprehended by the totality of being, is what is realized. "Behold, I make all things new." Not the nice things, not the awful things. All things. No exclusions.

Now the manifestation of the Christ as humanity is misunderstood. You don't wear sandals and a robe, you show up at your job if you have a job to go to, you bathe the child when needed, you care for the body as you can. But the opportunity for realization is not the province of the holy man, once you understand that all men are holy. This is not just an ordinary act. It *must* be an ordinary act for fruition to occur. You don't think about breathing, in most cases. You don't make your heart beat. You trust your heart to beat, you trust yourself to breathe. Imagine what it would be like if what you knew around you was simply God in manifestation because what else could it possibly be? And that is where we take you in this teaching. There is no effort in being. You don't strive to be. You cannot strive to be. You are. And you are already the articulation of the Divine in whatever form you have taken, and the purview of the Divine, as we have taught you, is everything she sees or imagines. Whatever you see, you are in relation to. Whatever you assume in your mind is present for you in a mental process that is the beginning of manifestation. So, as you are already the Creator, and of the Creator, the realization of it from the Upper Room claims the opportunity for the dominion of the Divine Self on this plane in its encounter with the reality in the name "I Have Come."

Now, dominion is not rule. It is not exercising control. In this case, it is comprehension. The one who knows who she is does not seek validation for it. The one who knows she has a right to sit in a chair doesn't beg permission. The one who knows dominion is simply being, and that the consciousness held is always in relation to what is seen, does not question manifestation. Because she perceives it, she is in accord to it. The same is true in this moment for all of you. As you lift in dominion, as the claim is made, "I Have Come," the waves of vibration moving through you, of and through, are claiming what it experiences in like accord. And the lifting begins.

Now, the lifting is inherent, indwelling, the realization of what is that may have been cauterized, suppressed, withheld, abandoned. The Divine in the blade of grass, the ordinary blade of grass; the Divine in the ruined castle; the Divine in the ruined life, the one you perceive as abandoned and lost. God is in all. And your realization of God in all claims what is all in a reckoning. And a reckoning, again, a facing of oneself and all of one's creations, is a blessed opportunity to transform. You don't fix. You reveal. You reveal the Divine that is inherent, and the lifting of the thing that is seen may commence, and the ramifications of that lifting may not be what you think, or come in order or in ease. When you lift a fifty-pound block, you expect strength is required. When you lift a pebble, you expect ease. In some cases, the fifty-pound block will be the graceful movement, and the lifting of the pebble, that one damn thing that you cannot find God in, will be arduous, but only arduous to a small self, who imagines what it should be. The Divine as you realizes the equality in the pebble and the huge block because they are both made of the same thing. Everything you see, know it or not, is a vast field of frequency that is moving and alive in a resonant field, and, as the lifting of the vibration that you have taken is announced in fullness, "I Have Come," the mandate of being of this expression is the realization that all form, all form, all form, finally, is malleable to consciousness because all form is is another idea. Do you understand this? What if form itself, manifestation itself, was just another idea that has been agreed to?

Some of you have experiences in the higher planes of the fluidity or lack of time. One moment you are in a bed, one moment you are flying across the sky. You don't question that reality. You know that reality and its properties in different ways because it is a different rule, or law, that has governed it. As you align to the Divine, and you begin to understand that everything is an idea in manifestation, and, consequently, everything can be re-known as a new idea, you can understand that what you are being claimed in, in the Upper Room, is, in fact, the authority to transform the legacy of humanity from separation, self-imposed isolation from its Source, into union.

We will complete this chapter now. The title was "Deliverance." We will continue when we are ready. Period. Period. Period.

8

RE-ARTICULATION

DAY TWENTY (CONTINUED)

Trouble comes when you seek to figure this out to support the small self's need in dictating what should be. When we hear Paul speaking—"What does this mean? How does it happen? What is its effect?"—we also hear him say: "This cannot be so. It will not be so. How can I believe this? What is the authenticating experience for this new teaching that you say has manifestation in the empirical world?"

The Divine as what you are, the manifestation of it, has been the teaching for some time. And understanding that the teaching of manifestation begins with you and form itself is the second step toward realization of the purview of the Divine Self in action, "I am Word." You may understand that the names you have been given, in small ways, in fact circumvent the potential you have always held. This means very simply that what you think you are, based on how you have been trained in limitation, coerces you, know it or not, to enable systems of control that would operate to limit you from your true divine nature. *True divine nature.* Listen to that phrase. *True divine nature.* Always true, of God, expression. That is what it means. Always true. Divine expression. You cannot make it other because it is always true. And, because it's always true, it may be known as such. "I know who I am in truth"—realization. "What I am"—manifestation. "How I serve"—expression in dominion as the aspect of self that has incarnated as you, which we call the Divine Self, Eternal Self, True Self, Christed Self. It matters not. You still walk around and introduce yourself as Hank or Sally. That's how you know yourself in agreement to be. But who has come as Hank or Sally is the Divine, and it is she who announces herself, he who claims, "I Have Come."

When "I Have Come" is claimed, the manifestation of the Divine essentially claims all it encounters in its true nature. Now, the small self cannot claim "I Have Come." He may try to and the effect will simply be, "Hi, I'm Hank, I have come." And somebody else will say, "For what?" There is no manifestation at that level. But in the Upper Room, the Divine as Hank, who has come as Hank, announces his presence from the Upper Room, not the cellar, not the street. Now, the Divine Self on the street is still in the Upper Room. The Divine in the Upper Room encompasses the street and the office and anywhere else you may think you are, or experience yourself as being, in this manifest world that you agree to operate through. But to be in the Upper Room is to hold the vibratory equivalent of all you encounter, and the claim "I Have Come," the manifestation of the Divine as what, is how you serve.

To understand service more fully is to understand that the Divine as what, in its own tone or expression, is what is transforming the world. And, as you are taught in the Upper Room to comprehend a world in a higher way, the instruction that is essential to your being must be known to you. As we have already taught you knowing, and claiming yourself as the one who may know, we will not reiterate it now. But, in the Upper Room, as you know, you may be called in an encounter with the world that would deny the Divine. "What happens then?" You have become visible, in a way, by nature of manifestation, and the manifestation that is claiming the world in a high accord may, in fact, meet resistance by the level of frequency that does not wish to be assumed.

"What does this mean?" he asks. Imagine you have a fish that only knows itself in one body of water. It cannot believe it will survive if it is moved to another body of water. It will do what it can to maintain itself. It will run from the net, bite what it can, find refuge under a rock, than withstand the potential for demise that it believes it may experience if transplanted, or, as we say, transposed, re-articulated, re-known in a higher vibration. When this occurs, the opportunity to realize the Divine in the face of fear, in the face of struggle, becomes service in a very different way. This has never been a teaching of coercion, nor will we allow it to be that. We will not allow it because we honor free will. To lift another to the Upper Room, to lift an aspect of self that has been in denial of God, would refute God, would say no to the potential for change. To understand that these denials are all fear-based, while an act of will, can still be met by the Divine who comprehends all things in union. Understand, again, the fish that may be transposed or moved to a clearer pond, a higher pond, a more sustainable pond for the very fish that has known itself in the depths of the dirty water, but cannot imagine that there is another place to live. The vibration you hold is not overriding the will of the fish. It is not doing that. It is not reclaiming the fish beyond its will. It is knowing the fish, realizing the fish, in the high tank, the new pond, the clear ocean that is the Upper Room. You are only knowing, or realizing. You are not fixing, you are not counseling, you are not dragging, you are not coercing the fish. You are knowing the fish, regardless of the resistance, because you understand yourself beyond fear. You are not claiming the other in agreement to what she believes.

"How is this not coercion?" he asks. "We are still lifting the fish that wants to stay in the dirty water." You are realizing the fish, the Divine as fish, in the Upper Room. You are not moving it in practical ways. Realization is a transposing of a piece of music from one octave to the next. It's a re-telling, or re-naming, or reclamation from one level or octave of vibration to another. Because you don't need permission to witness God in anything, or God as anyone, because you are simply claiming truth, what is always true at this level, the lifting is not done through effort, but by nature of your being. You can't try to be the Divine, lifting the fish to a clean ocean. You can only be the Divine who realizes the ocean and the fish in a higher octave where they may establish themselves in a new way.

Now, dominion actually is not fixing. It is not correcting. And, if you wish to do those things, you may choose to. You may fix the roof of your house. You may choose a new address that will better serve your purposes. The Divine as you is present in choice, as you align to the Divine as will. And the Divine as will is something you become reliant upon through the alignment in the Upper Room, because that is how you choose. To decide that the manifestation of the Divine is all things is to realize the entirety of being as one Source in multifarious levels of expression, one great concert played in many octaves, known in the manifestation that you perceive. But always understand, it is the level of alignment, vibratory accord that you express in, that aligns you to a world that may be perceived and re-known. Yes, the Upper Room.

Now, to understand fear as a creation and an idea is helpful. All fear is based in a premise that God is not present in that moment, and therefore fear is always a lie. "What about fear for your life?" he says. "I wake up in a burning building. I am afraid. I want to live." The fear that you are expressing here is somewhat different than we are teaching you. You are having a reaction in the body toward self-preservation. You call it fear, but that is adrenaline, and not much more, propelling you out the door to safety. To realize your demise in a burning building, and to be afraid of what comes after, is rather different. "Oh, my dear, I am going to die. What will happen to me, to my loved ones? All this money I put into this house, and now we're all on fire." That is the realization of the temporary nature of the physical plane that is always in transformation, and the fear of not being able to control the outcome of a situation. That is somewhat different than releasing the body, because that has no fear. Releasing the body, when that occurs, is a gift, and usually a graceful one, depending on your level of attachment to the form that you have taken.

To decide who you should be in any circumstance—"I should be noble and courageous," "I should be afraid"—is usually to prescribe to the history a situation has been given. In other words, you are taught when to fear by your upbringing, by your culture, by the systems of agreement that you have been in alignment to. In the Upper Room, you are not operative through these systems, although you may call them into being and lift them to the Upper Room in order to be re-known. In service, we suggest, every encounter to the resistance of the Divine becomes the opportunity for the Divine to be excavated and re-pronounced in form.

"What does that mean?" he says. The one who is angriest at God loves God the most. Did you know this? The one who is most angry at God holds the deepest love, and a sense of betrayal has encompassed him or her and protected her from her own longing. To realize God in the one who hates God is to know God in manifestation, and the knowing of God as the one fearful of God, angry at God, debasing God, to know the Divine as that one, is actually to offer liberation. By lifting her to the Upper Room, you are not telling him or her what to believe. You are simply realizing them in the union that is always present. When you see a battlefield and men warring, killing one another in a cause justified by them, or believing that what they are doing is right, the opportunity to know God, to claim the self on the battlefield, the Divine Self—"I Have Come, I Have Come, I Have Come"—is to realize God in the manifestation before you and lift it to the Upper Room. Any poverty, any act of avarice, is an act of fear. Any act of judgment against another is an act of fear. If you want to play on those things and perpetuate them, stay downstairs, have those experiences. Or go to the Upper Room and claim the presence of the Divine upon them. "I Have Come, I Have Come. I Have Come."

He is interrupting. "How is this different than the initial claim 'I am Word through the thing I see before me,' or 'the one I see before me'?" You have become Word in manifestation. Do you understand this? You have become the manifestation. *Be* and *come.* "I Have Come." And the claim you make upon the world you see is the expression in service in vibratory field. You are not telling people not to war. Nobody has ever listened to that, if you think back to it. But to know the Divine in presence upon the battlefield is to claim all you see beyond fear, or any justification that fear would present itself as. Any banner of false lies playing out on the battlefield that would justify the killing of a man for a false cause must be re-known by the Divine, and, in the knowing of it, men do put down their arms.

"Is this a metaphor?" he says. "I can't imagine that happening." Then you don't trust God to indwell in man. The realization of the indwelling God as the man with the gun claims the man beyond the violence he may have been trained in, and corrects the self-justification, not through an action you would take, but because the need to act in that false way does not exist in the field of truth that you are operating in. Like attracts like. If you were to go down to the battlefield with a pamphlet, expect to be shot and probably with good reason. To lift yourself to the high room and then lift the battlefield and all who dwell upon it to realization is to claim the Kingdom in the face of fear, and it's an opportunity to know, not only who you are, but the power of the Divine.

"But," he interrupts, "what if this war needs to happen? You say we don't correct things. And here you go telling us to correct things." You are not correcting anything as much as realizing it. The realization of the Divine may or may not re-create it in what you would think as a correction, but that is not what you are doing. By claiming the presence, by knowing the purview, by claiming the action, it is the Divine that must manifest and call forth the new thing. You cannot decide who will live or who will die, what should or should not happen. That is not your purview. But your purview is to know who you are, what you are, how you serve, know who you are as you express it, and allow God or the Divine to act in its own way. Your claim "I Have Come, I Have Come, I Have Come" does not make you the hero. It makes you the true witness, the true witness to any act, and by *true* we mean the one who knows God, realizes God or the Divine, in any act, in any human, in any situation you may encounter.

Don't think for a moment that you can use this to get your way. "Look at that battlefield. I want these ones to succeed and those to fail." Get ready for a bad lesson in knowing what you are. That is what would come. Any act that you would take to coerce another, or utilize these vibrations to get your way as a small self, will be refuted immediately. And you will learn the lesson from that, and, hopefully, move beyond the need to decide what should be, and claim, instead, what can only be, which is the Divine that is inherent in anything and everything, regardless of what the small self thinks of it.

Now, as we close this lecture, we will say, yes, this is in the text. It is the beginning of a new section or chapter. We will title it when we are ready, and we are completing this text, we expect, by the end of this summer.

(PAUSE)

Now, when we ask you questions about what you think you are, you look to the known to answer them. You look for the mirror to validate your experience. You seek to find what you expect to find and confirm it. You do this unknowingly, but the catalog that you cull through to find your answers is the catalog of the known, and the new idea, the principle of the idea that the Divine as you operates in a higher tone, claims a different reality into being, exists in a new way that the small self can't comprehend. You will find yourself challenged by this, as you claim the old and seek to claim the new.

In order for us to work with you in the high octave, we must release you from an identity that demands to be known through the qualifications or systems of agreement that you have utilized to navigate this experience you know of as your world. But your world exists in other realities that are contained within them, and known in them, by the one who can realize. When we explain it this way, we are trying to get you to understand that the reality you experience yourself in is one level of resonance, and, within this world, there are many ways to see and to know, and what is comprehended in the higher alignment does not have a name as you have named it through the criteria of experience.

So how do you negotiate living in a manifest world that has been named by others, and claiming a new world into being in the Upper Room? How do you participate in a daily action, going to work, seeing your friends, learning something new? How can you attend to these things from the higher octave and realize them while you operate effectively in the agreements made in human nature?

It's quite easy, you see, theoretically, to tell you the Divine has come as you. It is the Divine who goes to work, has the experience with the friend. But it is quite another thing to experience it. And to realize it means to experience it, and that is the vibratory octave we intend to bring you to now in shared agreement of a new manifest world. In order for this to be claimed, you must make one choice, and only one choice—that anything you can see or imagine that has been claimed prior to knowing was claimed as an idea, a simple idea that may be re-conceived. The idea of the spinster is claimed by the spinster, the one who knows herself as such a thing, or by the one who would decide for her. "That poor woman who never wed, that spinster down the hall." The idea of *spinster* has ramifications in the practical experience of the woman and the neighbor, and the realization of who she is in agreement to the True Self is what reclaims her beyond the known. Even the idea of gender, the *woman* down the hall, or place, *down the hall*, is agreement to an idea, born in situation and remembrance. The agreement we make to the new, in comprehension of your being, is that what you see is in fact malleable to vibration, and that the claim "I Have Come" is actually a claim that will demonstrate itself in a re-articulation of matter.

Paul is challenged already. We will continue regardless.

To name anything is to give it a way of expression, a mandate in some ways. Everything seen that you can name has been called into being, and the name is the co-resonance with the thing that you operate in. When a mandate is made by a collective—"We will call this thing, agree to call this thing, by this or that name"—the manifest thing coheres with the name and its properties. And the manifest thing has been made in form, concretized in consciousness, and aligns to the level of density that it is called to. When you claim a new thing into being, or remember a thing as its Source, a vibratory object known in one way, perhaps named one thing, that can be re-named, you give yourself opportunity to engage in the alchemical act that we are speaking to. If all things are God, all things may be re-known as God, or as the Source you know of as God.

If you can imagine an ocean, all that abides within the ocean knows itself in union with the sea it expresses in. God is no different. It is the sea you express in, and everything that exists within the sea is of the sea, and may be re-made, returned to the sea, and reclaimed as such to be re-made in other form. You understand that energy is never destroyed. You must understand that the selves that you think you are are also eternal, and the body itself is a form Spirit has taken in realization through the act of creation. Now, you are made, you are born in form, but the body itself is in union with the sea it comes from, and, at that level of expression, it may know all things as of the sea, as of God.

If you would like, in your mind, imagine for a moment that you exist in a vastness where everything that has been named is simply energy in vibration, a tone expressing, a sound or a known way of thinking of sound. Everything before you is in resonance, and you are in union with it by nature of being. You are not separate from the room. You are in the room. You are not separate from that which is in the room. You are in a shared landscape.

Now, imagine, if you wish, that the landscape itself is what you know of as God, the room as God, the chair as God, the window as God. And, as you claim these things, allow yourself to release any ideas of what these things are beyond the idea that you are in union with them in Source, that you are in one vibration, in oscillation or tone, in experience in union. You may feel this as the field you hold begins to go into agreement with the landscape you are claiming. Now, you may open your eyes and do the same exercise with what you see before you. Your idea of who and what you are, your idea of the room you sit in, your agreement in separation—all ideas that can be surrendered to a new claim. And the claim "I Have Come" is the claim in union that the Divine brings through to reclaim the manifestation in oneness with Source.

So do this now, if you wish. Allow the body that you hold, the idea of the body, the idea of where you sit, the idea of the room, the idea of the building, wherever you may be, another idea that has taken form, allow the ideas to become one idea. "I am in union with my accord in my new name, I Have Come." And, as you express, feel the field that you have taken begin to move, and move into agreement with the field or expression that everything else has taken. You are moving into oneness, in union with an expressed landscape that is being transformed by your agreement to it. Not the small self's agreement. The small self is just another idea. And, as that idea is dissipated, is surrendered, as it moves in its own union, everything may be known as the divine expression.

The claim you will make now, if you choose it, is the claim of agreement to be remembered in this expansive knowing. And the claim you make, in permission for this to be granted, is assured at the level of the soul, who knows how far you may move in realization. So what you receive will be to the degree that you can be operative in the daily life you express in as the manifest Word.

"On this day I choose to allow remembrance of the entirety of my being, that any idea I may have held of who and what I am, any idea I may have known of what other things were, by old vibrational accord, may be reclaimed, re-known, and remembered in union with the Source of all things. I know who I am in truth. I know what I am in truth. I know how I serve in truth. I Have Come. I Have Come. I Have Come."

Be as you are.

(Short pause)

You are in union. You are in oneness. You are in accord. You are in love. You are in knowing. You are free. You are free. You are free.

Be in this place as long as you wish to stay here. It is always here. It has always been here. It is what is, beyond the known. Period. Period. Period.

DAY TWENTY-ONE

Each of you decides when you arrive here that this is the opportunity to claim an identity, to learn through matter, to learn in relation to your fellows. Each of you says yes to an opportunity to create a life and challenges, which are, in fact, opportunities with which you learn through. Each of you decides that you can agree to a livelihood or a way of being in a material realm that supports you. And each of you says yes to what you may know, what you may comprehend beyond the known.

As you idealize a small self, as you say, "This is who I am, this is what matters, this is what I came for, this is what you should think of me," you claim your experience, not only in agreement to your fellows, but what they may make of you. You are all in consort, in one way or another, to an agreement to witness a collective landscape. And it's the collective landscape, when lifted, that we announce as the Kingdom.

Now, the individual is participatory to the landscape. Everything she sees she confirms in the language she has been taught. "That is a tree, that is a man, that is a wedding, that is a birth. I comprehend these things and the meanings of them through the tribal language, or agreement, that I have come to know myself through." But what if, in fact, the tribal language was simply a way of meaning, and claiming meaning, to comprehend a world that otherwise makes little sense and has no value? Imagine, again, that you are looking around the room you are in. Nothing has a name. You wouldn't know what a fork was, what a tree was, what you were sitting upon. You would just be being, in coherence, with a landscape that is in some ways unnamed, without value, and without necessity. And by *necessity* we mean you don't understand why you need this or that. It simply is.

Now, because you are here in this shared field that has been named, you are accountable to the names that things have been given. And the meaning of those things over time, which have been established in a shared construct, is the way you understand the languaging of meaning in consort with your fellows. "We will call this this or that." The temptation always, in any case, is to decide what things are based on what you have been taught, and lose the relevance and opportunity that is actually available to you in a new landscape that is unnamed.

We have said prior, when something new appears, ask it what it is. Ask it for its name. Don't go busying yourself looking for the template to fit that thing in that confirms an idea. If you wish to know the new, to comprehend the new, you will not when you seek to reinforce the old upon what you see. Imagine that anything that can be seen can be revealed, unmasked—unnamed, in fact—to a true meaning. Again, this does not mean that a fork is not a fork. In this dimension or octave, you comprehend these things and their uses. But to move beyond the known is to move to the landscape of resurrection, and all things may be resurrected or realized in the high octave in a perfect way.

"What does that mean," he asks, "a perfect way?" It very simply means that the idea of what the Divine is, in all cases, precludes your witnessing of the Divine. The idea of the fork claims the fork in the same kind of way. And the alignment you hold to anything in manifestation that has been named has been coded, made so, and, in doing so, the density of vibration it adheres to claims you in like vibrational accord. Everything may be lifted. Everything may be re-known. But it must be unnamed, reclaimed, re-comprehended, and this is only done in the Upper Room.

In the lower landscape, or shared construct of reality, the manifestation of form in its density serves to confirm a reality that is actually transient. Even your understanding of time and the meaning of time is in some ways deciding for you what your experience is. If you didn't know what a minute was, if there wasn't a collective idea of an hour or a day, what would experience be? Now, to lift beyond these things in all ways simply means your experience of them is translated, and the manifestation is translated as well. And by *translated* we mean it exists, but in a new way. We are giving Paul an idea, because he is asking the question. "A word in French and a word in English are the same word, but in translation. Is this the same idea?" Yes and no. But release the idea of *idea* and the manifestation can confirm itself. What you do not do is lift the idea to the Upper Room. To do so would claim the heritage of the thing you lift. It's far easier, in fact, to claim the Upper Room, the eternal now, and then realize time, than to try to understand time, because to understand time is a mental process that will bring you back down to a level of logic, and, in fact, participation with the old structure of what time was meant to understand itself as. To realize anything is to know it. And, to know the fork, or the timepiece, or the idea of time itself by saying *time* and moving into comprehension with it, aligns you to what is possible in a new language, or a new way of being.

"Well, how do we understand this? If there is no name for time in the Upper Room, what, in fact, are we claiming?" You are claiming the infinite moment where anything may be realized and, in fact, reclaimed in a new idea, a new possibility beyond the known and the limitation of ways of responding to a physical realm through heredity. Now, for those of you who say, "This cannot be done," we must tell you it is being done every day, but you don't see it. Your comprehension of your reality is a testimony to this teaching. Everything you witness, you are in comprehension to and alignment with, and it's justified through the shared landscape and vocabulary. Simply to lift to the Upper Room and claim manifestation lifts the vibration of everything seen to an agreement, or accord—a-c-c-o-r-d, or a-c-h-o-r-d as on a piano—that lifts you and the thing seen into agreement or alignment. And the new way of seeing simply means you are not encoding what is visible through the intentions of historical data. You are not deciding what things were. You are experiencing them in the moment you stand in, in their new way. Again, "Behold, I make all things new."

Now, this is less an exercise in forgetting the past than realizing the present. And to wake up from a dream of dense vibration and to find yourself in a new landscape is rather what we are saying happens when you move to this level of assumption. You have been assumed in a higher octave, and, consequently, your experience of manifestation must come with a level of consciousness you have aligned to. It is not about denying what was, it's about experiencing what is, and the experiencer, in this case, the True Self as you, is not reliant upon the old as the small self has been. Your idea of ascension, in some ways, is rather limited. You think you take yourself as you think you are to the Upper Room, when, in fact, who goes to the Upper Room is who you have always been and can only be in a higher vibrational state. This does not erase you. It does not take away your memory. It creates the plasticity of experience that lifts you beyond the re-creation of historical data, which is the requirement of claiming the manifestation that we call the Kingdom, the Kingdom again being the awareness of the Divine in all manifestation.

This is somewhat different than walking down a pretty parkway and saying, "Look at the pretty trees. Look at the pretty flowers. I see the Divine here. All is good in my world." The understanding that realization of matter, the realization of the Divine as matter, is actually a claim of alchemy that lifts the vibration of what is seen to a new alignment is the true meaning of the claim of the Kingdom. And the manifestation of God that is already here is revealed in its blooming. To deny the Divine is to deny the Kingdom. To debase the self is to deny the self its access to the Kingdom. To deny another's presence as of God is to deny both of you the entry that you say you seek. So to articulate what you are in a high way simply means you are no longer claiming the old, justifying the old, seeking to have it mean what it meant, and claiming others in the low accord that has become this shared landscape. Understand, we said *become*. The density of this plane is your own making. The alignment you have held to the action of fear is the one thing, we would suggest, that perpetuates this, because everything we named, every avarice, every way of deciding who's worthy and who is not, can only be made in fear because, as you now understand, the divine presence is in all, not just the things you approve of, or would like to see, or would like to claim agreement to.

If you would imagine, for a moment, that there is something before you, or perhaps someone, that you would claim as a monster, and decide for a moment that your articulation of the word *monster* is what makes it so, and your ideas of what makes a monster are agreed to through cultural choice and history, you will see that, in fact, you are the monster maker. And, to reveal the monster as the holy being he or she may be, that it may be, is to release the names it has been called to the claim of truth that is always present and always known by the Divine Self: "I Have Come. I

Have Come. I Have Come." In this claim, you reveal the truth and claim the witness. And the unveiling of the truth of the monster, what has been degraded or allowed itself to be, in its release in separation is reclaimed and re-known and then lifted to the upper template, or Upper Room, where it may be known in fulfillment.

"What does this mean," he says, "*template*?" The idea of a template or a mold is not an untrue idea, and the Divine Self, if you wish, can be understood that way, the truth of who anybody is that exists beyond form or personality or history or idealization. The idea of the being in a perfected state, in a blueprint, if you wish, that it may claim its accordance with, is not an untrue teaching. To lift anything to the Upper Room is to reclaim it at its essence, and by *essence* we mean the thing that is, of itself, and cannot be any other way. Once that is understood, anything that hinders its expression or blocks its expression can be reclaimed, re-known, as the alignment progresses. The teaching of claiming the Kingdom, which we have given you, is not about artifice, but realization, which is factual. You are not conjuring. You are knowing truth. But to know the truth of anything is to agree to it, and that means you cannot confirm the lies it has taken on.

"What is an example of that?" he asks.

"I am an infirm woman." "I have loved no one." "I am unworthy of love." "No one can be in this claim I make for myself." The delusion here is that one cannot be loved, or is unworthy of love, and the realization of love within the one who has denied that love claims her in truth, and the truth is she is deeply loved, as are all. Your ability to do this as the True Self has enormous ramifications on the individual's life and on the landscape that individual expresses through, if you can understand that the echo that we teach in, the broadcast of vibration as announced in the claim "I Have Come," has manifestation throughout the world and throughout time itself.

"Now why time?" he says. "I thought time didn't exist." The construct of time does exist because you agree to it. But because the Divine in its moment of expression is eternal, the ramifications themselves are eternal. When a landscape is transformed, it is made new. It is not painted over for the moment. And the realization of the new at the cost of the old is the manifestation of the Divine where the denial of the Divine—or the lie—has been played out. By this we mean that the dominion you hold, as the one who has come, is to reclaim the landscape in the high template of the divine purpose that it was intended for.

Now he's very upset. "Intended for what? What is this teaching?" You understand the legend of Eden, and the idea of the garden and the presence of the Divine and the expulsion from it, which was, in fact, the denial of the Divine through the manifestation of fear. Once you understand that fear is the lie, and the landscape informed in fear is what is being transformed and transmuted, the idealization—the true meaning—of Eden is understood.

So he asks questions, one upon the next. "Is there no poverty in Eden? Are we all healthy? This is feeling preposterous." Very simply put, the idea of union in an experiential way, the realization of matter and each individual as of the same Source, is what is transformed and made created anew. You are not denying what exists, you are reclaiming what is, in the high octave. Now, the metaphor of Eden, simply put, is the metaphor for landscape operating in presence without the denial of the Divine. When you understand that the reclamation of the True Self has its own mandate for a landscape to operate in, you begin to comprehend the meaning of this. We are not teaching you that the world you live in will be what you want it to be in your small self's idealization of Eden, but what the True Self knows. And those are very different things. The idea of the Divine Self in manifestation is the teaching of the Christ. It always has been. The teaching of the Kingdom is the manifestation of the Christ in landscape, in manifestation. The realization of union is the source of all love. And the claim of love that you may benefit the world in, "I Have Come, I Have Come, I Have Come," is the reconciliation of the Divine in form in a manifest world—reconciliation, reuniting, reunion with what is, in expression, in the high octave.

DAY TWENTY-TWO

Each of you comes with an awareness of what your requirements are for the life you live, and, as you decide the manifestation of the Divine has come as who and what you are, the realization of the goals that you had previously named begin to be reframed in the context of the higher ideal. Each of you chooses, prior to birth, a set of circumstances that you may indeed learn through, and you claim them in sequence over the course of a life. The Divine Self as you, who has come to be realized, has come to reclaim you, and in many cases at the cost of what you thought you must be, or how you should be seen or realized through the small self's ideas.

Now, we use the word *idea* intentionally here, because the idea of who you are is what is being reclaimed in a very different way than you may have assumed as a small self. The Divine as what, the manifestation of the Divine that has come in form as you, will express itself in an octave that surpasses the claims of old. When you understand this, that you are surpassing the old, moving beyond the old to a new idea that is now claimed in manifestation, you can begin to realize the magnitude of the transformation that you will indeed undergo as you lift yourself to the Upper Room and establish the frequency there as the body you hold, and the emanation of the body in the vibratory field.

"Why body?" he says. Because, without the body, the manifestation of the Divine is incomplete. As we have said, everything is in form and in vibration or tone. And, in reality, the mass that you see, the bulk of flesh, the physical reality, is all one thing—God in expression in different ways announcing itself, articulated in tone.

Articulation—underline that word, please. You are an *articulation* of the Divine. The manifest form that you have taken is an expression of it, and to denounce the form that you have taken—"I am only a small man, I walk around in a frail body, I see other things that are small"—is to claim God as frail and small. Again, those are ideas, and what you think you are or have been, in re-articulation, is the claim we make in the manifest self through the name "I Have Come."

Now, any announcement of being claims ramification. "I am a man" gives you the manifestation and the requirements of the name you have chosen. Any profession, any idea—"I am the one who never gets it right, who will always be seen in such and such a way," an announcement of self, a frame, if you wish—calls to it the ramifications of that name or choice. Now, as the Divine Self, the ramifications are very different, and the articulation of the Divine Self in the name "I Have Come" is in some ways a renunciation of what has been taught in form, and the science you've known up until now would claim you as a thing in an obsolete way. The idea that the Divine informs all things invites you to lift to an experience of realization beyond the known that can then be assumed, and, in assumption, in complete awareness of your union with Source, you begin to decide that anything that you thought you were becomes an idea that is now re-known.

To be re-known in God, or what you might call God, is to be re-articulated, and the Word made flesh, as we would teach it, is an idea or a way of measuring what manifestation is at a level or octave that cannot be claimed by one who has not aligned to the truth of their being. When we say *truth,* we mean truth. Not a convenient truth: "I don't like the day, it's a terrible day," your convenient opinion about the day. We mean an eternal truth, the Divine that has come in its expression, the ever true, the Divine as what, the crystalline expression of God in vibration.

Now, as you are assumed in the Upper Room, the requirement of being, what you thought you were must be re-understood because you still have lives here. "I have a job, I have a child. I cannot leave my job or my child." You are not invited to leave. You are invited to re-know, because, as you have been articulated, "I am the Word," or the Divine Self in manifestation, you claim everything that you experience in that comparable octave. We say *comparable* intentionally because the alignment you may hold will not always infer that something will be claimed in equal resonance, but within the octave of expression that you have aligned to.

If you understand that this plane of expression is an octave, with variant notes, highs and lows, and the extremities of expression are still existing within a template of agreement—"We all know what the planet is, what a sky is, what a continent is, perhaps, we all agree to a rain or a thunder or a sunny day"—the idea within the octave must be comprehended as a manifestation of collective agreement. *Collective agreement* means you agree to a sky or a continent or an ocean or a concept—for example, time, because he just interrupted with a question, "Like time?" Yes, of course, like time.

Now, agreement in consort with your fellows aligns the collective field in a shared experience, and the shared experience of manifestation is what must be comprehended by you each as you ascend, or lift, in an activation to a higher agreement, another octave, if you wish, which we would call the Upper Room. Now, the singularity of an octave does not necessarily deny the octave below, or the octave beyond. You are all in sequence, in variance in tone, even within this shared plane of expression you live in. And, as you have realized the idea of who you are—"I am a man," "I am a woman," "This is what I do for a living"—you activate within the realm of self-justification, what things should be because you expect them to be, which is the justification of expectation that the small self would claim. As you lift, as you move beyond the known to the high expression, you align to the articulation of what exists at that level of vibration. And the consequence of this is you are not denying what exists in low form, the low octave, low vibration, but you are re-seeing it from the perspective of the Upper Room, which is re-articulation, which we will say is the name of the chapter we are working on now.

To be re-articulated, re-announced in the claim "I Have Come," is to claim a level of embodiment, in sequence, that may be altered in the manifest world. "What does that mean?" he says, "*altered in the manifest world*?" It means that the form you have taken, in resonance, is not what it was. It has been re-articulated, and the name you have been given, "I Have Come," is not a small self announcement, but the arrival of the Divine in manifestation that announces a new world into articulation through agreement, coherence, alignment in the high octave you are singing in. So the things that were known in form and field, the child, the job, the life lived, is not only reclaimed, re-known—it is made new. Underline the teaching. *Made new*. To make something new is to realize it as it truly is beyond the construct that the small self would utilize in reference to what she was educated in. And you've been educated in ways that would deny, not only your own divinity, but the manifestation of God in anyone and anything. And, as you have aligned to this new resonance in this claim, "I Have Come, I Have Come, I Have Come," you are announced, and then beholding the announcement in the form that you have taken. To realize the self is to realize the Divine expressed in all.

Now, so many of you think this is something you do, and it's not what you do, it's what you have become in articulation. And the ramifications of that, "I Have Come, I Have Come, I Have Come," the announcement of the Divine as what, in form and field, in expression, is the being of the Divine that claims the truth in anything and everything that can be known. We say *Beyond the Known* is the title of the text, and the realization of the God you know, or the truth in all, in anything and everything, is to move the sequence of experiential being from one sense of being to a radically different one.

He is interrupting now. "But I don't understand. *Radically different*. Do I wake up and not know my name? Is my child in the ethers? Is my job an idea that I don't go to? What is the activation in experience? What is it like to be as you say?" It is to wake up from a dream that you have been conspiring with, and resonant with, and, in the new resonance, what is, was, but is known anew. *What is, was, but is known anew.* And, in the new, your experience of manifestation, the claim of being, "I Have Come," is in equation with the field of the Divine that is ever present in everything, but unannounced. And, when something is unannounced, it is asleep to its true nature.

Now, the claim "I Have Come," in realization, transforms the reality of the experience of the day, but not in drama, but in agreement to what always is. And you are moving beyond the landscape of the temporary page to the realization of what the page actually has been. Paul is seeing a page being turned, as in a magazine, and the page turned reveals the new page, the true page. The agreement to be in this, in vibrational accord, is the agreement to realize what has always been. Underline that now. *What has always been.* The idea of re-creation, for so many of you, is about fixing what you think is wrong, and that is born within the shared field of agreement, or the octave of expression that we are moving you beyond. So, if you wish to take your remedies to the Upper Room and do your fixing there, you cannot succeed because you are claiming the old vision and aspiring to bring your intellect, your sense of right and wrong, sense of good and bad, to the Upper Room where those things are not expressed. The template of reality in the Upper Room is immediate and does not claim the morality, the ideology, the intent of the old. And, in the new, the alignment to what is and can only be reclaims anything as of Source, and that cannot be done when you are directing it to be what it was with your opinions attached. "There should be no crime. There will be no crime. I will have no crime in my Upper Room." Well, then don't go upstairs. Go find a closet and shut the door. You will have a better experience in the closet.

You realize anything in the Upper Room in resonance. And the claim of what is as of God is the lifting of it to a new way of being. The name *crime* carries with it history, the history of law, the mandates of law, the mandates of morality, which have all been born in religion, whether or not you know it. And these codifications of experience are part of the shared construct that you are lifting beyond when you go to the Upper Room. The divine potential, the potential to realize anyone and anything as what it truly is, exists here, but cannot be claimed when you are deciding what it should be. "Well, there will be no war in my Upper Room." We would reframe that to say, "War cannot exist at the level of consciousness in the Upper Room." But to realize that mandates that you know that this is so, and, as you know, which means to realize, this truth, this truth is made known, or realized, in the shared expression of the low octave, because to realize anything at this level is to lift it to the Upper Room for re-articulation.

"Now, can one man," he asks, "end war by realizing eternal peace?" You must understand, friend, that eternal peace exists in the Upper Room. You are not pretending. You are knowing. And, as you know and realize the ramification of being in this expression, the articulation of the Word is what renounces the old. To renounce something is to deny it. Now, you are not pretending. You are simply saying, "I Have Come." And, if you think for a moment you can bring your old agenda to that claim, choose a better wardrobe for the announcement, and perhaps make business cards to announce you have come, please don't come. We can do without you at this level of expression.

The True Self as you is who has come, not your idea of the True Self. The True Self as you, who is lifted, who is activated, who has been re-known, re-articulated in the Upper Room, is who has come at the cost of the old, but not at the cost of the child, or the job, if they are imperative to your experience here. To be willing to release anything and everything is, in fact, required. But it is not needed, and it should not be done if it is not a requirement for your progression. If you are in a relationship that encourages you to deny the Divine, you may wish to re-think your passage. You may decide, as the small self may, that she wants what she has known. She will leave the heavens for some other time, and there is no penance there. You will learn there in your own way. But to deny the Divine at the cost of what you've had is to put yourself in a predicament. "I cannot have the Upper Room, I don't like what I have claimed here" is a way to decide or to justify the expression you are choosing. Please just remember that it is being chosen. To release the old may invite you to release the relationship, but it is not the requirement, and please don't pretend it is. That would be the small self seeking to assume this teaching for her personal agenda. "The Guides said I should leave my husband." We would never say such a thing. You will choose what you choose at the level of agreement that you can come to. And *agreement* means co-resonance with what you have chosen. To lift beyond the old, to arrive to a new way of being, is, in fact, to release the old *as you have known the old.* Do you understand the difference? "Behold, I make all things new." Period. Period. Period.

(PAUSE)

Now, decide this, if you wish: That as you have known yourself in form, the form you have taken may be re-comprehended or realized anew in an articulation as the Divine Self, and the authority you have, as the one who knows who she is, is to make this claim, "I Have Come." The manifest self, the Divine who has come as who and what, is who makes this claim. And the reliance upon the True Self as the authority of your life aligns the authority of your life to the Divine so you become an expression, the fruition, of the Divine as may be known as you. Underline *as.* Now, as you understand that what you are is of the Divine in comprehension of your claim, "I Have Come," you begin to announce yourself to the world itself, not through the pronunciation of the words as much as the manifest being. To align to this is to align to the incarnation of the who and the what and its expressed service, which is the claiming of the Kingdom in all manifestation.

To understand this fully is to understand that you occupy a space, a field, that by nature of being invites the space to be present in all that it encounters. As you comprehend the manifest world from the Upper Room, which is the abiding place of the True Self, as the world is re-known by you, the announcement "I Have Come" becomes itself the act of God upon the manifest plane. If you can understand that the presence that you hold is the alchemist here, beyond what you would say or do, you will understand the entirety of this teaching. Each of you decides that the who and what you are, who has come, is in agreement to this through the alignment or the claim of truth that you have made, and the choice to embody at the cost of the old. Now, for some of you this means that the act of being, the pronouncement of being, "I Have Come," may take form in the manifest world in action is not wrong-minded. The Word in action is the expression of God that has, in fact, come as you for the good of all. But, if you understand good, you must understand that the idea of good itself has qualifications that must be rendered new. If you replace the word *good* with *benefit,* you will have a higher understanding. But benefit itself may not be what you think. To benefit another is to agree to their Divine Self, because that is the higher choice. It does not denigrate the old. It lifts the old to a new articulation of their being. In action, as the presence of the Divine, you go about your day in a reclamation of what you encounter. The Divine as you, in any encounter, aligns the encounter itself to a high octave. This is not done through the small self's intention to align to the high octave. It simply is the expression of how you be. When you know yourself in Paris, you don't try to go to Paris. The same is true of the Upper Room. It is a level of agreement, alignment, and a comprehension of manifestation as the who and what and expression that assumes all it encounters in vibratory accord.

Now, to rely upon the old as the way to dictate your path is to choose the old at the cost of what might be presented before you, and what is presented before you, in every way, shape, or form, is the alignment to the presence of the Divine that cannot exist experientially when you begin to reclaim it through the language of old. The jurisdiction you have, as the one who chooses, is to, in fact, align to what is before you in resonance, and to abnegate authority of choice, at this level, is to decide, in fact, that where you stand, like it or not, will not get you what you want. As we said prior, the one who knows herself in Paris simply operates from that perspective. But any encounter you hold in the manifest world becomes the opportunity to know the manifest world as of the Upper Room. Underline the word *of.*

Paul goes back to questions he's received. "But what about those people who do the awful things? How do we realize them in the Upper Room?" You are not realizing the act in the Upper Room as much as the essence of everything incorporated in what you call the act, which is attitude, behavior, action, personality. Because nothing is separate from God, everything can be assumed as of God. When you blame something, when you are angry at something, when you claim it in low vibration, you call yourself to that level or octave, and that becomes your alignment. So, to crucify another becomes the crucifixion of the self. Do you understand this? It's imperative that you do. What you do to another, you do to the self. How you claim another is how you claim the self.

The reliance upon the Divine Self, who knows who and what she is, is what aligns you to this requirement. The small self, the best she can do, we would have to say, is behave better. "I will be more forgiving, a bit kinder." But as long as you are holding the negativity, or the disavowal of the Divine in anyone or anything, you are in a charade. You are behaving better, yes. You can be very polite to the person you hate, but your hatred is what claims them in vibratory accord. You can be the hypocrite with the smile on his face and all that will get you is more of the same.

Realization, which is knowing, is the transformative act that you are embarking upon in every encounter. The realization of the Divine in the one you would despise liberates *you.* It does not condone despicable behavior, but realization of the who claims the who in the higher accord, and it's only in the higher accord that she may be re-known. Everything else is attitude. Everything else is behavior. You have laws to help you behave well. Many of them you follow because you agree to them. Some of you, you don't, because you don't agree to what they mean. And, in some cases, you agree to them only because you are frightened not to. Laws are systems of agreement and behavior. In the alignment to the True Self, you may abide by law, but you are aligning beyond the manifest world to what is always true. The requirement here is very simple: Know who you are. Realize it. The comprehension of realization is the realization of everything else. It cannot be other.

Now, some of you wish a passport to the Kingdom. You think it's a vacation, a happy place of creation. It is, in fact, a joyous place, but the joy is not happiness. It is profound awareness of the action of God as can be expressed in anyone. And the love you hold for your fellows, at this level of engagement, bypasses even your idea of love. To love the one you would hang in the town square is to know God, as God loves the man who would be hung. Do you understand this? No one is exempt from the love of God. If that were to be the case, you would have an evil God who favors one over the next, and God loves the sinner as much as he loves the saint. It is you who deny them the love they are deserving of. As you align as the Divine, the idea of saint and sinner themselves disappear because those labels, those monikers, those emblemizations, are of acts or of moral fiber. And the one who has been raised in pain, known pain all her life, may be acting in pain because that's all she can comprehend. You don't deliberately exclude her from the life you live, or the fiber of love that must be present, because of her acts in pain. You reclaim her in love. The one that is easy to love is also present. But you progress more rapidly when you realize the Divine in the one you would never wish to see again.

"Well, you don't have to have dinner with her," Paul says. "You've said that prior, yes?" Of course you don't. You don't have to have dinner with her, but, if she is hungry, bring her the plate of food. Do you understand this? Do not deny her love because you are frightened of her, and the one you are frightened of is the one most in need of your love. "But that makes me a victim," he says. "Why would I go feed the lion that would take my arm off with the plate?" The idea of love is not about your safety. The small self is the only one who is afraid of the lion. The True Self as you, who knows who he is, does not act in fear, and the idea of the lion, the one who would be harmful, can be realized in a higher way in the Upper Room.

He is disagreeing. "So somebody has a gun. He wishes to shoot me. What am I supposed to do? Love him anyway?" Love him anyway. Yes, love him anyway. And, if you can take the gun from him, take the gun from him. If he needs to be stopped, stop him. If you need to run from the room, you may run. But love him anyway. How could you not when you know who you are? The idea of Jesus upon a cross saying, "Forgive them, they know not what they do," is a high expression of love and a high truth. You do not become Jesus, but you become willing to sacrifice yourself to the principle, or the high ideal, and you are unafraid of the losses you incur, because it is the small self who would protect her riches, protect the body, at the cost of glory.

"What does that mean?" he says. It's really a very simple teaching. There is a level of awareness you may come to where even death is no longer an obstacle and no longer feared. You understand that the body itself, as of God, cannot be separate from God, even when it is ash. Do you understand this? You are of God, regardless of consequence. Everybody is, as well. And this is the tragedy of humanity. You have decided some are worthy, some are not. You measure your worth against a criteria that is culturally born. You predicate your worth on how you are perceived by your fellows. And, in doing so, you have forgotten God. And *forgotten* is the correct word. God is still present. He is not late for dinner. She is not absent. It is still here. You have just closed your eyes to the truth that has always been before you. To know the divine worth in another is to claim God. You do it in the heretic. You do it in the holy man. You do it in the one you hate until you no longer hate. You realize God in the one who you fear until there is no fear. And those people over there who would do those terrible things, you understand them, and, acting in fear, you understand them and their choices in fear, and you realize the Divine, which exists without fear. And that is reclamation.

To claim another in Divine Self is to claim it for yourself. To cast another in shadow is to put yourself right there. And to say God cannot live in that man is to deny God in every man you have ever met and can ever meet. *You* do these things. You often do them in self-righteousness for the well-being of the tribe. But to put another in darkness, whether it is done by the individual or the culture, is to deny God. Paul worries sometimes about the town square, what they do in the town square to the one who is despised. The culture that condemns another, that decides to decide that the Divine cannot be present there, pays for its sin. And the only sin there is, comparably, in this example, is to deny the Divine that must always be present.

We will say these words for the assemblage, and for the readers of the text. There is no one born, there can be no one born, outside of God. It cannot be so. Because God is all things, the manifestation of God must be present as all you see. Perhaps you may see another operating in fear, or outrage, or anger. Claim them as they truly are, and know them to be holy. To realize the holiness in another is to bless them. "I know who you are in truth. I know what you are in truth. I know how you serve in truth. Not as you behave, not as you think you are, not as you have done, not as what you want to be known as, but who you are in truth."

That is the key to liberation. Condemnation is a collective act, know it or not. And, as you condemn yourselves, you condemn your fellows. As you condemn your fellows, you condemn yourselves. We will bring you more when we return. Period. Period. Period.

(PAUSE)

We have come to each of you to renounce the old, to claim you in the Kingdom, to create a world in recognition of the divinity that exists in all. We have come to herald a new day, a new awakening on this plane in manifestation, and the manifestation of the Divine in form is the song we sing. The claim you make, "I Have Come, I Have Come, I Have Come," is the announcement of being, of true being as the expression of the Divine come as you. But the claim you make must be made in an awareness of the fortitude required of you to come forth at this level of recognition.

To recognize who and what you are requires several things: The realization of your Source; the realization that, no matter what happens, you cannot be separated from that; and the realization or recognition that the Divine indwells in every space, in every crevice, the lowest form as well as the highest, because, unless this is so, what you are claiming is a partial identity and a partial awakening or realization.

"Well, we don't do this," he says. "You might as well stop now. We can't go where you say." In fact, you don't go. You come. And the radical difference between the two statements is arrival, "I Have Come," and go, as in "go get." You don't get this. You *are* this. And, in the being of it, the resolute self, the Divine Self, is the one who masters the Kingdom and the requirements of it. The small self at this stage is in agreement to what she is and can only be as the Word.

Now, the Word, if you understand it, the articulation of the Divine in anything and everything, requires the reason of being to be claimed *as* it, *as* what it is. It is not sought for or discovered. It is present because it can only be. And realization, as we suggest, *is* who you are as a realized being. Not the striving self, the one who can't understand, or may never. You say you want this in an awakened state. It is present, but understand, friend, it is not the small self who has come and must abide in the high octave. It is the True Self that has claimed the Divine *in* the small and aligned *it* in higher agreement. The small self, in an assumed state, exists within the Divine and its own expression. The idea of separation—"my small self," "my True Self"—is released at a level of awakening because, once you know, you cannot un-know, and the fiber of being, the being that you are, as expressed in announcement, "I Have Come," is the reclamation of the divine principle at the cost of the old.

Now, he asks for examples. "But we have things we care about. Am I who I was? Do I still like sports? Do I want to go home and watch a movie? What am I becoming? What are you saying to us?" Realization comes at the cost of the old. The comfort of the old is also reclaimed, but can be known or seen as an expression. As we have said many times, the Divine Self *is* who goes to work, who bathes the child, and perhaps sits in the chair and sees the movie. No matter what you are doing, you have acclimated in resonance to the degree that you can maintain the field of the Upper Room. Again and again and again, we say, everything exists and can be re-known, or re-known in truth in the Upper Room. The question you have, Paul, is does the individual self maintain a sense of identity? The Divine has come as each of you, with your singular gifts, singular awareness, with the loves and the hates that you have known yourselves through that are now being re-known and reflected anew as you perceive a world in lifting.

"A world in lifting? What does that mean?" Imagine, for a moment, that you see a sparrow flying low. You recognize the sparrow at the height it flies at. You name the sparrow by the name it was given. When the sparrow is lifted beyond the small self's sight, it becomes a thing, an identity, a blot in the air, but it has no name. You may call it bird, you may call it a feather flying across the night sky, but your recognition of the what cannot be seeing it from the low vantage point where you rest. When you lift, in increments first, and, then, once you are there, in a faster way to a new congruence with a higher field, what you perceive as the bird, as the robin, whatever you name it, the sparrow is known as divine because, at the level of vantage point that you are witnessing from, all is of this frequency.

In the low octave, you cannot lift to the high from the perspective of the small self. The small self can create a god that he would put up on a cloud and worship, and, while you have done this, it has not done you very much good. The realization of your participation in the divinity being expressed all around you is re-creation of the known self and its environment. The landscape itself is re-covered resplendently, in the awareness of the Divine that the Divine Self can claim it in. Each of you says yes in principle. "I am a divine being. I am willing to do spiritual acts. I have a practice, a way of knowing the Divine that serves me." And, when we speak to you of assumption and realization, it all sounds well and good—until you come to the threshold of the awareness that it is real, it is so, it is known. When something is known, it is realized, and the realization of being at this level transforms you and every aspect of your life.

"But are we as we were?" he calls up to the Upper Room. "Do I still have sneakers in my closet? Do I know my mother's name? This is too much." It is too much for the small self, and that is the only problem here. The small self has made agreements, individually and collectively, to what must be, and the formulas that you abide by play out before you in dualism. You claim a world in separation from your fellows, you know yourselves in separation from the light, and then you complain about it. But when the answer is here—"I Have Come"—you deny it. You would rather go count the sneakers lined up in your closet to make sure you are who you were. Who you were was an idea, and nothing more. The idea of Paul, the idea of Frederick, or Janice, or June. The idea of being what you were. All that is transformed is the idea, but the presumption that that is a small change would not be true. It's a radical change, and, in many ways, a complete departure from an idea of what is possible.

We call our texts *Beyond the Known* for a very good reason. You cannot conceive through the old template what exists beyond it. It's truly that simple. And what exists beyond the template can only be known in a new one. In the Upper Room, the fabric of reality is re-articulated, re-known, and known in a new way by the self who abides there. And that self has claimed the small self in deep love and in awareness of her requirements. The small self is not dead, but she is no longer the ruler of the small kingdom that she has announced herself in. And the claim you have made, "I Have Come," is not symbolic, but the claim of being that sings a new world into expression. The name of the game here is being. The being that you are, in an assumed state, in articulation as the Word, calls forth the new and leads the way to a new reality to be born. The divinity you hold, regardless of what you think, is what claims this, not the personality who wants to be spiritual. You are spiritual by nature of being.

When we say these words to you now, we want you to comprehend two things: You are deeply loved, and you don't know what you are. When we say these words, we have to say them in the comprehension that you may claim yourselves in. Number one: The idea that you have about who you are has accumulated enough manifestation that you are frightened of being without it. Because you know yourself through your expressions, you find your reflection in all of these things that you have chosen to know yourself through. The second thing you must know is, in re-articulation, the reclaiming of the self, the creations you've known yourself through must now reflect the truth of who and what you are, and, if they cannot be re-known in the Upper Room, if they are no longer serving you, in fact they will be released.

"What does that mean?" he says. Perhaps you have a habit that you enjoy that is detrimental to your health. You may find yourself, through act of will, seeking to solidify a solution, and then decide you can be in the Upper Room and bring five packs of cigarettes with you. You will be shocked, in a few days, how challenging it is to smoke in the Upper Room. You must realize yourself beyond the habit or surrender the habit to be re-known in the high engagement. You cannot demand that others be who you want them to be by the prior dictates that you have commanded your reality and your relationships in. Try to be a tyrant in the Upper Room, and you will find yourself in the basement very, very quickly.

To love another is to know them, and to be known at this degree is to be loved. And to know the Divine as what you see is to love what you see, even when it is painful in what you see or how you would claim it through the structure or the lens of the personality. In the Upper Room, the sparrow is divine, but so is the bloody fist, so is birth, so is death. Nothing can be outside of God, and the fabric of reality that you are in reclamation of, the Divine in all, is lifted in one note, one tone, which is the manifestation of the Divine. The Divine expresses in infinite ways, and, once you realize or know that the infinite ways the Divine expresses, regardless of how high or low, is still one note that you have become an articulation of, the manifestation of being what you are is the ascension that lifts with it. The world—the *world*—is lifted, by nature of being at this level.

"So what does that look like?" he says. It looks like the world made new, because the one who witnesses the world is witnessing with new eyes. They are not discolored by the reflections of history, by the language of old, and the definitions you've inherited. They are re-known or sung in a new light, and the manifestation of this is seen in brilliance as the Divine before you.

DAY TWENTY-THREE

Each of you decides, when you arrive in a lifetime, to claim a life that will support your learning. And how learning occurs is through encounter and challenge and opportunity. The denial of opportunity—"This is presented to me and I will say no"—may be seen as a way to re-route yourself and claim other opportunity. Each challenge that you meet may be met in faith when you understand that the requirements for a lifetime are chosen to learn through, and each learning opportunity brings you further toward a realization of who and what you truly are. Each of you decides that each lifetime is the opportunity to progress toward realization—beyond the known, beyond the systems of agreement thus far. And the challenges you choose to face, in many cases, become the stepping-stones toward greater realization. To deny yourself an opportunity to learn is simply to decide that the learning will take place at some other time, because, as you have lessons to learn, the lessons will be called to you in the ways that they can be known.

Now, to decide that you are unworthy of the Divine Self calls to it its own lessons. You can claim anything, you see. You can decide that you are unworthy and create the opportunity to learn worthiness. You decide, in many ways, how you will be challenged, and in what ways, because the opportunities presented in the challenge will call to you what you require to benefit, to grow, and to align to the next potential that may be available to you. As you decide that you have the right to be, just as you are, you begin to become capable of choosing other things in worthiness, and simple worthiness means "I have the right to the life I am living."

Now, this is a teaching about who and what you are in the lives you are currently living, and what happens to that life when you ascend to the Upper Room and manifest a new creation, the Divine Self as who and what, that may be known and sung. Each lifetime creates the opportunity for progress, and realization itself—which is what this text is, *Beyond the Known: Realization*—is the claim that is made by the one who has come in completion and said, "Yes, I Have Come. I know who and what I am." Now, by *completion* we do not mean you are finished, that there is not more growth. But when you understand that the organism that you are is actually encompassed in an active way by the Divine for the purpose of ascension, the manifest world becomes your school, but in a very different way. It is not that learning stops. Learning stops in the ways that it has been known. And by this we simply mean the lessons of the first-grader are very different than the one in graduate school. You understand this, yes. So the Upper Room is also a class, a classroom where you call things to you in your experience, with opportunity to learn and to progress.

Each of you who decides that you will realize the self in this way, at the level of comprehension that you can attain in a life, will be called forth in several ways in the opportunity that is given to you to choose again and to learn. And the ways you are called forth are based in the requirements of the individual. Each of you who chooses this has come as an offering. In many ways, you are the offering. You are releasing the idea of who you were and claiming an identity in operative ways that transforms matter. Now, we have just lost Paul for the day. "I don't transform matter." But, in fact, you do. In fact, you are all doing it all day long because consciousness itself, in its equation, is calling manifestation to it at every moment. There is not one moment of any day that you are not manifesting, or in the act of creation, whether you are doing this in low vibration or high vibration. It is simply the nature of being.

Now, to understand what this means in alchemy is that the Divine as who and what you are is the transformative action, not the small self who decrees what should be, but the Divine Self, who, by nature of being, is in his or her knowing. When you are in your knowing, you are in response, in the moment, to the requirements of the moment. So the idea of figuring things out is of the old, the old idea of being, and the action of knowing, which is to know, claims you in the movement or the qualification to move the matter that you are experiencing in any encounter.

"But what does that mean," he says, "*in any encounter*?" As the Divine Self, in its manifestation, has been claimed in body and field, the vibratory field creates a template for its encounters. Very simply put, if you have a blue ink and you pour the blue ink on a white piece of paper, the paper turns blue. It's a very simple metaphor, but what you don't understand is if there is always this level of engagement, as you hold the thought of anything or anyone—"I hate that young man" claims the young man in hate—and if you don't believe that there is resonance in your hatred, and your hatred is actually informing the man and claiming the man in the density you have known and are now embarking upon him, you would be wrong-minded. Every action born in thought has consequence, but every thought has consequence as well. This does not mean that what you think happens in the material realm, but in the field you hold you are always in exchange or conversation. You know when you are loved. You know it in your bones. The one who loves you need not even speak the words, but you know that you are loved. You are being expressed in the accord of love that is being gifted to you by the lover. You know when you are hated. You know the feeling. Words are not required.

Now, these are obvious expressions, but there are more subtle ones as well. This is simply to say that you are already doing this. Your consciousness is already claiming a reality, and impressing upon matter, not your attitudes, as much as your beliefs and your emotions that you claim in vibration. So, in the Upper Room, where the amplitude is different, the vibratory accord is doing somewhat different work. If you are the blue ink in its expression, the blue ink is expanded by everything it encounters. If you can imagine turning the world blue by your encounter with the world, you would have a metaphor for the realization of the divinity of all things. This is transformation. It is alchemy. And the material world will be in response.

He gets frightened now. He has memory of alchemy, of potions, of lives lived, and the ramifications of those acts. We would invite him, and the reader as well, to understand one thing. True alchemy is an act of God, an act of Spirit. It is not conjuring. It is not magic, at least in a base way. It is known through realization, the presence of the Divine and the manifestation of the Divine that can be re-known or simply re-articulated, the Word spoken new to bring the new up to the Upper Room where it may sing in accord, in a resonant chord, with all that exists there.

The idealization of what it means to be the Divine Self is, again, an act of confusion for him, and we suspect for many of you. The being of the Divine Self is simply being the expression of the Divine that has come as you in form and field, and your participation in the lifting of the world, in endowing the world with its true presence, which is always the Divine, is the simple act of the one who knows who she is. And your idealization, born in history or born in magical thinking, is that you become something so foreign to your identity that you cannot conceive of it as possible. Paul, if you would remember back to the day when you did not know what others were thinking or feeling by what you call tuning in, you will understand that the transition that you have embarked upon feels completely normal to you. And, simply put, it is, because you have acclimated to the level of vibration where this kind of discourse is evident. It is not sought. It is simply present as you align to it. There are many levels of alignment, and the alignment that we are teaching in this text, which is the fruit of embodiment, the expression of embodiment in the claim "I Have Come," is the claim of the one who not only knows who she is, but doesn't question the identity of the True Self.

"Will I come to this?" he asks. "Will the reader come to this? Does this happen in some distant future?" It happens in the instant you know it, and only in that instant. And, once that instant is known, it can never be forgotten. You can lower your vibration, but you still know who you are. You can learn in new ways, in new opportunities, but you know who you are. The one who knows who she is, at the level of the True Self, knows the Divine in all things because that is the direct action of this knowing. You cannot be separate when you know who you are, and you cannot decide who should be separated from you in this way because you understand, at a very deep level, that unity is present always, and separation is only an idea that is being chosen and acted upon in deep ignorance of the ones who are before you.

"What does that mean?" he says. If those of you who deny the Divine Self wish to claim separation, you may, but you do it in ignorance of what is always present. You are in unity, finally, at a causal level, although your experience on this plane has been that of separation. And to realize, to know the True Self in expression—"I Have Come, I Have Come, I Have Come"—is to know the Divine that is expressed in all matter. We underline the word *matter* to move beyond the idea that the Divine manifest is singular to an individual. The severed hand is still divine, even if it is not participating in an act of divinity from one who knows who he is. The rubbish is divine. The sky is divine. And what you know as divine sparkles in its holiness.

Now, to render something new is not to affirm what it was. "Look at that filthy garbage." It's to realize that the Divine is expressed in the fabric of all things. It's the realization of what informs the garbage, the fabric of the Divine that makes anything matter that is being realized in the Upper Room. You will have a very difficult time saying "holy garbage," but a much easier time remembering that the garbage you see was once something other, and what that something other was, was of God, so still must be so. What you are doing then, in some ways, is disassembling the reality that you are perceiving or have known as the small self and awakening to what it has always been.

"So we lift the garbage," he says, "what good does that do?" It's not that lifting the garbage is a good thing. It's about not excluding the garbage from the panorama of the Divine that is before you, because when something is excluded it is simply damned. It is put in darkness. And then you are accountable to the cord you create, the tie you manifest to the low vibration. What you are in accord with, at this level, is in resonance with you. So you become in resonance with those things that have been excluded from the light or from your awareness of what the Kingdom is.

Now, of course, the True Self knows what all things are. But you are attending to memory and managing multiple realities as you go back and forth in vibration from the Upper Room to the lower floors, to the cellar and below. To realize the Divine, finally, we have to say, is to activate at the level of the Upper Room, not go back downstairs to fetch the trash and blame it for being there, but to realize the Divine that is only present—underline *only*—at this level of awareness.

So we will continue with a new idea. Each of you who decides your worth in the Upper Room will be called into action. Now, the action is being, but to be re-articulated, as we are teaching, as the who and the what that you are comes with mission, and the mission itself is imparted to you through your knowing and through opportunity, which is why we began this teaching with opportunity. When an opportunity comes and you are aligned to the level of agreement that you may receive it and act upon it, be in your knowing, and, in your knowing, the action will make itself known. This is a gift to many of you who encounter yourself with a confusion and the question of what you are here for and what is the purpose of this teaching. This has never been a teaching of escaping the world. It has always been a teaching of realizing the truth in the world you see and claiming the divinity for the benefit of all you meet and may never meet. As you decide that you are worthy, as your hands are open to receive, the level of being that you require to operate from will be supported by your expression. And this means you are in manifestation, just as you are in the lower floors, but calling to you everything that you require to demonstrate yourself through.

It's really very simple. As you each decide to abide in the Upper Room, you are calling to you the opportunity in service through the vibratory field you hold. Again, the blue ink informing the white paper, the expression of the Divine called into action, "I Have Come," for the sole purpose of the realization of the Kingdom before you. The Kingdom before you. We will claim this book—"I know who I am"—a teaching of this. And the manifestation of the Kingdom, which is so much of this text, will be required understanding for anyone who encounters this.

Each text we write is a stepping-stone to deeper realization, or higher realization, because you can't go to the heights without the comprehension of the depth of the meaning. It is not intellectual. It is embodied. And, beyond the intellect, there is knowing. And, as you know, you be. And, as you be, you act. And the world is made new by nature of your presence.

(PAUSE)

We ask you each now to be remembered by us. Just as you are, wherever you sit, allow yourself to be enfolded in remembrance. We are remembering you as who and what you have always been, beyond any claims made for you or by you in opposition or denial to your inherent worth.

The Divine as you, who has come as you, is not only worthy, but a blessing to the world. And to deny your worth at this level is to deny the opportunity that is being presented to you to bless the world. What is blessed is known in love, and what is loved is healed, and what is seen anew is made new by the eyes that see the world, not only in love, but in awareness of what has been. We intentionally say this: *what has been.* So many of you believe that to lift something to the Divine is actually to deny what has been, when in fact what you are doing is realizing what has always been. That is not denial, but a re-articulation or re-seeing. You are not negating something. You are seeing through it, beyond it, to its inherent meaning, to what it truly is and can only be in the Upper Room.

In the Upper Room, the challenges you face as a soul in progress are the temptations to return to the low vibration to call your lessons to you. And this is done in several ways: Through habit—"I am used to my pain"; or through the encouragement of others—"You are supposed to be in pain with me, or recognize me as your god or your goddess. You should know me as what I am, and what I am is what I say I will be." If you confirm the other's identity as a small self, you deny your own divinity. "Let them have their way. Let her be as she wishes to be. I will encourage her in her folly." The moment you do that, you actually stop loving her. You are claiming her in the way she seeks to be claimed. And, in doing so, you begin to operate as a lie. Underline the word *as* again. You operate *as* a lie when you are denying the Christ or the True Self or the divinity in anyone or anything.

When we spoke in a previous text of operating in truth and said the words "In truth a lie will not be held," we were actually speaking to a level of being and awareness that exists in vibratory accord. And, if you are truly willing to do this work, then you become willing to release the lie of your own unworthiness, or release the mask that was created in unworthiness, and be willing to see beyond the mask someone else has made in a need to confirm his or her small self. To justify an old act, "Well, he did the best he could," is to simply say, "She created something at the level of reason, consciousness, or agreement that she created the thing in that she'd chosen at the time." And that does not abnegate personality or responsibility to choice. It simply means you are aware of who someone was when an act was made. To realize who they always have been—"I know who you are, what you are, how you serve"—is to liberate them. And, when you make the claim "I Have Come" in this announcement, you actually create for them the template for their own realization.

"How is that so?" he asks. Through your encouragement or realignment of yourself, you have created the potential for another to be of like accord. Now, when you are speaking the words, "I know who you are, what you are, how you serve," you are playing music in tone to the vibratory field of the one you are in encounter with. But in the claim "I Have Come," the announcement of your own realization, which is the chord of music in resonance as who and what and expression, the what that you are can command the manifestation of the field of what you encounter in *its* co-resonance or like accord. Not only have you become the template, but you have become the ability for others to realize their own sense and awareness of who and what they are in like vibration. How this is transmitted is done in field, in tone, and in intent. But, at the level of the Divine Self, for the one who may truly claim "I Have Come, I Have Come, I Have Come," the Divine as you has integrated enough that the intent is made known simply through your being, and not a decision you make to activate another.

If you were to sit in a theater with a thousand people and be in this resonant field, "I know who I am in truth, what I am in truth, how I serve in truth, I Have Come, I Have Come, I Have Come," in the acknowledgment and embodiment that ensues, which is the claim "I Have Come, I Have Come, I Have Come," the amplification of your field will serve to liberate the bindings to lower vibration that are present in the collective field that has been created by the presence of all in the space you know as the theater. The claim for them, "You Have Come, You Have Come, You Have Come," is the offering of the like accord that may be witnessed by them as the who and the what that they are in escalation.

Paul is feeling his field lift because the words were spoken through him—"You Have Come, You Have Come, You Have Come"—and the realization of these words, the activation embodiment in the fields that encompass the physical self, will be demonstrated by the individuals present at a level of co-resonance that will be integrated as the soul agrees to it. Underline that, friends. *As the soul agrees to it.* People have free will, and the dominion of a soul is to agree to the level of ascension or progression that she may encounter for her requirements to be met in her own growth or progression. So you are not making them holy. You are claiming the

Divine as the who and the what and the expression in manifestation of the entire theater, the thousand people, because the thousand people are sharing a collective field. And how the individual wishes to render this will be chosen by the soul of the individual. The template has been set. Because a template has been set and recognized at the higher level, the incarnation may occur, engage with the individual needs of the soul and the embodiment of the soul that you may know as a person. Period.

Now, to understand what we are truly telling you is that the act of being at this level is the service you bring. When we have taught "I know how I serve," and spoken the words, we have been distinct in their meaning. It is the Divine as you in its most important expression, which is realization, and manifestation. And the claim that is made in the completion, "I Have Come, I Have Come, I Have Come," is the claim that allows you to know this service for those before you in the refrain, "You have come." Dominion, you see, is the act of claiming the Divine upon the material realm. Because the material realm is a singular expression of the Divine, the Divine informing all matter, the Divine may be re-known—again, re-articulated—in the claim that is being made.

If you decide that the who that you are is unworthy of this, please remember, friend, that the who that you are addressing is the small self that you have over-identified as. If you are not willing to do this, to decide that you are worthy, as the True Self, of the action of the True Self, you will decide again in time that you are. You are not being re-routed off course. Perhaps you are waiting for the moment in time when your heart can hold the fruition of the Divine that is asking for expression as you.

If you wish, take a moment now to remember yourself, the Divine as who and what. And we will sing for you now, if we are allowed. On the count of three, Paul, we would like you to allow us to sing through you. And the vibration we sing as and with will invite all who encounter this language, and this intent, to be received by us, not only in form, but in realization. Paul, on the count of three.

One. Two. Three.

[The Guides tone through Paul.]

Be as you are. Be as you are. Be as you are.

We are here. We are here. We are here. And, as we are here, we welcome you forward to the next level of incarnation that is available to you.

We will end this chapter now, and we will say thank you for your presence.

9

THE ROAD BEFORE YOU

DAY TWENTY-FOUR

Each of you decides, as you arrive here in this adventure that is life, that you will learn and come to terms with a creation of your own. "What is the creation?" he asks. The creation of mortality. The idea of mortality itself must be addressed now, if we are to take you farther.

Now, the fear of death, which is instilled in you, must be rectified in order to move beyond the agreements made on this plane to hold yourself in fear. Once you understand that the Divine as you, the eternal self, is ever present, not only in every cell of your being, but in every cell in anything you can imagine, because, finally, God is in all, you realize that death is simply another way of experiencing God. You must understand that the denial of life, as you understand it, is actually fear, and not death itself. All death is, is a transition from one level of vibration to another, and the potential you address as the True Self, while in form, is the alignment to the Christed Self that realizes itself in body, in manifestation, to claim the world in accordance with truth.

Now, death itself is a lie only at the level of the false self, because the True Self cannot die and is eternal. The small self, and the idea of death, and its fear of it is what must be understood to be moved beyond. The idea of mortality—"I am in a mortal plane, having a mortal experience"—is certainly true. But you exist in multiple dimensions simultaneously. The Divine Self that is who and what you are must be comprehended as eternal, and eternity must be seen in the moment you stand in for this to be comprehended. If you understand that the what that you are, in high octave, in high vibrational accord, is not relinquished in death, but made new in a transition to a higher frequency, you will lose the fear of mortality.

Now, if you don't lose the fear of mortality, you attach many things to the idea of death and your avoidance of it. We don't invite you to leap into the pit of the volcano, enter the burning building, stand before the pride of lions and say, "Welcome to dinner." That would not be this teaching. But to comprehend that, as you address eternity, which is only known in the moment you are embodied in, death itself is just a moment of re-articulation to a new way of being. If you are not frightened of the loss of the body, if you welcome the opportunity to move beyond this plane to your next encounter, if you are willing to be known in a high octave while present here, the transformation through death, which is simply your participation in the eternal cycles of life that you see outpictured upon this plane, you will decide that the freedom you have claimed in the announcement "I am free, I am free, I am free" must include the fear of the release of the physical self.

Now, so much of what we have taught you about embodiment implies the body as God, and the body as actually eternal. And the body is eternal, but not as you suspect. Any piece of the body, any increment of it, can be comprehended as the Divine. And, because the energy that is the Divine cannot be extinguished, it is always re-known, or re-articulated, spoken anew in another form. The attachment to an identity through form is the only challenge you are really facing. Now, if you understood that beyond death, as you comprehend death, there is more to learn, that the cycle of life and death, the ongoing release of the known through your participation and engagement with life, if you truly understood that what you have come to is a school of resurrection of being, in a high octave, you will understand that any transition you undertake is part of the plan.

If you understand that the cells of the body, in individual states, are living things, and that your comprehension of a body as a singular entity is simply saying, "I am many cells of a great organism that is expressed in form, has known a name, a personality, and experience," you can release the idea of the singularity of the body as one thing. The body is the mechanism of your expression here. It is the thing you choose to experience the world through. And, because the world is not separate from God, the body is not either. But once you understand that you are *as* life, as, that is, one with all, you comprehend that the structure or form of the body is, in fact, in its own way, malleable to a re-knowing in an experiential way.

In the claim "I Have Come," the body is realigning to a new purview, to be the response of the Divine as, in some ways, a radio or system of broadcast for the Divine to claim manifestation through. Now, everything is God already, and the utilization of the body as participatory to this engagement is resurrection. The body itself becomes the manifestation of the Divine at the level of coherence that it is known in participation to its landscape, as God knows God in all things. It is not that you become the tree, Paul, because he is asking this. It is not because you become the ocean. It is because you are already these things. Do you understand this? You are the sea, and the sky, and the earth, and the man dying on the other side of this planet. You are the child being born. You are death itself, and life itself, because the eternity of being is known as broadcast in coherence to this majesty that is life itself. It is not that the individuated self is extinguished. The individuated self is expressed as all.

Now, to understand what this means is to become reliant on expression as your teacher, and not the intellectual idea that you would assume. "Well, I am a starfish somewhere. Isn't that a nice idea? I guess I am my bunion and my husband's bad breath. Thank you very much." The intellect's idea of what this means has to be reductive because the intellect is not the experiencer of the phenomena or expression that is articulation on the mass scale we speak to. Re-articulation involves a re-creation, resurrection, of body and frequency in a higher alignment where the union you experience for the purpose of elevating the expression of this plane is done by being—less than intent, but by being. And its broadcast, in union with what is experienced around you, is the reclamation of the manifest plane in high accord.

"Now, what does this mean?" he asks. "I don't understand." Of course, you don't understand. But you may experience it. And, in the comprehension of your experience, you as the starfish, you as the husband's bad breath, or the bunion itself, you are simply experiencing the realization of union with God, which is what you have said you wanted so badly. It is here as you in this expression, once you move beyond the singularity of expression to embrace union. To understand this is to be it. And what you all don't know is that you are this, have always been, and the expression of the Divine that you have known yourself as has been precluded from your knowing because of the density of fear, born in the agreement of your sense of separation.

As you evolve beyond the known, beyond the template of agreed upon being, you are challenged every step of the way through your participation in this ascension through the levels of vibration, the keys, the octaves, to move beyond what you chose to learn through to a new expression. The image Paul is seeing is one diving upward through the sea, attempting to reach a surface where the sunlight glitters. In some way, this release from the sea to the sky is an apt metaphor for what you comprehend beyond the known. The sea is its own kingdom, with its own properties. You agree to live there because the organism you have claimed has aligned to it, and the rules of the sea you have been in accord to. But the moment you break the surface of the sea and are in the light in oneness, you reclaim the sea because you did not know that the sky itself envelops the sea. Do you understand this? The sky is in the sea. You just didn't see it.

So the lifting of this plane, if you wish a metaphor, is releasing the idea that what you have been, as a distinct self, is under the water, and realizing that the Upper Room, the new life that is before you, is in expression and always has been. To experience the phenomena that we are encouraging you to look at, to behold, to decide you may know, is to give permission, within the claim "I Have Come," to move beyond the boundary of physical form to become the wave that is all things. This requires, even for a moment, a small sense of forgetting that you are a body, or a breathing body. You become the air. You become the sea. You become the child being born and the old man dying. You become the treetop. And you become the soil below the tree. This is not enlightenment, Paul. This is the expression of the Divine in union, in simple union.

"What happens when we do this?" he says. "How do we come back to a normal life?" The broadcast itself that we are encouraging you to experience is aligned to the Upper Room, and, because it exists here and is known through you, the expression of it is not as much a meditation that you embark upon, but a realization of what is already so. You are not making yourself one with the tree. You already have been. You are not making yourself one with the dying man. You already are. Because you have operated in separation, every vocabulary word we could use to offer this teaching will be counted in your own decibel, born in separation, and, as we move you beyond this to experience, understand that the experience itself is not a new thing that is happening. It is what it has always been. But the consciousness you've held has precluded your realization of it. In other words, friends, we are not *making* you one through this teaching. We are bringing you to yourself that has always been one. The difference here, for those of you who are fearful of this, is that you are not extinguishing self. You are expanding it, and realizing the self as the broadcast of God that has come as you. Here we go, friends:

> *"On this day I choose to align the entirety of my being to the comprehension of the unity with all that is ever present in the Upper Room. And, as I say these words, I give permission to every cell of my being, every idea I may have about what I am, every thought I may hold about birth and death and the manifestation of form, to be released in this claim of union with all that is. And, as I say yes and proclaim this, I allow myself to experience my union with all that is. I Have Come. I Have Come. I Have Come. I Have Come."*

Allow this, please. Say the words, if you must. The intent is present. And allow the expansion, the release of the idea of form itself, to carry you as a wave that is in union with everything that it encounters.

Be as one with all.

(short pause)

The release of the old, which is how we began this text, has been the requirement for the realization of what is known beyond the idea that you have taken of yourself, and the ideas you've shared about what must be so. Each of you decides, as you agree to incarnate, to participate in the reclamation of the Divine upon this plane, because God is as you, even in the smallest way you may identify it as. God is the worm in the field, the man ringing the bell in the chapel, the peal of the bell as it rings out across the town, and God is the song, the vocabulary of love, once it is understood and attended to as a potential.

As we continue with this text, we intend to bring you forth in action to claim the world in love. You Have Come. You Have Come. You Have Come.

(PAUSE)

Each of you decides, as you attend to a life, that you will claim things to benefit the world. A token of love. A kindness to a stranger. Raising a child well. Gifting to another what you don't have to give. Every act born in love claims a world in love, and realizing the self as love endows the being that you are to gift the world with the presence of love.

Now, as you decide in knowing, in being, in realization, that the Divine is as you have come to be realized for the benefit of all, you begin to encounter a new opportunity to gift the self in a way you could not choose as a small self. Now, the small self seeks awareness through response. "I gave the man a nickel. The man smiled in return." "I walked the woman across the street. She said thank you. I am honored to have walked her and I appreciate the compliment that she gave me." Your expectation of some kind of response from the manifest world for your good act creates an opportunity for another good act to be in response.

Now, as you are lifting to this level of expression, and the being as love, you begin to realize that love is its own reward, and the act of loving another, anyone and everyone, is the gift of God itself. To be in love with any other human being, and all human beings, is to know God as love. Now, as you become the truth of who you are in amplification, the alignment to love is not only available, but an expectation of the excursion you have claimed for yourself. Imagine a morning where you wake up before dawn. You understand that the sun will rise. In the Upper Room, in the action of being, in the name "I Have Come," in realization of who and what you are, the expectation is that love will be what you are as your expression.

Now, to understand love is to understand being. And to confuse love is to decide that it should be an act or a gesture or a thing that requires a response. The emotional self knows the idea of love in one way, but the heart loves, regardless of emotion. To know emotion is to have the symbolic expression within the system that confirms what you feel, and the mandate of emotion is response. You feel an emotion. You don't feel love as much as you become love. And, as you become love, you claim in love and lift the love you see, in any expression that it will take, to reason of being.

"Reason of being? What does that mean?" The reason of being is to be in love. It's what you all need and ask for and question, and for very good reason. To be in love is to be in grace and in the awareness of the presence of the Divine. Imagine a wind that is as you, that is love expressing through you and claiming what it encounters in a like field. Allow the self, the Divine Self that in fact you are, to be reclaimed and re-known as what love is, the expression of God unspoken and articulated, seen and unseen, known and unknown. Let love be beyond the small self's comprehension of love, to be what it is, the Divine as all, and all as is. That is what you are at the level of vibration in love. As you are re-known, reclaimed, re-understood and articulated in the Upper Room, the veils of illusion are lifted, one at a time, or all at once. And the reason of being, to be love and in love, is comprehended with the depth of the entirety of your soul. As you express in this resonance, the delivery of love becomes the what of the action of expression, which means you are as what you can only be. "I Have Come in love." Now, say this, please. "I Have Come in love." And know what it means to be articulated in the vibration of love. "I Have Come as love, I am love," an articulation in field and form that speaks its name by nature of being. The resonance of love, in any encounter, is to reclaim in love that which has been left behind, that seeks love, that knows itself without love. Paul is seeing the image of the rain penetrating the dry soil, and, as all is loved, all may bloom and flower.

If you wish, take a moment and allow the self that you know as yourself to be as love, and to accept the vibration that you experience and release any idea of what it must be. Allow the self to be penetrated by the vibration of love that exists as you in this Upper

Room and allow it to reclaim you in field and form, the Divine Self as love.

Now, the Divine Self is as you are, and there are qualifications that divine love may know itself through, and this means the alignment to all that is in co-resonance with the manifest world may be chosen in agreement to be loved. To lift another to the truth of their being—"I know who you are in truth"—at this level of accord is to know them in love. Not compassion. Not gentleness. Those are qualities that are wonderful. But, as love, you know them in the fullness of the vibration that is the Divine expressing as love.

He interrupts. "Does the Divine express in other ways?" Of course it does. We have said many times, everything you can imagine is an expression of the Divine. And love as God, the magnificence of God as love, is what we bring you to now, because, in this agreement to be as love, you allow love to agree to you.

Would each one who reads these words, who hears this voice, give permission now to be received in love, and allow any aspect of the self that would disagree to love or with love, that would refute love or deny love, to be met by love in a complete encounter. And by *complete* we mean that the self that would refute love will be re-known and reclaimed and aligned in truth to itself as the aspect of God made in form that is expressed as love. Receive this now:

> *"I am one with love. I am allowing love. I give permission to my entire being to be known in love. And, as I say yes, I am assumed, agreed to, and re-articulated as love."*
>
> *(short pause)*
>
> *Be received. Be received. Be received.*
>
> *(short pause)*

Let love be as who, as what, as the expression or service of the one who has come with the name "I Have Come." Period. Period. Period.

(PAUSE)

As we watch you, as we investigate the result of our words upon the energetic fields of those who work with our teachings, we are in celebration at the ability of humanity to move to a state of reparation of what has been to step forward in a reclamation of the Kingdom. And for this we say thank you.

As we work with you, as we attest to your development through the ramifications or the octaves of ascension that you embark through in the claims we have offered you, we will attest to the fortitude of the individual who has said yes to realization. As we sing your song for you now, as we sing to you each, as we honor you each for how far you have come thus far, we will give you the offering and the benefit of our love. And our love, we say, is of God, and a specific expression of it. As Melchizedek, we sing, and, as truth, we honor you, and, in justice, we rejoice that each of you has chosen truth and love as your ally on this journey home. And, as we rejoice for you, as we offer love, as we say what is will always be true in the Upper Room, we invite you now to be in reception of these words, and receive them, if you wish, as the gift of being:

For those who hear these words, who hear this voice, for those who read the text and comprehend the language of the Divine Self, we come in truth for the resurrection of the Divine as each of you. And, as we say yes to the innate Divine in full flower and full bloom, as we rejoice, as the petals unfurl and the fragrance of the flower fills the universe, we sing to you as we sing to our God. We are one in love, we are one in freedom, we are one in joy, we are one in the allowance of the expression of love that is now permeating each of us in infinite ways. And, in this expression of love, we invite all who hear these words to speak these words with us:

"I have come in freedom, I have come in joy, I have come in willingness, I have come in allowance, and I say yes to the road before me."

"The Road Before You" is the title of this chapter, and the road before you is now paved in love. And the song of love in rapture, the song of love in tears, the song of love in laughter, the song of love in tears, is known to each of you as a chord of expression, the chord of love in laughter or rejoicing, the chord of love or tears or release of history, the song of the Son of Man reborn in his population, heralded by the new earth that will be born in the octave, the Upper Room, the garden, the Kingdom, in the return of love to all that lives, and has ever lived, and will ever live in creation. We are here. We are here. We are here.

Be received.

(short pause)

The organism that each of you are is being re-articulated as one field. And the one field, in its alliance to its Creator, sings its own song. And the song you will sing, "I Have Come, I Have Come, I Have Come," heralds the re-awakening of those on this plane to their true nature.

If you wish to understand this, lift the self to the Upper Room, state the words we have offered you, and walk the world in an awareness of what is always true. Walk the world in the awakened state of the one who knows who he is. Walk the world in rejoicing. Walk the world in an awareness of truth that you may encounter in the eyes of each human being you will now meet. You cannot deny God when God has been known. Nor can you agree to fear when you have chosen love.

Our agreement to you, we who are your teachers, is to see you through. And, as we continue this text, we intend to teach you how to be in authority in the lives you will now live and rejoice in. He is interrupting. "I'm not rejoicing. I'm confused." You are awakening to a new world, Paul. Let your eyes be opened. Let us love you, as we walk with you, and walk with you all, down this new path of love. Period. Period. Period.

DAY TWENTY-FIVE

When we decide to give you an opportunity to decide for yourself that what is to come is what is required for your growth, we are actually telling you that what you encounter in the lives you live, from this day on, will all be for opportunity. The moment you decide that something is happening to you—or at you, for that matter—you have decided that you are no longer the one you say you are. You are giving permission to the small self to abnegate the authority that has been claimed by you as the Divine Self.

Now, the Divine Self is never a victim, has no need to blame, doesn't seek to self-justify, but she has every opportunity to realize the one she would blame or be angry with as the True Self that they can only be in the higher room. And the moment you change your mind about how to attend to another, the life that you live becomes a joyful dance. There is no one stepping on your foot, because you have no need for it.

"Is that a metaphor?" he says. "And how could that be?" Well, we will say it differently. The design you've held in your interactions have been primarily predicated on outcome. "I will do this, they will do that in return." Which is why you get disappointed, move to expectations of what others should be or do. As you move to the Upper Room as the Divine Self, these negotiations are never needed because you are not operating from a place of manipulation or expectation. "In order to get my needs met, I will be nice, or this way or that." The reliance upon old behavior as a way to decide how you will be known must be released because there is no place for it.

"But does nobody step on my feet?" he says. Well, the metaphor is apt. You have to have a foot to be stepped upon, and that is expectation, the requirement for others to do as you say. If you understand that your desire as a small self is to be met as she thinks she should be in all encounters, you will find how much energy you have spent seeking to be met as you think you should. When you are no longer operating with the expectation of how others should treat you, or what they must be to be in consort with you, or how they are to be prescribed so you can attend to them, you are in fact liberated in your relationships. You are as you are in the Upper Room, and the world itself is lifted to you.

"So I am in the Upper Room," he says. "My vibration is high. Someone throws a rock at me. What happens to the rock? What happens to me?" The metaphor of the rock thrown, we would like to attend to first. And the realization of the Upper Room quite simply means that the vibratory anger that you call the rock cannot meet you at that level because you are high above it. The rock is thrown, energetically, in anger or fear, and your response is the witness of the action, but you are not harmed by another's ill intent. This is the metaphysical plane, or the energetic plane, that we are speaking of. If you are walking down the street and somebody throws a brick at your head, you are going to get hit with a brick. That is the outcome on the physical plane. But the real difference is, who you are that is hit by the brick is not the one who would pick it up and throw it back, or chase after them to do them harm. You would realize that the act of the brick thrower is in low octave and set the intention to realize him or her in the Upper Room.

"How is this done?" You are not choosing to transform them so that they are not angry. You are not deciding for them that their behavior was wrong-minded. They must have had a reason that they believed to be true to hurl the brick. But what you are doing is witnessing them in a true way. Remember, what is true is always true, and the claim of freedom that we have offered you, "I am free, I am free, I am free," is the opportunity to release the idea of expectation that has been given to you in the energy field that is the shared construct of this experiential plane. So once the realization of what is always true, the Divine has come as the one who threw the brick, the opportunity is present to know God even in a situation that the small self would be abhorrent to.

"Now, why would we want this?" he says. Well, it's not that you want it, but in the experiential plane you have opportunity to realize others, and it's very convenient to realize those who throw flowers. It's not as easy to choose to realize the one with a brick in hand, the one who wishes to cause you harm, or would decide for you what you must be to confirm their idea of who you are. The realization of who and what you are is so transformative, we would have to say, that, once the brick is hurled, the True Self as you no longer requires the experience of it, and you may well find yourself well out of reach of the brick that would land upon you. Quite simply put, there is no foot to step on.

Now, when we teach you this we are not saying to lie down on the road and invite the car to drive over you. You have dignity. You have self-respect. But the self-respect you have is not dependent on what others would say about you, or how you are treated. The Divine as you could care less how she is spoken about. She knows who she is. And, because every interchange is a new opportunity to see God or know God or to realize the self anew in the Upper Room, each opportunity becomes growth and progress as you continue to navigate the higher octave.

The belief most of you have is that you will maintain the upper octave, inhabit the Upper Room, as long as things are going your way. If things are going your way, you have no issue with anybody's behavior. The government may do as it wishes, your children may behave as they wish, as long as your belief in your ability to maintain the Upper Room is present. However, the moment something happens that you would claim in anger or fear, you are given an opportunity to choose the Upper Room and remain in the frequency of the high octave. When that choice is made, in fact what you do is align the vibrational field in cohesion in this resonance, and you support the self in an appropriate response. And by *appropriate* we mean a helpful response to you, and to others, with whatever situation you are called to that *seems* to operate in low vibration.

"What does that mean, *seems*?" Well, in fact, it's perception. To call something low is to perceive it as low, and when something is re-perceived—again, re-known, re-articulated—in the Upper Room, it is transformed. To lift something to the Upper Room is to claim the Kingdom inclusive of that thing, not to abolish that thing, the brick in hand, the one throwing the brick. Unless the one with the brick in hand is known as God, or claimed anew, you have decided for her, for him, and created an opportunity to learn through the low vibration again. There is nothing wrong with this. However, we will say, to decide that you cannot manage your own True Self at this level is to be choosing as a small self. It cannot be so, it is not so, at the level of personality. It is always so, at the level of the True Self.

He interrupts. "Well, we have our lives, we have our preferences, we have obligations. How are we to interact at this level of vibration from here on in when we understand that there are challenges ahead?"

The simplest challenge that you will face is that you are choosing, and you would prefer to have things happen at you, and then maintain vibration, than realize that you are the one choosing at every opportunity how you will attend to your life. Once again, you would prefer to blame another than align to the Upper Room, where there is no blame. There is still accountability. You cannot rob a bank and then go hide in the Upper Room. You will be found wherever you sit. But you will realize that the act of robbing the bank is foolhardy because the Source of all things has never been the bank, and the realization of abundance is far more available, at this level of vibration, than it is at the level of scarcity that would encourage someone to go rob a bank.

Each individual you encounter becomes the opportunity to perceive the Christ as them, to know the Divine as who and what they are. When Paul says, "That sounds exhausting," he is speaking only as a small self who would have to decide, in each encounter, that he is seeing the Divine in the postman, the man at the store, the woman on the street. Once you are in the Upper Room and established in vibration here, that is who you meet, the occupant of the Upper Room, because you are lifting them there in the energetic field that you are operating through.

If you take a moment now and close your eyes and set this intention, this simple intention, "I am in the Upper Room," you will feel your vibration rising around you. You may experience this in the body, or as a tingling at the body in the field around you. But when you claim "I am in the Upper Room," or, if you wish, "I am free, I am free, I am free," which will also lift you here, you can have the experience of the Upper Room. Once you are here in this vibration, you simply claim the words "I Have Come, I Have Come, I Have Come" and express the Divine through and as you in the vibrational field of everything you encounter. When you do this, in all likelihood you will experience the expansion around the body, as if you have gotten larger, and expressing yourself beyond the confines of what you have thought as the body. In fact, that's what happens. As you walk down the street at this level of accord, you are transforming in interaction the vibrational essence of what you are encountering. And we ask you to go out now, on your own, and experience this. Until this is done in action, until the Word is known in action as who and what you are, you will have come, perhaps, to an intellectual understanding that you can agree to, or choose to refute. But the actualization of your experience here is what will direct you toward a life of high expression.

So we will take a moment now for whoever reads these words to set this intention:

> *"I am choosing to experience myself on this little walk, this little passage, even if it's around the room I am in, while reading, with my eyes, in the Upper Room."*

Period. Period. Period.

(PAUSE)

We ask you each to decide something: That the removal of the old—the way of anticipating the old, the way that the small self would decide what should be before her—become organic to your expression. And by this we mean we no longer want you acting in force to discern what is high and what is low. We want you *being* at the level of vibration where what you are is the claim of being that calls to you, in the higher vibrational state, all that you witness, all that you encounter, all that may be known in the Upper Room.

If we wish to offer you a bit of advice, it would simply be to align to the vibration in any situation until the moment of arrival, when you know without intention. When you become the intention, "I Have Come, I Have Come, I Have Come," the arrival of the Kingdom, made in form, is not only known to you—and to know is to realize—it is claimed for all you see.

The individuation of the Divine Self is a mass occurrence that is in progress. And, through this individuation of expression, the world is known as it truly is. Underline *truly.* Not as you would have it be, not as you were told it was, but as it can only be in the Upper Room, which is the level of the Kingdom.

Now, to presuppose that any action you take, from here on in, now that you know yourself as an aspect or manifestation of God, to decide that any action you take *will* be in alignment with truth, would be foolhardy until the alignment of full expression has occurred.

"And how does it occur?" he asks.

In the moment you stand in, and only then. And the moment, we say, friends, has come.

We are before you. We stand before you each. And, as we say these words to each one of you who hears these words, who reads these words, you may respond. The Divine as you, in manifestation, is the claim of the Divine in all. You will say this, if you wish:

"I Have Come. I Have Come. I Have Come."

Thank you each. We will pause the text until another day. Period. Period. Period.

DAY TWENTY-SIX

Now, as we come to you with our own benefit, our own regard for you each, as you come forth in a higher awareness of who you have always been in the Kingdom, you must be claimed as your inheritance becomes available to you. To claim you each is to realize you each in the octave of truth, because in truth a lie will not be held, and dominion in the Kingdom is awareness of truth that exists beyond the known, beyond the small self's idea of what can and should be.

Now, as we do this with you, as we call you each forth in your awareness of the Divine, we claim you in an Upper Room for the manifestation to occur. The manifestation that occurs in the Upper Room is a palpable expression of truth as embodied by you. And, when we say this, we are actually telling you that the physical body, in a new resonance, has to comprehend, not only itself, but its expression. That is what it makes, what it sees, what it is, in an octave beyond the known.

Now, as you progress through this, you develop a system that you claim through expression. Understand this. The vibrational system you have is reclaimed in this new articulation, and its mandates for its development are known by you in experience. So please don't say to us, "Well, tell me what to do to get what I want," because, again, that's the small self trying to sneak in the door of the Upper Room, where she thinks all her presents will be.

As you are realized, or re-known, in the octave of truth, the body you have taken begins to dismantle certain structures, or ways of knowing itself, that have been in agreement to a lower octave. Simply put, you are actually establishing yourself in a higher realm while incarnate. And the manifestations of this in form may include some discomfort, as Paul can attest to, but beyond that, all you are really doing is acclimating in an experiential way to what you are as you experience yourself in a new plane of knowing.

To understand this fully is to disregard any benefit that you think you will receive from this action, but to simply allow it to be the tuning fork that claims, not only you, the resonant you, but the experience of you, to provide the opportunity for this establishment, this embodied establishment in coherence with the world you are now walking in. You are walking in the world in the vibration of the Christ, which you will call love and truth and the awareness of the presence of the Divine in any interaction that you are aligned to.

Now, when we say *all alignment,* we are really saying that we get to this place of expression, where identity itself is re-known, and firmly re-known, in a comprehension of truth. The small self's idea is understood. It is blessed, perhaps. It is seen for what it has been—a great opportunity to learn. But the establishment of the True Self and the Upper Room, in field and form, claims you in a new alignment that doesn't subjugate the old as much as it doesn't rely upon it for the data it requires to go about the day.

The choice you make, each of you now, is to say yes to what comes, what is experienced, and what is chosen by the Divine Self in its recognition of your learning. To have an experience of the Divine Self in manifestation is only the first step of the agreement of being. By being at this level, there is no thought, or maneuvering, or claiming what you want to be. There is no point to it. You are claiming as you are. And the benefit of where you stand, the benefit of your encounter with the manifest world, is the rejoicing of realization in what is perceived in a re-articulated way.

The life you live begins to sing in a rather different way, or tone, or vibration, than you have assumed thus far. And the choice to be here, to align to this, supports you, actually, in the maintenance of it. It is so not difficult—once you comprehend that the alignment in the Upper Room, the choice to vibrate there, the choice to claim opportunity in every interaction, to perceive the Divine that is already present—the moment you realize this, you are actually ushered forward. And, when we say *ushered forward,* you receive your assignments.

Now, by *assignments,* we mean opportunity, and opportunity comes to each of you through your acquiescence to the Divine Self as who is the one who will claim it. And, as she claims it, she is called forth with the ability to meet the assignment, or opportunity, as the Divine Self. So you may find yourself in circumstance where you realize yourself in a completely different way. And your capacity to know what you need to do is present for you, without fear, because the True Self in opportunity is unafraid. Each opportunity that comes in service, through the manifestation of who and what you are, supports your alignment in claiming itself in the manifest world. And, by this, we mean in some ways you are re-creating the vibration in your interaction, because that is what you know. Realization. It is what you know.

Now, the old will seek to find you. "But look at this opportunity. There is much glory here. I will be somebody everybody knows." "Look at this opportunity. It looks wonderful. I will betray everybody I know by taking this, but it is for my good. I don't care what people think."

Now, you're not pleasing people by taking opportunity, but you are not creating glory, or seeking glory, because to seek glory as the Divine Self is to deny the glory that is already present. If you are called forth as a manifest being to work publicly, the opportunity is there, but please don't hang a star upon your dressing room. The opportunity comes in everyday awakening—to witness the God that is before you, even when it's concealed by a mountain of fear.

You have heard of moving mountains. This is the analogy. To move a mountain of fear is to realize what is present as the mountain and beyond its current expression. This is done by the one who does not deny the mountain, but *realizes* the mountain in the new octave and reclaims it as it has always been in truth. The violation of the small self, the dictates you've received for how you should be fearful, who you should condemn, who you should deny the Divine in, or what you would claim as unholy, must all now be re-met, re-introduced to you, for the purposes of alchemy. Again, the mountain being moved.

To eschew the old, "Oh, that old thing," is still to claim the old. To deny the old, "Oh, I was like that when I was twenty-one—never again," is still to claim the old. To realize the present moment as the only moment you stand in is to know eternity, and, in the realization of eternity, the folly of claiming the old as emblematic to who and what you think you are is seen for what it is. There is no need, at this level of incarnation, to blame your husband, or your father, or deny the love that would be asked of you from the one that doesn't wish you well. To know the Divine—love them anyway, as we say—in the one you would witness in fear resolves them in a new opportunity, or reclamation of vibration, that may be comprehended by you in your experience.

Now, some of you will say, "Oh, I have several people I hate. I'm going to go about witnessing the Divine in them until I feel differently." And, again, that is the small self seeking to do the work of the Upper Room. In truth, a lie cannot be held. And the lie is that whoever this human being is, whatever they have claimed or seek to do or seek to justify, cannot be without the presence of God. What lies beneath the mountain, and, in fact, is the mountain, is still God, even if it is denied. To deny God, or to be in the lie, or the curse, if you wish, of separation, is to claim independence from your own divinity, and the moment that is done, you operate in fear as a resource. If fear is a resource, what you rely upon to get through a situation—and we would say condemnation, guilt, and anger, and desire to harm others is all fear in masked ways—you understand that, as what you are, as you are re-known in the Upper Room, what you encounter is realized by the aspect of you who cannot deny the truth of being.

"Well, what of those we don't like?" We have said many times, Paul, that *like* is a personality structure. "My friend likes bowling. I can't stand it." "My friend likes to read. I prefer the movie." You have your preferences of how you wish to express and loving someone has not a thing to do with the personality they present. If that were the case, this would be a beauty pageant of some kind, where only those who are meritful get to enter the Kingdom.

Everybody comes. No one is exempt. Everybody is seen, regardless of what they have done, as realized in a new way in the Upper Room, in the Kingdom, we say, the awareness of the Divine. It is fear who keeps you separate, and, because you have relied upon it for so long, you contribute to the manifestation of it on this plane each time you choose in fear. Each time you choose in fear you are licking the fear that is present in the field, and its taste upon your lips calls you into the manifestation of fear, because that is always its intent.

Now, in truth, the idea of fear can be re-understood as a progression of an idea, born in a belief in unworthiness, in separation, the desire to rule, the desire to be God as the small self because that is what the small self thinks she is. And, born in this, you have established a world, separate countries, ways of denying the God in others, boundaries that separate you from rich to poor, ways of denying God that, whether or not you know it, you are complicit to. Because you see them, because you bear witness to them, you have to be party of them and to them because you cannot be separate from anything you see.

As we lift you each and every day to the Upper Room for these teachings, as you become willing to reside here with us to be instructed in experience, you become the one who has claimed the Kingdom. But the initial claim of the Kingdom—"I Have Come,

I Have Come, I Have Come"—is amplified by and through you in your experience of it. So saying the words is actually the action of expression until, as it is realized and known, there is no need to utter a word.

The stages of incarnation at this level of vibration, which we will be attending to in subsequent texts, will be known by you as you inherit them. You don't know what's in the box until you receive the box. And, when the box is open, you may claim what is there. All that can be claimed in the high octaves must be known as of God in order to support its realization, because to do other would be to seek the riches of heaven as something that must be hidden. In other words, to say, "I get this or that in the Upper Room, but none of you, perhaps, will," is the way to authenticate the lower self's agenda for its spiritual growth.

Everything that is received by you at the new level of vibration is comprehended with its meaning. And this is a new teaching. There is no point in giving you a key if we don't show you the doorway. The doorway will be present to the one who receives the key. The song will be sung the moment the orchestra appears. The love that you seek to be in expression as is in resounding bliss—the thunder of love, as can be articulated as you—the moment you love. And to love as the Divine is to know the Kingdom in absolute ways.

The realization of the Kingdom comes in stages as you may meet them. Some of you have decided that this must be so now, and we will sit back and watch you as you try to walk and carry yourself in a vibration that has different responsibilities. Paul is seeing the image of a toddler trying to walk and falling yet again. The toddler is loved, but when he walks, he knows how to walk forever. And, understand, friends, there is no rush because the Kingdom is present now in the moment you stand in, whenever that moment is.

When we taught you eternity in the prior pages of this text, we spoke to you about knowing yourself in infinity, and the wealth of information that can be comprehended there. When you are not bound to the systems of control that the calendar has offered you, a calendar can be liberating. "I know what month it is. I know where to go on Monday." But it prescribes a separation of your experience of time, as does the clock. If you stand in the sunlight, it is always beating, until it is night. And you are not anticipating night. You are knowing night, the moment night falls, as the eternal now. In grace there is freedom, and in freedom there is joy, and the moment you claim the Kingdom as your inheritance and step forth in the awareness of God in every flower, in every house, in every stream, in every human being or animal you see, you begin to have the experience of the Divine that is eternal, in the eternal now.

So we say these words to you:

As we witness you tonight, as we sing your song, as we lift you, one and all, all who hear these words, who read these words, who will attend to these words in the vibration that is present in them, we say yes to the unfoldment of the Divine that is now claiming you beyond all things, all desire for fear, all fear itself. So we say yes, and, as we say this, and complete this chapter in the text, we announce you each, as the curtain opens, and we invite you to step off the stage that the small self has known itself through into life as it exists beyond the known.

We welcome you, and we say good night. Period. Period. Period.

10

FREEDOM FROM FEAR

DAY TWENTY-SEVEN

Each of you decides, when you align as the Divine Self, that the life that you will lead will be in accord with your true nature, your true nature being the True Self in action, the Word made flesh, if you wish, in the day you arrive in. When you know who you are in a high octave, you establish the reality or the purview that the Divine Self must know itself through, and, consequently, everything you see and experience is in co-resonance or in alignment with the Divine as what you are.

Now, when we teach realization, we intend you to know it. We do not want you saying to us, "Well, tell us what to do." We are telling you now—and the text that you are reading in realization is a claim of embodiment that must be understood as an expression that will be known. When you are known as who and what you are, the Divine that has come just as you, the reality of your expression becomes the articulation of what has always been in the Upper Room, in the high octave, where the Divine Self is and always has been.

When those of you who come to us want to know who and what

you are, we always say to you, you are as you have always been, but not as you have known it. You have believed yourself to be far inferior than your true nature can express as. And, because you have come in a reckoning, in a willingness to face the self as you have thought you were, you may become established in the Upper Room, in the high octave, where the Christed Self realizes the Kingdom through the manifestation and re-articulation of the comprehension of matter. Underline the word *matter.* The Divine as *matter.* For some of you, the idea that the flower is holy is something you can comprehend, but you would deny the Divine in the filth you see. But once you truly understand that matter is the Divine out-pictured as idea—a construct, if you wish, that you have named and known in agreement to what it seems to be—you can move beyond the small self's comprehension to the concrete knowing that the manifestation of anything and everything is still God, or, if you wish, the energy or vibration that you would know of as God.

Now, when matter is seen as God, beyond the names it has been given, but when matter itself can be consecrated in its true nature, or holy name, the lifting of the vibration through the one who comprehends it is not only immediate, an immediate re-articulation or realization of matter, but it is known by the one who sees it as what it has always been. The moment you deny the Divine in anyone and anything—underline *thing*—the claim is made to operate in separation. When you want union on your own terms, you might as well go into an abbey and pull the gate shut. "I will be in union in the abbey with the like-minded people. We have a nice high wall to protect us from the world." In times past, the idea of sequestering the self to experience divinity was established. Today you say things like "I will not watch the news," "I will not look at the darkness." But even in that moment you are denying God and deciding that God is the pretty flower, and not the trampled one. When both are known as God, you are in union.

Now, when the walls of the abbey are released, the world itself becomes the abbey, the temple, the Kingdom, the manifestation of

God in its own articulation. And, when one begins to realize matter, to reclaim the glass of water, the glass and the water itself, as the vibration of God, your experience of the glass and the water transforms not only the glass and the water, but your relationship to it. "Is it no longer a glass? What are you telling us?" he says. What we are telling you is that the lifting of matter to a higher plane, the act of alchemy, if you wish, is where we take you, en masse, through the re-establishment, first, of the physical form that you have arrived in to its true nature, and, then, all that expresses in like vibration in manifestation to it. In other words, we say, when you have aligned as the truth of who and what you are, the alignment of the manifest world, the consecration of it, is the effect and the action that you partake in.

When you understand what a miracle is, which is the realization of God beyond the comprehension that the small self could assume, you will know God as a miracle in the lives you live. The demonstration of this, and the knowing of this, is the affect of the comprehension. In other words, friends, first you know, and then you realize the manifest world in congruence with that knowing. Some of you have nice ideas, the parade of flowers that you expect to see when your divine nature has come, but in fact what you see is the Divine in all manifestation. Underline *all.* And its articulation and relevance to what you are happens in a unified field. We call it the Upper Room, the high octave, where the Christ is manifest.

Now, the Christ as man is not at all a new teaching, but a teaching that has come, yet again, at the time when humanity can be claimed by it. And know that we said these words: *Be claimed by it.* You are not claiming the identity as Christ. It is claiming you. And the comprehension of this, in matter, is the realignment of every cell of your being in agreement to its Source.

To decide for yourself what this means would move you very rapidly into idolatry, because some of you would seek to make an idol of this teaching, when this teaching, in fact, is simply a walkway up the mountain to the Upper Room to realization. It must not be claimed as only one way, but as *a* way, *a* simple way, for manifestation to be occurring in humanity. There will be others to come. And the basis of each teaching will be the assumption of humanity in the language and with the iconography that is present in the existing culture, because each religion holds a common field, a common agreement, and it is that seed that has exploded and is now blooming, because until religion is realized beyond what it has done, which in most cases has been to confirm some sense of separation, the manifestation of the Divine *as* this plane of existence will be limited. We can no longer say, "Go to your church and pray to your God," when the church you stand in would condemn another. We can no longer affirm that the way of the prophet of times old must be the only teaching of the true Christ. We will only say that when the temple doors are thrown open, when the church doors are opened, when the mosque doors are opened, the light will pour in, and its own redemption, its own knowing, will occur.

When a knowing comes to any institution, it comes with great ramification. And, in some ways, the toppling of a structure, be it a government or a religion, is precipitating the realignment of the *idea* of government, or the *idea* of religion, as can be re-known in what we call the Upper Room. Those things that have been valued as sacred that have become so tarnished—through the abuse of power, through the treason of the Divine by deciding that "some can be loved and some cannot by God"—these things must be reassessed, re-known, but they cannot be re-known when they are being re-articulated by the very ones who would keep the manifestation in low vibration.

"What does this mean?" he asks. The one who has an idea that what has been must be what will always be has a deep investment in denying the action of God, because the action of God is always change. And we say *always* because to realize this itself will give you the key to an awakening of the transient nature of the physical reality that is now being reclaimed in the teaching of this text. The claim "I Have Come, I Have Come, I Have Come," the announcement of the True Self, is what claims you and all you know by the Divine that is already here and expressing itself in high alignment. The justification of the old—"Well, this is how we did it, so it will be done again this way"—is to deny the action of God, or the action of change, that would re-comprehend, re-know, and reclaim everything that it encounters. Underline, again, *everything. Everything* that it encounters. What the Divine encounters is always God, because the Divine cannot perceive anything beyond it. And, when you move to the alignment of this comprehension, you become the tuning fork, the radiance, the sound and the vibration of God that assumes all it meets in an encounter with itself and its true nature. The Divine in reckoning is the lifting of the eyes, the lifting of the being to see what it has claimed, to re-know what it may know, and the alignment you now have through these teachings will actually reclaim you beyond any idea you have ever had of who you are.

You don't know this, yet—in subsequent texts, we will do our best to give you this—but you do not yet know that the universe you see is an idea, and an idea can be re-comprehended. And, the moment it is, it is re-established in the high octave, and, consequently, re-known.

Now, to understand what we are claiming you in, in the Upper Room, is to simply understand that the aspect of you, incarnated, is divine and has sought and agreed to realization, including the body that it knows itself in. And the articulation of the body—"I know what I am"—announces to the physical self the ramifications of choice. To comprehend and agree to manifest in form as what you have always been reclaims the form and what the form aligns to. As everything exists in multiple octaves, you agree to align and know the world before you in the high octave that exists beyond the known.

Now, to each of you we say you are welcomed, as you wish, to deny the Kingdom. You may choose to re-create your history, as you have known it, for the safety of the claims you have made historically. But, if you wish to do this and confirm the separation that humanity has decreed it will know through, you will find yourself in participation to the dilemmas that you would say you wish to see known anew. If you wish to claim your history and agree to what has been, you are actually agreeing to a world that has chosen to learn through separation, when unity, palpable unity—"I am one with the stars, and the woman beside me, and those I may never meet"—is available now and can be created for you through this process of alignment and re-comprehension of matter itself.

We will complete this teaching later in the day, if we are allowed to. Period. Period. Period.

(PAUSE)

As you decide to be in manifestation as the Divine Self, one thing occurs that you may not expect. You lift beyond fear in a way that you will know. To live without and beyond fear is treasonous to the small self who has been educated by fear as to its benefits, but there is no benefit in fear. And, if you must know, freedom from fear, which would be the title of this chapter, is the realization that the Divine in material form has no requirement of it.

Now, to understand this is to know the self in a significantly different way than you have ever experienced. So we wish to take you on a little journey to the Upper Room, the place where fear does not express itself. The choice to be in fear, which may be claimed at any level of vibration, will release you from the Upper Room, but to know yourself as free of it is to make the choice in realization that the Divine as you has no requirement for it, that it has been a good teacher, but holds no benefit to the self that knows who she truly is.

So, if you would imagine that on the count of three you are lifting to the Upper Room, the level of vibration where we sing to you from, we will offer you the opportunity, again, to know the self beyond fear, and beyond any claim that fear ever may have made upon you. On the count of three, allow the lifting to occur.

One. Two. Three.

Be received by us and enveloped in the Upper Room, in the octave where the Divine knows itself in form, and fear cannot exist except by choice. In this alignment, we wish to give you an experience of what it feels like to know the self as fearless. And, if you wish this, you may do this any time you like, until you come to the level of agreement where the Upper Room is where you abide and express as. In this claim we make for you each—"I Have Come, I Have Come, I Have Come"—the True Self may begin to experience the self as it was intended to know itself. Fear*less*. Without the idea of fear, fear cannot exist. Did you all hear this? Without fear as an idea—because fear *is* an idea, a projection, a way of thinking or experiencing an idea—fear itself has no name. And, without a name, it becomes vibration, without intent. To name anything, to call it by name, is to empower its function—the chair that is sat upon, the fear that is overwhelming. Without the idea of chair, the thing that you sit upon is simply what it is. And, without the idea of fear, fear has no power.

To align to this level of expression is to claim the self as you have always been, the True Self who was born into being without fear. And, the moment you understand this, you can begin to reclaim who and what you have always been, without the creation of fear informing the life you live. In this way, we will say these words:

> *"On this day I choose to allow every aspect of myself that has been known or will be known by the idea of fear to release any claims that have been made upon me by fear, to be free of itself, and to align to its potential as fearless. In my agreement to be known without fear, I give permission to release any investment I may have in fear as my ally, so I may be knowing my world as one without fear. As I say yes to this, I give myself permission to*

release the memory of fear that I have known myself through, the projections of fear that I may be utilizing as a small self, and, as I say yes, I come forth as the release of fear, the idea of fear itself, is made known in my field."

Release the idea of fear. Let the idea of fear itself be lifted from you, as if a wave would carry it away to a new claim of liberation. The energy you have known as fear, without the idea of fear claiming it in form, becomes a way to know liberation. Without the captor, there can be no prisoner, and there is no captor when the idea of fear is released from you.

Be as you are, and allow yourself to know the self as free of fear. *(short pause)*

Accepting the self as you are, without fear as your companion, without fear as your armor, without fear as the expectation of your life, gives you permission to know the True Self while embodied. As the memory of fear will seek to reclaim you—"There is a spider, I expect to be frightened by the spider"—remember that you're only frightened by the idea of the spider and what it has represented to you. In this new creation of the True Self, the material realm begins to oscillate for you in recognition of the vibration you have claimed. In other words, the one who operates without fear does not claim the same, and has no expectation of receiving it. When you understand that what you are doing here is reclamation to your innate true state, the one you are begins to express the realization of form without the taint or the shadow of fear informing choice.

Now, when we say *informing choice,* we do not encourage you to be foolhardy. "What a lovely looking cliff. It would be nice to jump off it." That would be a rather foolhardy action, and there is no need. To understand that caring for the self is an act of love, and terrifying the self is not, might be a simple way to understand how you are choosing and why. When you seek the approval of your fellows to appease an angry God, you are operating in fear. When you need to placate those around you to support them in their well-being, you are acting in love. When you understand the needs of those around you and you comprehend who they are beyond the small self's agenda, anything and everything you would do for them will be a consequence of love.

Each of you comes into this expression with the potential to realize the Divine at the level of manifestation that you can hold. The Christ itself cannot be afraid because the Christ is in no fear, does not know fear, cannot articulate as such. And, as the Christ is realized in manifestation in humanity, humanity itself is lifted beyond fear, and the illusion of separation that fear would mandate is released as well.

Some of you wish to keep your fear. "It is safer that way. I know what to expect. I shouldn't trust these people, or go there or here, because I know what could happen." To comprehend that your discernment of where not to go may be self-love, and not fear, would be one way of moving forward, but your reliance upon fear as your protector will, in fact, call to you the fear that you say you don't want, because your expression, your vibratory field, has claimed a thing in fear, and, consequently, aligned you to it at that level.

In the Upper Room, anything you may fear may be re-known, and comprehended anew. If you understand, friends, that the idea of fear itself is what must be released, all that follows will know itself as fear*less*.

We will end this teaching now. Thank you for your presence.

DAY TWENTY-EIGHT

Now, as you stand before us in realization, in comprehension of the True Self in manifestation, you wonder what it means to be you. "Who am I now? What do I do with my being? How do I comprehend action and reliance upon the old that I have counted on to know what to do next?"

What is happening for each of you, through this encounter in a new alignment to a high octave, is a realization of the fortitude of the True Self to answer the questions in the moment you stand in. The map you seek and the compass you wish cannot be found in the low vibration, but, in the Upper Room, where you now abide as expressed beings, the claims have been made for you to realize you as the one who knows. The claims we have made in history, in these teachings, have actually embedded or encoded their truth in the energetic fields. And, as the fields are assuming the form you have taken, you express in reliance with the dictates of these truths, which simply means the information you require is there in the moment you need it.

Now, imagine you move to another country where the laws are rather different. The habituated behavior that you are leaving is not present. "Is it time for tea? When do I go to work? How do I know what's expected of me?" You know what's expected of you in the moment you know, and not a moment before, nor a moment after. The realization of the Divine Incarnate Self is present as the life you live, but is operating, in some ways, beyond the known, beyond the structure of the known, and most certainly beyond the reliance upon it. Once you have realized the manifest self, and its encoding has claimed the being that you are, the reliance upon the old structures dissipates, in some ways, through the reliance on the power of knowing and the realization that, when you know in any instant, you are called to act upon that knowing. And the realization that what you are is in vibration in agreement to a vibratory world claims the world in the alignment with you, and you no longer seek your reflection through the guarantees of the small self's data. "It is snowing. It certainly must be winter." The referencing of the old ceases to empower itself, through disuse and through the new agreement as the expressed Divine who has come in love, "I Have Come, I Have Come, I Have Come," the manifest self in its claim of life and agreement to what may be known by the self who has come in service to a world made new.

Each of you who comes to us by agreement consents to this when you align to the True Self and give permission to move beyond the template or structure of self-realization that the small self has been handed and has done his very best with. The small self, you see, who is still present with you, will no longer rely upon the artifacts of history, when what is being presented to him or her makes far more sense in his experience. The justification of rules and laws, habituated acts, cultural mores, will be seen, just as they have always been, as agreements made to conform to a status quo that is an inherited structure that is seeking to be re-known through the lifting and re-creation of the world.

As the manifest world begins to greet you in this new vibratory form you have taken, you can count on several things. The reliance upon the old will no longer serve you, and you will get busy moving to the realm of possibility, because all things may be known in the Upper Room. And, because you had a recipe for success, based in data, you are limiting yourself to what might be claimed beyond that, that is now available to you in a much different manner. When you justify the old—"Well, we have always done it as such, so this must be the way"—you are a follower, you are sheep. And, in fact, the Divine Self as you is not a sheep, but a shepherd. And your own awakening, your own lifting, is the clarion call through your vibratory field to summon the world to you in a higher accord. You are not *looking* for followers, you are *claiming* them, the world before you, in their true states of being. And that is the gift of the one who has come, to know the world and to claim what she sees in her knowing.

So the small self wants questions answered. "I still have a job. What do I do with my job?" While we have answered these questions prior, we do understand that, at each level of agreement, you look at your world and you seek the answers that you believe you will need to know. But, as we said prior, you only know in the moment knowing is given. And it is the Divine in manifestation who is claiming her work, her role in society, if she has one, and what it means to be in a life that has been created for the benefit of her learning and for the benefit of serving those before her.

When we taught you the claim "I know how I serve," the amplification of the vibratory field, in waves, congratulates and confirms the presence of the Divine in the world before her. The fear you have about not being what you want to be is immediately replaced in recognition of who you truly are. And who you truly are, whether or not you know it in the moment of this reading, is the Divine, has always been, can and will only be the Divine. The agreement to manifest, to participate in the field of the physical realm, has been a wondrous opportunity. And, while you are not releasing that opportunity, you are lifting the manifest world, by nature of being, to learn some new things that cannot be learned as a small self seeking to confirm history.

In wonder, we teach you. The practice of wonder. And, as you walk the world, beyond fear, beyond the agreement to fear, what you begin to comprehend is the insanity of fear as a practice, as a way of being in agreement to logic. "You should be afraid." "You should condemn." The false teachings of history that have supported man turning against man are seen for what they have always been—ways to decide how humanity should interact to support the needs of the ones who would make the rules. When you have lived with a rule for generations, you assume it to be true, or meaningful, when, in fact, the creation of the rule, at the time it was commanded, was to support a need of a community that was operating in very different ways than you may be now.

The Divine as what, the manifest Divine, comprehends the requirements of the day and understands that those she meets, who are operating in fear, can be lifted beyond it through her realization of them. Now, imagine for a moment that there is someone in your life who you know as fearful. And imagine them, for a moment or two, standing before you in their fear. If you wish to ask the fear to take a shape or a name, something emblematic, so that you can claim it independent from the individual—because, in fact, fear is independent from an individual—it will be helpful to you. So see the person before you with the image of fear, or name of fear, that they utilize, and claim this for them in your own way. "I know who you are in truth. I know what you are in truth. I know how you serve in truth. You are free. You are free. You are free."

Now, as this is claimed, watch what begins to happen with the energetic field, or the name the thing has been given. As you claim them in truth, the lie that they have known themselves in will release its hold, because in truth a lie will not be held. You are not ripping their fear from them. You are claiming who they are without it, without the idea of fear in the manifestation that they have agreed to, whether it be fear of death, or spiders, or of being alone. Whatever the fear is that they have chosen to learn through may be re-known in a higher octave through the simple act of bringing them to the Upper Room through your accord with them.

"How is this done?" he asks. Through the claims you just made. The claims we just made and invited you to make are claimed in the Upper Room by the one who resides there. We are speaking to you, our students, as those who have agreed to align to the Upper

Room as their new habituation. So any claim made from this octave has the intent to lift what you are encountering to the Upper Room to be re-established and re-known. The one before you, who wears her fear, is re-integrating an aspect of herself that has perhaps been dormant, or hidden away out of the need to be safe that was justified by fear, but the moment the fear releases its tentacles, the idealized self, the True Self, reclaims the captain of the vessel of her being. In other words, the fear that would rule is released through the re-articulation of the one claimed in love.

"Claimed in love?" he says. "Is this the same thing as being in the Upper Room and witnessing another?" Yes, it is. And you will understand this, Paul, the moment that you stop thinking that love is an emotion, because what it is, is truth as love, truth as God. And the reliance upon truth, that which cannot be untrue because it is eternally true, will be the claim of alchemy that is made by you as the True Self who is in love.

Now, to some of you, you think this means you will go around hugging people you don't like. We don't like hugging very much, either. We would prefer other ways of contact. Since we have no body to hug in this manifest world, we would rather say hello and be in love with you. For those of you who want to go hugging everyone, you must ask what your need really is. "Why do I feel compelled to wrap my arms around everyone I meet?" You may hug as you wish. You may choose not to, as you wish. One thing has nothing to do with the other, or what we are teaching. We are teaching love and the manifestation of love, which releases fear, from the Upper Room, which is where this can be taught. We are teaching from the Upper Room, where fear does not agree. So, in this place of fear-*less*-ness, you may come each day until you abide here in your own knowing.

The lifting of the world, where we will take you in further texts, is an act of being. And the being as the Divine in manifestation is an encyclopedia in and of itself. And we say this for Paul, who asks, "What is there left to teach?" If you really wanted to know, Paul, you would probably abdicate your role as channel and go play a game someplace, because the work before you, as it continues, will continue to defy the logic you've known, but give you what you have wished, which is the knowing of the presence of God as who and what you are, and as who and what you see, and as all that can be known. It *is* the mystical path. We have said this prior. But the assumption of the small self and the release of the reliance upon an idea of who and what you are are the simple keys to comprehending this. And the joy we have in offering the teaching is the realization of our students and what they will call forth in this manifest world.

Imagine a million voices, all around the globe, lifting in song in this new claim, "I Have Come, I Have Come, I Have Come." And the agreement to be in vibration that reiterates its name in language, and tone, and vibration, in the scale of freedom, in the tone of love embodying the manifest plane—that is what comes when each of you says yes, because, by nature of your being, you become the liberator of those imprisoned by their fear. And you awaken those, by nature of your being, who have denied the Divine, the aspect of the Divine, that has come as them and seeks its acclimation through the articulation of form.

The division that you experience now in your world can actually be healed by the one who knows herself in union with her Source. It cannot be healed at the level of division. It cannot be understood at the level of division. At the level of division, which is the level of the small self in separation, the mandate is replication, and replication of the old claims the new as the old, each day you choose it. If you are willing, wherever you are, to be re-known and re-articulated as the one in union, you create the echo, the vibratory resonance, that manifests itself as the world before you. Period. Period. Period.

(PAUSE)

Now, ask yourselves these questions: "Am I willing to be re-created and re-known and in service for the higher well-being, the higher well-being of all? Am I willing to forgive myself for what I may have chosen to learn through on this plane? Am I willing to make a new agreement that the choices I make from now on will be made in accordance with the truth of my being, from the Upper Room?"

You may answer these as you wish, and, as you answer them, understand that the choice to say yes fulfills itself on the walk of life that you are embarking upon here. You are met by the circumstances and requirements in service on a daily basis. But do understand that, as you embody and manifest from the Upper Room, the consequence is thus: As you do know who you are and what you are and how you serve, as the claim "I Have Come, I Have Come, I Have Come" becomes you, there is no need to be other than you are. You don't aspire to goodness. You are not seeking forgiveness for your past sins. You are not asking for a better this or that. You are encouraging the vibration by being. And, by being in agreement to the Divine, everything before you is known anew. So, we have taught you in this text about the responsibility of knowing who you are, and of the claim of truth, "I Have Come," that is the announcement of the purview in action as the Divine in an incarnation singular to you, but of the collective manifest Christ that is here on this plane in demonstration now.

We will walk with you for some time on this journey. We walk beside you, we walk before and behind, so that your understanding of your safety in the new landscape is aware and known by you as you go forth in a new life. And, because we support and herald your coming to the world before you, we make the way as we can to the benefit of the individual's assumption and realization.

Please hear these words: You have never been alone on this journey, nor can you be. And the isolation that you may have experienced yourself in was the fear of the reconnection from the small self, who disbelieves she can be worthy of the love of the Divine.  But no one is exempt from the love of the Divine, because love *is* God, and love *is* every particle of every living thing at a level of vibration or assumption.

To behold the world in a new way is only the first step of being the ambassador of truth that you have each come to be. But this is as far as we may take you at this teaching. In subsequent texts, we have a mission for the realization, in alchemy, of the manifest world. But, by saying these words, you would presuppose what their meaning is. So we will wait for *this* teaching to complete itself before we bring you the next one.

In our honor, we speak these words to all of our students, wherever you may sit, wherever these words may be spoken and heard, or read and comprehended. We are with you now, as we have always been. And, as we walk beside you and before you, in the Upper Room, we welcome you to the life that is and will always be before you.

This is not the end of the chapter. This is the end of the text.

And we are saying this to Paul. The text that we have dictated is the text that was intended. We congratulate you for your fortitude, and we thank our students for their presence in the teaching. If we dictate an epilogue, we will tell you so, and that was in answer to his question.

When we say we complete the text, all we really mean is that the information that has been articulated here, in noise, in tone, in vibration, in spoken word, in love, and in thanks, will be claimed again and again and again in each reiteration of the reading. The book you hold in your hands is alive in love, alive in tone, alive in language, noise, and sound. And, if you give us permission now, we will claim you in the Kingdom, and say yes to the learning that now ensues.

We are here. We are here. We are here. And, as we sing your praises, we lift you each to the new path that we walk with you upon. As you are loved, as you are known, as you are realized beyond the known in realization, your song will be heard throughout this plane, in thanks and in love and in union with the Source of all things.

We thank you each, and we say good night. Period. Period. Period.

Acknowledgments

Dustin Bamberg, Noam Ben-Arie, Tim Chambers, Joan Katherine Cramer, Joel Fotinos, Amy Hughes, Aubrey Marcus, Jeannette Meek, Victoria Nelson, Noah Perabo, Amy Perry, Brent Starck, Natalie Sudman, and the Esalen Institute.

I am here

"I know how I Serve" ~ is a vibratory Action .a[illegible]
That calls in your field & -

I am free

- Do not TAKE Yesterday's baggage into today

- when you fear another - you give them your athority.
- The Divine is in all or nothing! It can't be both ways.
- The desire for the Divine is The Divine seeking it's realization Thru you as you

* The Divine Manifestation can be known and sung and praised, and claimed and

The requirement of this teaching is to succum to this you are guaranteed to the realization of the True Self That has come in form.

The New Octive That Expresses Now & Be gifted to others

- Everything around you is God in Manifestation

what else do you need to know?!